Radical Reformation Studies

Radical Reformation Studies

Essays presented to
James M. Stayer

Edited by

WERNER O. PACKULL and
GEOFFREY L. DIPPLE

Ashgate

Aldershot • Brookfield USA • Singapore • Sydney

Published by
Ashgate Publishing Limited
Gower House
Croft Road
Aldershot
Hants GU11 3HR
England

Ashgate Publishing Company
Old Post Road
Brookfield
Vermont 05036–9704
USA

Ashgate website: http://www.ashgate.com

British Library Cataloguing in Publication Data

Radical Reformation Studies: Essays presented to James M. Stayer.
  (St Andrews Studies in Reformation History)
  1. Reformation.
  I. Packull, Werner O.   II. Dipple, Geoffrey L.
  270.6

Library of Congress Cataloging-in-Publication Data

Radical Reformation studies: essays presented to James M. Stayer/
  edited by Werner O. Packull and Geoffrey L. Dipple.
    (St Andrews Studies in Reformation History)
    Includes bibliographical references and index.
    ISBN 0–7546–0032–7 (hardcover: alk. paper)
    1. Reformation. 2. Anabaptists. I. Stayer, James M.
  II. Packull, Werner O., 1941–   . III. Dipple, Geoffrey L.
  IV. Series.
  BR307.R33   1999
  284'.3—dc21   99–40592
                                                                    CIP

ISBN 0 7546 0032 7

This book is printed on acid free paper

Typeset in Sabon by Manton Typesetters, Louth, Lincolnshire and printed in Great Britain by MPG Books Ltd, Bodmin, Cornwall

Contents

Notes on contributors

Geoffrey L. Dipple is Assistant Professor of History at Augustana College in Sioux Falls, South Dakota. His research into Reformation History includes *Antifraternalism and Anticlericalism in the German Reformation* (1996).

Michael Driedger is a fellow at the Institute for Research in the Humanities at the University of Wisconsin-Madison.

Clyde R. Forsberg Jr is an Instructor in the Department of History at Trent University in Peterbrough, Ontario.

Hans-Jürgen Goertz is Professor of Social and Economic History at the University of Hamburg. Included among his publications of Reformation History are *Innere und äußere Ordnung in der Theologie Thomas Müntzers* (1967), *Pfaffenhaß und groß Geschrei* (1987), *Thomas Müntzer: Apocalyptic Mystic and Revolutionary* (1993), *Religiose Bewegungen in der frühen Neuzeit* (1993), *The Anabaptists* (1996) and *Konrad Grebel, 1498–1526 – Kritiker des frommen Scheins* (1998).

Taira Kuratsuka is Professor of Political Science at Meiji University in Tokyo. His research into the Reformation has focused on Anabaptist Münster, including 'Gesamtgilde und Täufer: Der Radikalisierungsprozeß in der Reformation Münsters: Von der reformatorischen Bewegung zum Täuferreich 1533/34', *ARG* 76 (1985).

Bill McNiel is an Instructor in the Department of History at Queen's University, Kingston, Ontario.

Werner O. Packull is Professor of History at Conrad Grebel College, University of Waterloo. Among his publications on the history of Anabaptism and the Radical Reformation are *Mysticism and the Early South German-Austrian Anabaptist Movement* (1977), *Rereading Anabaptist Beginnings* (1991) and *Hutterite Beginnings: Communitarian Experiments during the Reformation* (1995).

Sonia Riddoch is an Instructor in the Department of History, Queen's University, Kingston, Ontario.

John D. Roth is Professor of History at Goshen College, Goshen, Indiana. He also serves as editor of the *Mennonite Quarterly Review* and director of the Mennonite Historical Library.

C. Arnold Snyder is Professor of History at Conrad Grebel College, University of Waterloo and editor of the *Conrad Grebel Review*. His publications on the history of Anabaptism include *The Life and Thought of Michael Sattler* (1984), *Anabaptist History and Theology: An Introduction* (1995) and *Profiles of Anabaptist Women* (1996, edited with Linda Huebert Hecht).

Gary K. Waite is Professor of Medieval and Early Modern European History at the University of New Brunswick. He has published on the history of the Dutch Reformation, Dutch Anabaptism and the Spiritualist David Joris, including *David Joris and Dutch Anabaptism, 1524–1543* (1990), *The Anabaptist Writings of David Joris, 1535–1543* (1994) and *Reformers on Stage: Popular Drama and Religious Propaganda in the Low Countries of Charles V, 1515–1556* (forthcoming).

Acknowledgements

Behind every good book there are a number of great women, and this one is no exception. Patricia Halling has served as a diligent typist and proofreader. Cheryl Swanson's technical expertise was invaluable when the computer glitches became too much. Caroline Cornish of Ashgate Publishing was again a thorough and attentive editor. And a special thanks is owed to Sharon Judd, who was wrenched away from her quilting frame and the calf pens, and pressed back into service as an editor, proofreader and secretary. Without her efforts and expertise, the task of imposing some sort of unity on the idiosyncrasies in styles and programs of the essays contained in this volume would have been insurmountable.

Abbreviations

ARG	*Archiv für Reformationsgeschichte*
GZI	Lydia Müller (ed.), *Glaubenszeugnisse oberdeutscher Taufgesinnten* (Leipzig, 1938)
LW	*Luther's Works*, ed. Jaroslav Pelikan et al. (St Louis/ Philadelphia, 1955)
ME	*Mennonite Encyclopedia*
MGBl	*Mennonitische Geschichtsblätter*
MQR	*Mennonite Quarterly Review*
TQ Elsaß I and II	Manfred Krebs and Hans Georg Rott (eds), *Quellen zur Geschichte der Täufer* VII, *Elsaß I, Stadt Straßburg 1522–1532* (Gütersloh, 1959); VIII, *Elsaß II, Stadt Straßburg 1533–1535* (Gütersloh, 1960)
TQ Elsaß III	Marc Lienhard, Stephen Nelson and Hans Georg Rott (eds), *Quellen zur Geschichte der Täufer* XV, *Stadt Straßburg 1536–1542* (Gütersloh, 1986)
TQ Gespräche	Martin Haas (ed.), *Quellen zur Geschichte der Täufer in der Schweiz IV, Drei Täufergespräche* (Zurich, 1974)
TQ Österreich	Grete Mecenseffy (ed.), *Quellen zur Geschichte der Täufer* XIV, *Österreich III* (Gütersloh, 1983)
TQ Ostschweiz	Heinold Fast (ed.), *Quellen zur Geschichte der Täufer in der Schweiz II, Ostschweiz* (Zurich, 1973)
TQ Württemberg	Gustav Bossert Sr and Gustav Bossert Jr (eds), *Quellen zur Geschichte der Wiedertäufer I, Herzogtum Württemberg* (Leipzig, [1930], 1971)
TQ Zürich	Leonhard von Muralt and Walter Schmid (eds), *Quellen zur Geschichte der Täufer in der Schweiz I, Zürich* (Zurich, 1952)

Introduction

For three decades now James M. Stayer's name has been closely associated with the study of Anabaptism and the Radical Reformation. His
place among historians of Anabaptism was established in 1972 with the
publication of *Anabaptists and the Sword*. Hailed as a key revisionist
work at the time, it now belongs to the classics in Radical Reformation
studies.[1] Three years later the publication of 'From Monogenesis to
Polygenesis: The Historical Discussion of Anabaptist Origins', co-
authored with Klaus Deppermann and Werner Packull,[2] confirmed Stayer
as the prominent historian on the cutting edge of Anabaptist studies. In
addition to these milestones in Anabaptist historiography Stayer produced a steady stream of in-depth studies into a variety of topics and
individuals associated with sixteenth-century Anabaptism: the Swiss
Brethren, Thomas Müntzer, Balthasar Hubmaier, Wilhelm Reublin,
Melchior Hoffman and the Melchiorite movement, Bernhard Rothmann
and Anabaptist Münster, Menno Simons and David Joris. As these
names indicate, Stayer, like no other scholar in this field, is equally at
home in the south and the north. The fruit of these labours has been
gathered into rich comprehensive treatments of Anabaptism such as the
chapter on 'The Anabaptists' in Steven Ozment's *Reformation Europe:
A Guide to Research* or the entry 'The Anabaptists and the Sects' in *The
New Cambridge Modern History*.[3]

Stayer's distinguished contributions had as their aim nothing less than
to move Anabaptist and Radical Reformation studies to their rightful,
respected place in the history of the Reformation. This aim was evident in
his earliest articles on Thomas Müntzer as well as in *Anabaptists and the
Sword*. In the latter Stayer challenged the then current definition of
'Evangelical Anabaptism' and the apologetic tendency of the 'free church'
historiography to sweep unpleasant manifestations of Anabaptism under
the rug or out of history. At the same time he highlighted the plurality in
political ethic that existed within Anabaptism. His subsequent studies of
the interaction between early Anabaptists and Saxon radicals such as
Thomas Müntzer, investigations into the congregationalist roots of Swiss

---

[1] A.G. Dickens and John Tonkin, *The Reformation in Historical Thought* (Oxford,
1985), p. 232; James M. Stayer, *Anabaptists and the Sword* (Lawrence, KS, 1972).

[2] *MQR*, 49 (1975), pp. 83–121.

[3] 'The Anabaptists', in Steven Ozment (ed.), *Reformation Europe: A Guide to Research* (St Louis, MO, 1982), pp. 135–59. 'The Anabaptists and the Sects', in G.R. Elton
(ed.), *The New Cambridge Modern History*, II: *The Reformation, 1520–1559* (Cambridge, 1990), pp. 118–43.

Anabaptism, research into Menno Simons's place in post-Münsterite Melchiorite Anabaptism, and ultimately a re-evaluation of the relationship between Anabaptism and the Peasants' War, have greatly enhanced our understanding of the variety of the Radical Reformation, and its interconnectedness with the broader reform movement. In the last decade the benefits of this research became available in *The German Peasants' War and Anabaptist Community of Goods* and in the chapter 'The Radical Reformation' in *The Handbook of European History, 1400–1600: Late Middle Ages, Renaissance and Reformation*.[4]

But even this list does not exhaust Stayer's contributions to Reformation studies. With the temerity of mature scholarship nearing retirement he has ventured from the Anabaptist/Radical fringe to the bastion of the German Luther renaissance. With reviews and review articles and the perspective of a self-professed outsider he has dared to enter the minefield of Reformation orthodoxy.[5] Earlier he had subjected the Reformed tradition, particularly early Zwinglianism, to his critical scrutiny.[6] And he has been an active contributor to the ongoing debate about the nature and significance of anticlericalism during the early Reformation period.[7] His most recent book, soon to appear, turns Stayer's formidable critical skills on the influence of Karl Holl and others on Luther and Reformation studies. Like his earlier studies this assault on the mighty fortress of Lutheran prejudice will not fail to stir controversy.[8]

The essays in this volume, written by students, friends and colleagues of James Stayer, are tokens of appreciation to him as teacher, scholar

---

[4] *The German Peasants' War and Anabaptist Community of Goods* (Montreal, 1991); 'The Radical Reformation', in Thomas Brady, Heiko Oberman and James Tracy (eds), *Handbook of European History, 1400–1600: Late Middle Ages, Renaissance, and Reformation*, vol. 2: *Visions, Programs and Outcomes* (Leiden, 1995), pp. 249–82.

[5] James Stayer, 'Luther Studies and Reformation Studies', *Canadian Journal of History*, 17 (1982), pp. 499–505; 'The Eclipse of *Young Man Luther*: An Outsider's Perspective on Luther Studies', *Canadian Journal of History*, 19 (1984), pp. 167–82.

[6] James Stayer, 'Zwingli before Zurich. Humanist Reformer and Papal Partisan', *ARG*, 72 (1981), pp. 55–68; 'Review Article on Ulrich Gäbler, *Huldrych Zwingli*', *MGBl*, 41 (1984), pp. 116–21; 'Zwingli and the "Viri Multi et Excellentes". The Christian Renaissance's Repudiation of *neoterici* and the Beginnings of Reformed Protestantism', in E.J. Furcha and H. Wayne Pipkin (eds), *Prophet, Pastor, Protestant. The Work of Huldrych Zwingli after Five Hundred Years* (Allison Park, PA, 1984), pp. 137–54.

[7] James Stayer, 'Reformation, Peasants, Anabaptists: Northeastern Swiss Anticlericalism', in Peter Dykema and Heiko Oberman (eds), *Anticlericalism in Late Medieval and Early Modern Europe* (Leiden, 1993), pp. 559–66; 'Anticlericalism: A Model for a Coherent Interpretation of the Reformation', in Hans Guggisberg and Gottfried Krodel (eds), *The Reformation in Germany and Europe: Interpretations and Issues* (Gütersloh, 1993), pp. 39–47.

[8] James Stayer, *Martin Luther: German Saviour: German Evangelical Factions and the Interpretation of Luther, 1917–1933* (Montreal, forthcoming 2000).

and friend. Like Stayer's own research these contributions reflect a variety of scholarly interests in the Radical Reformation. Essays in Part One concentrate on the history of sixteenth-century Anabaptism, long the focal point of Stayer's scholarship, interest, research and impact. Part Two widens the scope to include the interaction between Anabaptists and other religious dissenters and socially marginalized groups. The final part focuses attention on methodological assumptions and presuppositions. The breadth of approaches and concerns revealed in these essays is surely a testimony to Stayer's own wide-ranging interests and influence on our understanding of the Reformation.

As noted, Stayer has been in the vanguard of revisionist scholarship on early Anabaptism. The jointly authored article 'From Monogenesis to Polygenesis' represented a defining document of revisionism suggesting generically distinct roots for Swiss, central-south German and Melchiorite Anabaptism. Almost twenty-five years after its articulation, the 'polygenesis thesis' invites and inspires interaction. The polygenesis model has not been without its critics, however, and a body of post-revisionist literature has grown up in recent years. In particular, Arnold Snyder suggested that while the notion of polygenesis highlights important differences in Anabaptist origins, it threatens to become a conceptual straitjacket when applied too rigidly in segregating the emerging Anabaptist traditions.[9] Recent research has moderated the influences drawn from polygenesis, emphasizing instead interaction between the various Anabaptist factions.

Two of the essays in Part One, those by Taira Kuratsuka and Werner Packull, concentrate on development, interaction and/or cross-fertilization in early Anabaptism. Kuratsuka, a political scientist, examines Hutterite communitarianism from the perspective of a utopian experiment. At times considered peripheral to the mainstream Swiss Anabaptist tradition, the Hutterite communities in Moravia have been receiving increasing attention from historians recently. The relative tolerance accorded the Anabaptists by the semi-autonomous nobility of Moravia turned this land into a major Anabaptist haven. Anabaptist refugees from various parts of the Holy Roman Empire brought with them distinctive Anabaptist traditions, and Moravia became 'the melting pot of early Anabaptism'.[10] Kuratsuka focuses not so much on the process of synthesis in Moravian Anabaptism as on its results, specifically the child-rearing,

---

[9] C. Arnold Snyder, *Anabaptist History and Theology: An Introduction* (Kitchener, Ont., 1995), pp. 402–4.

[10] Stayer, 'Radical Reformation', p. 261. The most detailed recent study on the Hutterites and their significance within the Anabaptist tradition is Werner Packull's *Hutterite Beginnings: Communitarian Experiments during the Reformation* (Baltimore, MD, 1995).

educational and marriage practices of the Hutterites. These he approaches from the perspective of 'distopian' authors like Huxley and Orwell. This perspective yields somewhat different conclusions than those reached earlier by Ferdinand Seibt. Kuratsuka suggests totalitarian tendencies and features in the Hutterite communitarian experiment.[11]

Another important centre for the interaction of Anabaptist traditions was the free imperial city of Augsburg. Here the famed Martyrs' Synod, a meeting of significant Anabaptist leaders, had convened in the fall of 1527. Augsburg, like Moravia, witnessed the clash of diverging Anabaptist traditions.[12] During 1527 and early 1528 Augsburg became a major Anabaptist centre, but persecution robbed the Augsburg Anabaptists of their leaders and drove the movement out of the city or underground. While historians have long noted the significance of Augsburg for the years 1527–28, subsequent years have received little attention.[13] Packull's essay addresses this lacuna in Augsburg's Anabaptist history in the context of the political, religious milieu of the early 1530s. In the wake of Charles V's abortive attempt during the Imperial Diet of 1530 to suppress Augsburg's Reformation, the Reformed gained the ascendancy over Catholics and Lutherans. In this climate Anabaptist fortunes revived. Pamphlets published in 1532 and 1533 respectively provide evidence of interaction between the Reformed and Anabaptists.

Among Packull's conclusions is the intriguing suggestion that the Anabaptist–Reformed discourse in the 1530s may help to explain some of the more 'moderate' positions taken later by Pilgram Marpeck and his followers who were active in Augsburg from 1544 to 1556. Like the Hutterites, the Marpeck circle was once considered peripheral to the Anabaptist story. It seemed that as an organized group Marpeck's followers did not long survive him. However, in the last half of this century the extent of the writing and publishing activity of the Marpeck circle, and its role in fostering dialogue between Anabaptist groups, has been slowly recovered.[14]

The influence of the Marpeck circle and its place in intra-Anabaptist dialogue is highlighted in the final two essays of Part One. Although focusing primarily on the history of the Swiss Brethren, Arnold Snyder and John Roth indicate the extent of Anabaptist cross-fertilization that

---

[11] Ferdinand Seibt, *Utopica: Modelle totaler Sozialplannung* (Düsseldorf, 1972), pp. 166–82.

[12] Hans Guderian, *Die Täufer in Augsburg: Ihre Geschichte und ihr Erbe* (Pfaffenhofen, 1984), pp. 40–44.

[13] For a recent treatment of Anabaptist fortunes in Augsburg after 1528, see Guderian, pp. 75–111.

[14] The most recent comprehensive study of Marpeck's life and thought is Stephen Boyd's *Pilgram Marpeck: His Life and Social Theology* (Durham, NC, 1992).

occurred even within this more exclusivist branch of the Anabaptist family. Snyder takes up Stayer's treatment of the Swiss Brethren political ethic. In *Anabaptists and the Sword*, Stayer interpreted the Schleitheim Articles of 1527 as establishing a radically apolitical non-resistance position as the norm for Swiss Brethren statements on the sword. Subsequent discussions of this topic by members of the Swiss Brethren, at least until 1560, Stayer's *terminus ad quem*, were considered little more than 'glosses on Schleitheim'.[15] Snyder shifts the focus to the 1570s and 1580s, that is after the Frankenthal Disputation of 1571. In manuscripts circulated among the Swiss Brethren during these decades he finds, if not a partial abandonment of the rigid stance of Schleitheim, at least a willingness to enter into dialogue on the question of the sword. And while the possible influence of the Frankenthal Disputation awaits further examination, Snyder provides evidence that the moderate positions articulated in the Marpeck circle were finding acceptance among the later Swiss Brethren.

John Roth notes a similar process of development by focusing on the hermeneutics of the Swiss Brethren, especially the development of their views on the relationship between the Old and New Testaments. In the past, the early Swiss Brethren have been characterized as New Testament literalists, a characterization Roth does not reject out of hand. He argues, however, that in the course of the second half of the sixteenth century, in the context of disputations with Reformed theologians, the Swiss Brethren were forced to refine and redefine their understanding of the relationship between the testaments. The results, according to Roth, were indicative of dialogue with the legacy left by Marpeck.

The cross-fertilization between Anabaptist groups in the sixteenth century is only one area of study of a larger phenomenon involving the interaction between various Radical Reformation groups. Stayer has consistently treated the Anabaptist tradition in a larger context. His recent reconceptualization of the Radical Reformation for the *Handbook of European History* describes the interaction of two movements: a spiritualist one arising among the Saxon radicals such as Karlstadt and Müntzer and a biblical literalist one associated with the Swiss radicals such as Conrad Grebel, Michael Sattler and Felix Mantz. In a conscious parody of Berndt Moeller's description of Luther's early relationship with Renaissance humanism, Stayer describes the relationship between Saxon Spiritualists and Swiss Anabaptist Biblicists during the early years of the Reformation as a 'constructive misunderstanding'.[16]

---

[15] *Anabaptists and the Sword*, p. 93.
[16] Stayer, 'Radical Reformation,' pp. 254–9. Cf. Bernd Moeller, 'The German Humanists and the Beginnings of the Reformation', in H.C. Erik Middlefort and Mark U.

The essay by Hans-Jürgen Goertz in Part Two revisits the constructive misunderstanding by re-examining two crucial documents: two letters written by the Grebel group in Zurich to Thomas Müntzer in September 1524. As Goertz indicates, traditionally these letters have been treated from two diametrically opposed perspectives. Either they have been read as evidence of dependence – i.e. that Müntzer laid the groundwork for the proto-Anabaptist movement in Zurich – or as a mistaken enterprise foredoomed to failure because it attempted to span the unbridgeable chasm between Müntzer and the Swiss Brethren. Stressing the desire for dialogue and the commonalities between the Zurich radicals and Müntzer, Goertz prefers instead to treat these letters as an attempt at 'fraternal conversation', aimed at clarifying points of agreement and resolving points of disagreement, between two groups of individuals pushed to the periphery by magisterial Reformers.

The other essay concerned with dialogue between Anabaptists and other representatives of the Radical Reformation is that by Geoffrey Dipple. But his treatment of Sebastian Franck and the Anabaptist Kingdom in Münster seems in some ways the reverse of Goertz's investigation. Instead of a conversation between dialogue partners, we have here the question of the influence of Franck, a quietistic and scholarly spiritualist as well as critic of the magisterial Reformation, on the apocalyptical and violent 'bastard line' of Melchiorite Anabaptism. The focus of the essay is on Franck's possible influence on Münster's chief idealogue, Bernhard Rothmann. Historians of Anabaptist Münster, Stayer among them, have previously noted the importance of Franck for Rothmann's justification of the practice of community of goods. Dipple focuses instead on the development of Rothmann's political ethic, taking as his point of departure Stayer's somewhat cryptic suggestion that Franck's ' ... anti-authoritarian reflections on sacred and profane history conveyed among northerners the radicalism of the south German Reformation'.[17]

In his characterization of the Radical Reformation, Stayer has taken a page from Hans-Jürgen Goertz and Adolf Laube, to argue that the Reformation involved not so much a process of radicalization from an initial, moderate Lutheran reform programme, but a process of moderating the initial, radical impetus by magisterial Reformers.[18] The relationship between the magisterial Reformation and the Radical is

Edwards, Jr (eds and trans.), *Imperial Cities and the Reformation: Three Essays* (Durham, NC, 1982), pp. 19–38.

[17] Stayer, 'Christianity in One City: Anabaptist Münster, 1534–35', in Hans Hillerbrand (ed.), *Radical Tendencies in the Reformation: Divergent Perspectives* (Kirksville, MO, 1988), p. 127; *Anabaptist Community of Goods*, p. 132.

[18] Stayer, 'Radical Reformation', p. 250.

probed by William McNiel's examination of the thought of Luther's erstwhile colleague at Wittenberg, and later radical opponent, Andreas Bodenstein von Karlstadt. Karlstadt's career may be characterized, to adopt and adapt Stayer's summary of Wilhelm Reublin's activity, as a 'picaresque journey through the early Reformation'. A Scotist theologian and doctor of both laws, Karlstadt joined Luther's reform movement in Wittenberg then severed his academic ties to become 'brother Andreas' in Orlamünde and, according to Luther, cleaned his pigsty in bare feet, only to return eventually to the ivory tower in Basel. McNiel's paper deals not so much with the changes in Karlstadt's theology as with continuity in his thought. Behind Karlstadt's theological development, he sees a consistent humanist methodology. McNiel's conclusions require us to rethink how we treat Karlstadt's spiritualism and supposed anti-intellectualism and in what sense Karlstadt was radical.

The final essay in Part Two tests the boundaries between the persecution of heretics and the phenomenon of the witch craze. Noting the temporal convergence of heresy and witch persecutions in the sixteenth century, Gary Waite asks the intriguing question: did contemporaries see possible connections between Anabaptist heresy and witchcraft? Noting that the same courts tried cases of heresy and of witchcraft, often one after the other, and that in some cases similar inquisitorial procedures were applied to both witches and Anabaptists, he leaves us with the tantalizing possibility that Anabaptist heresy was viewed as part of the same cosmic demonic threat that stoked the fires of the witch-hunts.

Essays in the final section concentrate on the paradigmatic assumptions that underlie the interpretation of the history of Anabaptism and the Radical Reformation. Is it possible to apply lessons learned in the study of the sixteenth-century radicals to the histories of other marginalized religious groups? The study of Anabaptism and other Reformation radicals has been aided by the sociological-typological interpretive categories developed by Max Weber and Ernst Troeltsch. Despite recent challenges to their continued heuristic value, the typologies of the 'church', 'sect' and 'spiritualist' continue to inform comparative studies. In particular, Troeltsch's characterization of Anabaptism as a form of Protestant sectarianism has found a sympathetic response among Mennonite historians, and subsequently has formed the basis for a significant historiographical tradition. Seen as an antidote to Luther's, Melanchthon's and ultimately Karl Koll's denigration of all Anabaptists as *Schwärmer* (religious fanatics) and descendants of Thomas Müntzer, Troeltsch's categories provide a less prejudicial criteria for distinguishing between Reformation radicals. Moreover, Troeltsch's sympathetic evaluation of the sectarian contribution to the modern Western liberal-democratic tradition endeared him to historians in the non-conformist, free-church tradition. Sonia Riddoch revisits Troeltsch's interpretation and evaluation of sixteenth-century Anabaptism and concludes that Troeltsch's views changed drastically from his early glowing statements in 1906 to his critical reflections six years later in *The Social Teachings of the Christian Churches and Groups*. Riddoch concludes that Troeltsch was not the champion of Protestant sectarianism assumed in some scholarship.

The final two papers in Part Three focus more directly on the application of Weberian and Troeltschian categories to the histories of religious groups. Michael Driedger attempts what must be the first comparative study of the Jewish and Anabaptist experience in early modern Europe. He finds one of the most insightful general interpretations of Anabaptist histories in Jonathan Israel's *European Jewry in the Age of Mercantilism*. While acknowledging obvious and significant differences between the histories of Jews and Anabaptists in early modern Europe, Driedger argues that the application of the Weberian typology has too often overemphasized these differences. Instead Driedger points to fascinating parallels in the sixteenth-, seventeenth- and eighteenth-century experiences of European Jews and Mennonites. Recognition of these parallels allows us to better contextualize the experiences of early modern Mennonites and to escape the ghettoization which threatens history writing on Anabaptism with its tendency to concentrate on its 'vertical traditions' of historical descent.

Clyde Forsberg's essay provides an interesting complement to Driedger's comparative study by examining parallels between the history of Anabaptism and that of North American Mormons. Forsberg suggests that previous attempts to understand apparent parallels between these two traditions have been hamstrung by the adherence to normative definitions of early Anabaptism and Mormonism. However, if one is willing to jettison these normative definitions, as revisionist historians of Anabaptism like Stayer have, the parallels between the two movements come more clearly into focus. Furthermore, an awareness of these parallels allows us to understand relations between Mormons and the heirs of the Anabaptist tradition on the American frontier in the nineteenth century.

PART ONE
Polygenesis and beyond?
New research into Anabaptism

CHAPTER ONE

The decline of Hutterite community of goods

Taira Kuratsuka,
translated by James M. Stayer*

As the Hutterites first enjoyed peace and prosperity under the policy of tolerance of the Moravian Hussite nobility, and as their 20 000 members lived in well-functioning order, the author of a chronicle of 1569 proudly declared:

> Think of the ingenious works of a clock, where one piece helps another to make it go, so that it serves its purpose. Or think of the bees, those useful little insects working together in their hive, some making wax, some honey, some fetching water, until their noble work of making sweet honey is done, not only for their own needs but enough to share with man. That is how it was among the brothers. So there has to be an order in all areas, for the matters of life can be properly maintained and furthered only where order reigns – even more so in the house of God, whose Master Builder and Establisher is the Lord himself.[1]

As can be seen here, Hutterite community of goods had absorbed a very strong utopianism. Even today we are deeply moved by the heroic martyrdom suffered by many Hutterites during prolonged fearsome persecutions, as well as their unbending religious conviction by means of which they were able to realize a utopian community in Moravia. However, the glittering surface of the utopia was always unavoidably accompanied by the dark counter-utopia which underlaid it. In order that the utopia might function as a perfect system the leaders had to rob the members, who worked as components of the system, not only of their freedom but also of their individuality and turn them, in a manner of speaking, into tin soldiers – otherwise the working of the utopia would be severely disturbed by irregular and unplanned behaviour of the members. Hence Josef Beck observed, 'The strict church discipline ... extended to the external appearance and activity of the community.

---

* Notes added by Werner O. Packull.
[1] A.J.F. Zieglschmid, *Die älteste Chronik der Hutterischen Brüder. (Ein Sprachdenkmal aus frühneuhochdeutscher Zeit)* (Ithaca, NY, 1946), p. 435.

... Everything, even greeting and kissing, was brought by them into the sphere of "public order" and regulated by ordinances.'[2] The elder, Andreas Ehrenpreis, who struggled in the seventeenth century to resurrect the disintegrating Hutterite community, preached to the faithful: '[The self] must be broken if we are to belong to the community of the Supper and to serve in communal work. Furthermore, the grain had to be brought together into one flour and one loaf. Not one grain could preserve itself as it was or keep what it had.'[3]

Although the Hutterites to a high degree were robbed of self-consciousness and given in its place the common we-consciousness of the utopia, these 'tin soldiers' were naturally human beings nonetheless. Again and again they weakened this utopia in order to fulfil the minimum of their human desires.

We must ask ourselves how the children were brought up in this community of goods, how they endured the upbringing and, finally, what kind of people they became. As soon as the communal school system began, it faced two substantial problems: the first was a terrifyingly high child mortality; the second was the cruel use of the cane on the children for discipline and the maintenance of good order in doing God's work.

The mortality rate for children was very high everywhere in the middle ages but in the Hutterite community it was extremely high. Naturally no statistics are available on this subject but a great many who left the community testified to the sad stories of their families: 'When she [a woman named Pirchner] came to Moravia they took her children and put them in school. In the course of six or seven weeks her four children died.'[4] 'Hans Braun came to Moravia with his wife and four children; three of the children died, of whom one was living apart from the parents in the community school.'[5] The reason for this was that many children were crammed together into a big room, indeed 'two or three, according to their size, sleep together'.[6] In this way they were very easily infected by various communicable diseases. It can be said with certainty that the children would not have been infected with these diseases had they been cared for by their families, particularly by their mothers. In 1556 leading Lutheran theologians composed a long document, recommending to the Count of the Palatinate severe

---

[2] Joseph Beck (ed.), *Die Geschichtsbücher der Wiedertäufer in Oesterreich-Ungarn* (Nieuwkoop [1883], 1967), p. xv.

[3] Andreas Ehrenpreis and Claus Felbinger, *Brotherly Community. The Highest Command of Love*, intro. by Robert Friedmann (Rifton, NY, 1979), p. 23.

[4] *TQ Osterreich*, III, p. 520.

[5] *TQ Württemberg*, p. 186.

[6] Ibid., p. 1106.

punishment for unrepentant Anabaptists: 'Process for dealing with the Anabaptists, proposed by some scholars assembled at Worms'.[7] In this document they levelled severe charges at the Hutterites on account of the death of numerous children.

> We also know that things are badly awry with the community in Moravia. It is particularly terrible that the young children are taken away from the parents in order to educate them in the same way under common supervision. And many children are killed by hunger and other kinds of neglect. To summarize, such a devilish communion is an impossible thing contrary to nature and law.[8]

In 1558 the Hutterite chief elder, Peter Walpot, and his councillors rebutted the charges in 'A booklet against the Process ... ',[9] but the charge about the death of Hutterite children was rebutted without substantive proof. Probably they wanted to avoid all further controversy over this sore point.

For ten years thereafter it became a pressing necessity for the Hutterite elders to take the required measures against the various communicable diseases. Many parents came to the schools in great anxiety to submit complaints about the health of their children. In a speech to the schoolmasters, dated 1568, Walpot said: 'It has often been the case that parents come to us and say "My brethren, I have committed myself and my children to the Lord and to the school", and then complain that one of the children has gotten impetigo in the school or some other ailment, be it on the eyes or the hands or the feet.'

When dealing with people whose children were sick or had died, the elders' words of consolation and their sermons about *Gelassenheit*, or Christian 'yieldedness', were inadequate in the face of parental sorrow and anger. If a panic broke out due to the death of a great number of children, many parents would rush to the schools to remove their children despite the vehement resistance of the elders. In this way the family, the suspected 'root of egoism', would reassert itself and the community of goods would be extinguished. Presumably on the basis of such considerations, the leaders concerned themselves with the deplorable situation of many children and considered what might be done.

Hence presiding elder Walpot published the school ordinance of 1568 accompanied by a long speech. Its primary content was the health care of the children, particularly preventive measures against communicable diseases and provisions for the care of the sick:

---

[7] Ibid., pp. 161 ff.

[8] Ibid., p. 166.

[9] Wilhelm Wiswedel, 'The Anabaptists Answer Melanchthon', with an additional note by Robert Friedmann, *MQR*, 29 (1955), pp. 212 ff.

> And when the children are brought to the school they should be carefully examined and if any one is found to have a contagious disease such as scurvy or the French disease [syphilis?] or paralysis, he shall be instantly separated from the rest in sleeping, in eating and in drinking, in washing, and everything. Also special brushes and combs shall be used for those having scalp eruptions. Those who have scabies shall be put together and not kept with those who are clean; likewise those who have scalp diseases.[10]

Other regulations of particular interest were that in arranging the beds the sisters should take care that 'the children who are clean are kept together and those who are not clean are kept together'.[11] Also the school mothers were instructed that 'when they reach into a sore mouth with the fingers, they shall be careful that they do not at once with unwashed fingers reach into a healthy mouth and thereby contaminate it too, but shall always beforehand cleanse the fingers with a clean cloth and water before they examine others'.[12] This ordinance also established various regulations for child care: 'The bed clothing shall be kept clean and shall be regularly changed, and when the little children get up in the morning, a sister, with two or three girls, must always be at hand on the stairway to see that no one falls'.[13] 'Also, together with the sisters [the schoolmaster] must pay attention to the children's shoes so that they do not have such hard shoes that make the feet sore.'[14] 'You should not bathe the children every fortnight, for this is not necessary, but bathe them once in four weeks and wash them every fortnight, unless there is a special reason or on account of scalp disorders'.[15] Obviously with such measures the Hutterites were not able to prevent various communicable diseases. Nevertheless, in relation to the primitive state of sixteenth-century medicine, their efforts were relatively progressive. Initially, however, their utopian communal way of life was the cause of the tragic deaths of many small children.

In the sixteenth century children were often caned by teachers in Latin schools and by their own fathers, but mother's love kept children from falling into despair. In the Hutterite communities, however, the mother was absent from the time the child was two; the children were abandoned to loneliness. There were only school mothers, sisters,

---

[10] 'Der Rede, so der Brueder Peter Walpot sampt anderen, mit den Schüelmaistern gethan: Anno 1568, Nemschitz' in *Selected Hutterian Documents in Translation*, J. Hostetler (ed.), vol. 1, (Philadelphia, PA, 1975), p. 22.

[11] Ibid., p. 10.

[12] Ibid., p. 24.

[13] Ibid., p. 22.

[14] Ibid., p. 8.

[15] Ibid., p. 12.

child-care maids, female custodians and so on, who served as supervisors of approximately one hundred children. True, it was preached to them that they should love the children as if they were their own. But the leadership, it seems, always directed the overwhelming majority of the members of the community to material production, hence there were insufficient personnel to care for the large number of children throughout the whole day and night. Therefore in good times and bad they had to discharge their responsibilities very mechanically, and because of the heavy burden of work they often erupted into anger. Walpot said to the schoolmasters:

> The schoolmaster is to be present in the school room not only for the children's sake, but also in order to give aid and advice to the sisters, for they need your oversight just as much as the children – since women are women and the weaker vessel – lest they in their annoyance and complaints go about among the children with canes as one does among cattle, when the flesh gets the upper hand and quickly becomes angry, as we have ourselves experienced.[16]

Often the children were treated in a similar way to that experienced by Japanese soldiers in the last phases of the Second World War:

> It has also occasionally been observed and experienced in the schools that a whole row or group of children among whom some talking has been heard have been taken out and all of them, the guilty and the innocent, punished one by one with the cane. This shall not be done any longer.[17]

The following remark shows that the children rebelled against abuses of caning: 'The children shall be made and accustomed not to fight against the cane but present themselves willingly; then one can always deal with them more gently than if they resist; resistance can not and shall not be tolerated'.[18]

How should the personnel cope with so many children, presumably educated in a large group rather than distributed into classes? They were virtually forced to use canes and blows. When we read supplementary paragraphs to the school ordinances added by Hans Kräl, the next presiding elder in 1578, it is clear that in the intervening ten years the cane and other types of physical discipline were even more misused:

> If a brother or sister would be rough, hasty or angry in disciplining the larger and smaller children, by striking and pushing; hitting the head, the stomach or the mouth – or attempting to hold shut someone's mouth; or hitting the person in bed with a pillow or

---

[16] Ibid., p. 6.
[17] Ibid., p. 32.
[18] Ibid., p. 16.

covers: such measures shall absolutely not be permitted to occur. The nurse likewise shall not begin at once to strike a child if it begins to cry at night, but shall diligently use other methods to quiet it.[19]

The decline of work morale among school personnel could no longer be concealed.

No one shall unwilling, with complaint or impatience, serve the needy ones of the Lord at this place, for there would be no blessing in such work and the children would in consequence have to pay for it with violence and rudeness in discipline. For where good will is lacking, there are improper words: 'You lousy children', etc., 'one must be continually occupied with you, one cannot do anything for himself', so that all who hear it would be grieved.[20]

In 1588 the presiding elder of the day, Claus Braidl, expanded the school regulations still further. Here one finds a shadowy side of communal life. For example: 'Anyone who brings wine to his children in school shall be reported ... . If anyone brings many gifts for his children, they shall also be shared with the needy and the orphans'.[21] But where, and from whom, did these parents get the wine and their many gifts? This question is also pertinent to another sentence: 'No distinction shall be made in food out of partiality or respect of person'.[22] One of the anthropological constants is that many sycophants of both sexes gather around every leader. In the Hutterite community the elders and their wives enjoyed various privileges. Those who flattered them got wine and other foods from the steward or his assistants and brought it to their children – secretly in the early days, and quite openly toward the end of the 'Golden Age' of the Hutterites. Similarly, people began to flatter the elders and their assistants openly in the schools, by delivering culinary delicacies particularly to the children of these leaders. Should we take the supplementary regulations of the presiding elder, quoted above, to be an expression of a certain degree of self-criticism?

Christoph Fischer, who as a Jesuit was certainly guilty of extreme partisan prejudice against the Hutterites, was nevertheless right to reproach them for the weaknesses of their school system: 'Only the perverted Anabaptists act against nature'.[23] Such a system could probably not survive very long. From Braidl's supplementary paragraphs to

---

[19] Ibid., p. 20.

[20] Ibid., p. 30.

[21] Ibid., p. 34.

[22] Ibid., p. 36.

[23] Christopher Andreas Fischer, *Vierundfunfftzig Erhebliche Ursachen/Warumb die Widertauffer nicht sein im Land zu Leyden* (Ingolstadt, 1607), p. 53.

the school ordinance, dated 9 January 1596 at Neumühl, one could get the impression that the schools threatened the Hutterites' very existence, although certainly the situation varied from school to school. The presiding elder wrote that 'charges have been raised that the children are allowed to be completely disorderly and that in some localities very poor school discipline is maintained'.[24] For example: 'that [the children] scatter, run hither and yon, or that one of them has a way of stealing out of school away from the other children'.[25] Hence the school personnel would organize many children into a regimented group and march them about in order to prevent the children fleeing. Fischer depicted this mockingly 'the children are chased up a small hill or massed by the gate, no differently than geese or cattle (except that the animals are freer)'.[26] Many parents began to take their children out of the school buildings and to give them so much food and drink 'that they passed it on to others above or below them'. The school personnel, too, was corrupted so that they would 'send the children far across the fields to their parents. They are suspected of doing this not without purpose, but when they can in some way manage to benefit from it'.[27] Likewise money made its appearance: 'Money received as gifts in the school shall be turned over to the steward'.[28] Who gave whom money, and for what purpose? The next sentence answered this question: 'Some children are secretly taken out of the school without permission, so that at times there are few children in the school (just the orphans and those without relatives)'. Many schools were closed, but at the same time we are presented with pleasant vignettes: 'Those who remove their children from school want to lay them down (in their own beds) and then get up and travel around with them among the people ... '.[29]

Ultimately the elders yielded to the strong tie between parents and children. In 1612 all elders agreed that 'the children should go home to their parents every four weeks'. In the Thirty Years War that began six years later, when almost all Hutterite settlements in Moravia were plundered and burned, virtually all the schools disappeared, since in the sources nothing more can be found about them.

Nevertheless, I suspect that the very reason for the existence of the schools came to be doubted by many Hutterites. In one source we find these statements: 'We see how many ill-bred children we get from our

---

[24] 'Der Rede Walpot', p. 36.
[25] Ibid., p. 38.
[26] Fischer, *Erhebliche Ursachen*, p. 54.
[27] 'Der Rede Walpot', p. 44.
[28] Ibid., p. 46.
[29] Ibid., p. 44.

schools, who are very difficult people to cope with in the community, also go astray in the world. They become evil people, and some of them come to a disgraceful end. Out of humiliation we do not speak of this to anyone'. 'Some of the children in the schools are so badly behaved that they are not allowed into the schools, and they are constantly running about and pestering their parents'.[30]

From this time on the Hutterite community began a very rapid decline. The process was accelerated by the Thirty Years War, in which virtually all the settlements were completely destroyed by armies on both sides – the buildings burned and plundered and many people assaulted or killed. The Austrian ruler robbed them through an intrigue of a buried treasure of 300 000 florins which they had diligently accumulated over a long period of time. All of this was very demoralizing but the loosening of interior discipline also contributed to the decline. In 1643 the presiding elder Andreas Ehrenpreis decreed that the Hutterite marriage system be enforced once again. He had become aware that many young men and women among the Hutterites were no longer tolerating the genuine Hutterite marriage system, which was based upon the arbitrary decision of the community elders. They were now being brought together with a love partner by a matchmaker. The matchmakers very skilfully manipulated Hutterite marriage assemblies, so that the elders, who did not know what was going on, ended up marrying the love-pairs that the matchmakers had brought together.

The Hutterite marriage system, which joined in marriage a widower and a young woman just past puberty, or a young man and a widow, or people who lived in settlements quite distant from one another, was probably designed with the intent that marital love should not surpass love of the community.[31] But young people, particularly young women, were dissatisfied with this system and eventually undermined it. They had probably witnessed heartfelt family love between parents and children (the sort of thing from which the school system was supposed to emancipate them), and found it very offensive when these families were sharply criticized and punished. Well before 1643 'illegal' marriages spread in the Hutterite community: 'Afterward in the marriage the elders were only deferred to for the purpose of confirming and promoting such disorderly coupling'.[32] Had freedom of choosing marriage partners and parents living together with their children been officially

---

[30] Karl and Franziska Peter (eds), *Der Gemain Ordnungen (1651–1878). Järliche Warnung an die vertrauten Brüder* (1980), pp. 59–60.

[31] Frantisek Hruby, 'Die Wiedertäufer in Mähren', IV, *ARG*, 32 (1935), pp. 1–40, 8.

[32] A.J.F. Zieglschmid (ed.), *Das Klein-Geschichtsbuch der Hutterischen Brüder* (Ithaca, NY, 1947), p. 217.

sanctioned, as is the case with Hutterites now, community of goods need not have fallen into decline.

Jacob Hutter and Peter Riedemann, among other major Hutterite leaders, on the basis of their theology viewed these pleasant human needs as egoism or selfishness, and wanted to replace them by the 'we-consciousness' that was forcibly created by collectivization. But the 'we-consciousness' formed in this way generally transformed itself immediately into an inhumane system of extremely petty rules, which eventually enslaved peole. Without breaking these rules, people could not fulfil their basic human needs. People who had been deprived of independent thought in the name of the community (which claimed to do what it did in the name of God), when they got into difficulty forgot their moral principles, stole the goods of the community one by one and sold them on the market. In sum, when all natural needs are labelled as selfishness and are suppressed or eliminated, sooner or later human beings rebel in order to survive, rob the community and totally destroy their system. We have witnessed such a phenomenon in our time, in the collapse of the communist regimes. This once happened in the case of Hutterite community of goods: 'In many ways community property was attacked, pilfered and diminished, so that many people entirely abandoned their consciences with respect to anything they had in their hands, be it steel, iron, leather, cloth, linen, hemp, wool, anything at all that the community had'.[33]

---

[33] Ibid., p. 521.

Appendix

There are two categories of utopia: the statist and the anarchical. The statist utopia invariably has two sides, the glittering surface and the dark underside. Seen from above, the statist utopia appears very beautiful and harmonious. But from below it is inhuman, like an army or a perfect, highly developed machine. This is the category to which Hutterite community of goods belongs. It is constructed from the standpoint of God in heaven by self-styled messengers of God and handed down from above to their faithful followers.

In contrast to the statist utopia, the anarchist or anarchical utopia in principle is without organization and system. In it there is only the private sphere, no *res publica*. This anarchical situation is necessarily impermanent. In it there is a war of all against all, followed by a dictatorship. From the time of Plato and Thomas More utopias have always been conceived and constructed from the standpoint of the ruler. But since the end of the nineteenth century we have begun to look at the utopian system from the inside or from below. This has substantially widened our point of view. In this respect we owe much to Zamyatin, Huxley and Orwell.

CHAPTER TWO

A Reformed–Anabaptist dialogue in Augsburg during the early 1530s

Werner O. Packull

On Sunday 5 March 1531 two Anabaptists, Hans Kentner and Jos Riemer, took the pulpit at the Preacher's Hall [*Predigthaus*] of St Ulrich in Augsburg, criticized the lack of change brought about by evangelical preaching, and made the case for Anabaptist beliefs and practices.[1] The action, reminiscent of sermon disruptions during the early years of the Reformation,[2] had been premeditated. Brothers and sisters had been invited to join Kentner and Riemer at St Ulrich. Evidently they expected a sympathetic reception from the audience.

The purpose of this chapter is twofold: first, to examine the circumstances that may have prompted the action of 5 March 1531; second, to explore the appearance of two pamphlets in its wake. The pamphlet, taking the Anabaptist point of view, carries the title *New Dialogue/ Question and Answer between a Preacher and a Baptist/Concerning Preaching/the Eucharist/ Baptism and Proper Christian Community/ Delightful to Read* (hereafter *New Dialogue*).[3] The *New Dialogue* appeared in 1532[4] and solicited a response of sorts from Wolfgang Musculus in a pamphlet entitled *A Peaceful and Christian Dialogue Between an Evangelical and an Anabaptist Concerning the Swearing of the Oath*

---

[1] Friedwart Uhland, 'Täufertum und Obrigkeit in Augsburg im 16. Jahrhundert' (PhD diss., Eberhard-Karls University, Tübingen, 1972), pp. 229–30.

[2] The action is reminiscent of the 'Predigtstörungen' during the early years of the Reformation. Heinold Fast, 'Reformation durch Provokation: Predigtstörung in den ersten Jahren der Reformation in der Schweiz', in Hans-Jürgen Goertz (ed.), *Umstrittenes Täufertum 1525–1975: Neue Forschungen* (Göttingen, 1975), pp. 79–110.

[3] *Ein new gesprech/frag unnd antwort zwischen ainem Predicanten und ainem Teuffer/ von wegen dess predigen/ Abendmals/ Tauffs und recht Christlicher gmain/ hübsch zulesen.* The pamphlet is found bound into a collective volume [*Sammelband*] of archival documents at the Stadtarchiv of Ulm. The Sammelband carries the signature vol. A 1208/I; the pamphlet is found on ff. 690–96. Prof. Dr Specker, Director of the Stadtarchiv of Ulm, graciously provided me with a photocopy and granted permission for its translation.

[4] I have dealt with the print history of the pamphlet in the introduction to a translation which appears in a collection of primary material from Marpeck's circle edited by Arnold Snyder. See *Later Writings of Pilgram Marpeck and his Circle*, vol. I: *Anabaptist Texts in Translation* (Kitchener, Ont., 1999).

(hereafter *Peaceful Dialogue*).[5] It is indicative of the religious milieu at the time that both pamphlets were composed in the genre of dialogue. Together they provide a valuable source of information about Reformed–Anabaptist interaction in Augsburg during the early 1530s, a period that has remained a lacuna in the history of Augsburg's Anabaptism. I begin with a brief review of Anabaptist fortunes in Augsburg up to the incident of 5 March 1531.

In my dissertation, supervised by James Stayer more than twenty-five years ago, I argued that Augsburg during 1527 and early 1528 was without question a major Anabaptist centre.[6] Over one thousand persons were allegedly implicated in the 'heresy'.[7] A congregation led by Sigmund Salminger and his assistant, Jacob Dachser, formed in early 1527. In the autumn of that year numerous Anabaptist leaders congregated in Augsburg for the so-called 'Martyrs' Synod'. A good number of these leaders had been won to Anabaptism by Hans Hut, whose controversial end-time predictions met with criticism at the Synod but nevertheless captured the imagination of a section of Augsburg's population. The arrests of the local leaders, Hut's death in prison, the failure of the apocalyptic forecast for the spring of 1528 and the draconian measures taken by the authorities decimated the budding movement. Hans Leupold, who had assumed the leadership after Salminger's and Dachser's imprisonment, was executed on 25 April 1528.[8] Many Anabaptists fled or were expelled from the city. By August 1528 Philip Plener, who had arrived from the Rhineland and taken lodging with Leupold's widow, declared a moratorium on further meetings in Augsburg's territory, ostensibly because dwindling attendance no longer warranted the residency of an Anabaptist *Vorsteher*.[9] Philip subsequently gathered a contingent of Swabians and Rhinelanders and settled in Moravia, but a small flock must have survived in Augsburg's territory. In 1529 or 1530 Hans Kentner, one of Philip's converts, assumed its leadership.[10] By February

[5] *Ain frydsams unnd Christlichs Gesprech ains Evangelischen/ auff ainer/ und ain Widerteufer/ auf der andern seyten/ so sy des Aydschwurs halben mit ainander thund* (Augsburg: Philip Ulhart d.A, 1533). It carries the date 28 July 1533 but circulated first in manuscript form. Wolfgang Musculus claimed friends urged him to have it printed. I used the copy in the microfiche collection IDC (KME 125/1).

[6] My dissertation was published as *Mysticism and the Early South German-Austrian Anabaptist Movement, 1525–1531* (Scottdale, PA, 1977).

[7] Karl Wolfart, *Die Augsburger Reformation in den Jahren 1533/34* (new edition: Aalen, 1972), p. 5.

[8] Packull, *Mysticism and the Anabaptist Movement*, pp. 93–128.

[9] Werner O. Packull, *Hutterite Beginnings. Communitarian Experiments during the Reformation* (Baltimore, MD, 1995), pp. 81–2.

[10] Kentner from Haldenwang in the Allgäu had been baptized by Philip in the spring

of 1531 attendance at weekly meetings held in the open outside Augsburg had swollen to two hundred. This renewed and growing interest in Anabaptism must have been one of the reasons why Kentner and Riemer moved their meeting for Sunday, 5 March 1531 inside the city walls to the Preacher's Hall at St Ulrich. A curious crowd gathered,[11] prompting the arrest of Kentner and the Anabaptists. The subsequent investigation by the authorities revealed that Kentner had established a small congregation in nearby Täferdingen and cultivated contacts with Anabaptists and sympathizers in Augsburg.

What then did Kentner hope to achieve by his action in March of 1531? He explained to his interrogators that he had been prompted by 'love of God and neighbour'. The brothers and sisters had gone public because they no longer wanted to spread the truth clandestinely as corner preachers [*Winkelprediger*]. To fully appreciate this statement it must be recalled that in 1527 Balthasar Hubmaier accused Hans Hut of teaching that 'the Gospel should not be preached in churches but secretly and clandestinely in houses'. The opinion that church buildings were 'temples of idols', spiritual 'murderers' dens' frequented by 'whores and pimps', was widespread among Anabaptists.[12] Why then did Kentner lead his flock to St Ulrich? The answer may lie in the religious changes and the religious climate that pervaded Augsburg in 1531.

Less than a year earlier, during the meeting of the Imperial Diet in June 1530, Emperor Charles V had suspended all evangelical services in Augsburg. Under pressure from the Emperor's party Augsburg's council had sent its evangelical clergy on leave.[13] Only after the Emperor's departure (23 November 1530) did evangelical fortunes revive. In January 1531 eight councillors of the old faith lost their seats. The 'Reformed' gained ascendancy among the pastors and preachers; Lutherans found themselves in a minority. Among the newly appointed clergy were four arrivals from Strasbourg: Wolfgang Musculus became pastor [*Pfarrer*] at the Church of the Holy Cross; Bonifacius Wolfhart preacher [*Predikant*]

---

of 1529 near Mindelheim, between Kaufbeuren and Kempten. He is described as a glass maker and was, no doubt, identical with the Philipite leader, Hans Gentner, who later joined the Hutterites. Riemer was a stone mason from Hesse, who had been resident in Augsburg since 1529. F. Roth, *Augsburger Reformationsgeschichte*, vol. II, (2nd edn, Munich, 1901) pp. 400–401; Uhland, 'Täufertum und Obrigkeit', pp. 229–30. Packull, *Hutterite Beginnings*, pp. 285–7, 348.

[11] Hans Guderian writes of a regular *Volksauflauf. Die Täufer in Augsburg. Ihre Geschichte und ihr Erbe* (Pfaffenhofen, 1984), pp. 79–80.

[12] Packull, *Hutterite Beginnings*, pp. 58, 173.

[13] Wolfart, *Augsburger Reformation*, p. 14; Stephen Boyd, *Pilgram Marpeck. His Life and Social Theology* (Durham, NC, 1992), p. 128; Guderian, *Die Täufer in Augsburg*, pp. 72, 88.

at St Ann, later at St Moritz; Dr Sebastian Meyer was appointed to St Georg[14] and Hans Heinrich became preacher at St Ulrich.[15] Musculus had served Martin Bucer as secretary and Matthias Zell as assistant. Representing a Bucerian orientation, he became the most influential theologian in Augsburg during this period.[16] His colleague, Wolfhart, has been described as a Zwinglian with Schwenckfeldian sympathies.[17]

The arrival of the Strasbourgers decidedly tilted the religious ethos in a Reformed–Zwinglian direction. As the controversy over the meaning of the Lord's Supper heated up, Augsburg's council sided with the Reformed–Zwinglians. Lutherans were forbidden to celebrate the eucharist at St Ann, where in 1524 Urbanus Rhegius for the first time administered the elements to the laity in both kinds. Eventually the Lutheran clergy was muzzled or driven from their posts altogether. Wolfhart's inaugural sermons at St Ann, focused as they were on the sacraments, did their part in turning opinion against the Lutherans. He allegedly emphasized the subjective inner to such an extent 'that many Anabaptists ... reconciled with the Augsburg church'![18] Not surprisingly, Lutherans considered Wolfhart a proto-Schwenckfeldian and friend of the Anabaptists.[19]

---

[14] Dr Sebastian Meyer, a former Franciscan, was driven out of Bern in 1524 and became preacher in Schaffhausen. He was present when Sebastian Hofmeister, another former Franciscan, met with Grebel, Reublin and Brötli. Meyer requested that Vadian send him the scriptural references used by the Anabaptists to argue for adult baptism. Hofmeister was subsequently banned from Schaffhausen because he rejected pedobaptism. He died in 1533. Meyer went to Basel, then Strasbourg and in early 1531 to Augsburg where he became a close ally of Musculus. *TQ Elsaß* II, p. 364 n. 2; *TQ Elsaß*, III, p. 495; *TQ Ostschweiz*, p. 17 n. 1, #16. I thank Prof. James Stayer for drawing this information to my attention. James M. Stayer, 'Reublin and Brötli: The Revolutionary Beginnings of Swiss Anabaptism', in Marc Lienhard (ed.), *The Origins and Characteristics of Anabaptism* (The Hague, 1977), pp. 83 ff, esp. 91, 98. Boyd was incorrect when he writes that these Protestant preachers were called in December 1531. *Marpeck*, p. 128.

[15] Uhland, 'Täufertum und Obrigkeit', p. 243. Heinrich was theologically closest to Wolfhart; he was considered by K. Wolfart to be 'von geringer Bedeutung'. *Augsburger Reformation*, p. 20.

[16] Musculus remained pastor at Holy Cross from 1531 to 1548. 'Musculus', in *The Oxford Encyclopedia of the Reformation* (Oxford and New York, 1996), vol. III, pp. 103–104. Wolfart, *Augsburger Reformation*, pp. 16, 20–21.

[17] Wolfhart's closest ally was Michael Keller, described as a fanatical Zwinglian. Wolfhart died in May 1543. K. Wolfart, *Augsburger Reformation*, p. 16.

[18] Emmet McLaughlin, *Caspar Schwenckfeld. Reluctant Radical. His Life to 1540* (New Haven, CT, 1986), p. 166 n. 25, pp. 168–70.

[19] James Thomas Ford of the University of Wisconsin at Madison described Wolfhart's views on the Lord's Supper as primarily that of a 'communal meal' instituted to commemorate Christ's love and fraternal love for each other. 'Augusta nondum est pura: The Eucharist Controversy in Augsburg', paper read at the Sixteenth Century Studies Conference, Toronto, October 1998. I thank the author for making a copy available to me.

Against the above background Kentner's action of March 1531 seems less fantastic. Given the religious climate in Augsburg and rising interest in Anabaptism, open debate or dialogue with the Reformed clergy must have seemed desirable and possible.[20] The city's councillors thought otherwise. Conversations between the Reformed and Anabaptists were relegated to prison cells. The Council entrusted Wolfhart and Musculus with the prison ministry and the ensuing discussions led to an agreement of sorts. Kentner and the majority arrested with him recanted.[21] In the wake of these developments Dachser and Gross, imprisoned for over three years, made their peace with Augsburg's clergy. Within a year Dachser was given a position at St Ulrich[22] and in 1534 was elected pastor to St Stephen in the weavers' district, where sympathy for Anabaptists had been strong.[23]

Not every one arrested in the aftermath of 5 March recanted. Those who refused were expelled. Among them was Bartholome Sixt, whose subsequent fate may be considered paradigmatic of Augsburg's Anabaptists during the early 1530s. Upon his expulsion Bartholome made his way to the community of Gabrielites at Rossitz in Moravia. Here a letter from Wolfgang Musculus was read to him in which Musculus chided him among other things for abandoning his sick wife and five children in Augsburg. Presumably Musculus used Bartholome as an example of Anabaptist irresponsibility. Consequently Bartholome returned to Augsburg,[24] but his plan to move the family had to be delayed because of his wife's illness. Imprisoned, he recanted, only to find himself under the ban of his former brethren. Messengers arriving from Moravia admonished him. Repentant he sought reacceptance and was reinstated into the fellowship, but he was still unable to move his

---

[20] Perhaps they knew of the disputation that had taken place in St Gall, 20–22 December 1530.

[21] The recantations took place in May and June. Eight women and six men had been expelled earlier. Among the prisoners had been a Hans Dorfwirt, a former priest baptized in Bern, who admitted to having baptized four or five persons near Strasbourg. Uhland, 'Täufertum und Obrigkeit', p. 241.

[22] He had been released on 16 May 1531; Gross on 22 June 1531; Salminger earlier on 17 December 1530. Wolfhart and Musculus were involved in Dachser's recantation which some considered a farce. Uhland, 'Täufertum und Obrigkeit', pp. 230–32. Cf. Packull, *Mysticism*, pp. 51–3; pp. 208–9 n. 47.

[23] Dachser was the only preacher elected by a parish in Augsburg during this time; he was chosen from among four candidates. In 1533 he had signed the names of all the preachers to a document that responded to Luther's attacks on them. K. Wolfart, *Augsburger Reformation*, pp. 64–5, p. 115, n. 2.

[24] He was back by October 1531. Boyd sought to identify the group of Anabaptists in Augsburg with whom Bartholome associated but failed to see the connection to the incident on 5 March. He makes no mention of Kentner. *Marpeck*, p. 133.

family. The threat of capital punishment led to a second recantation. His conscience troubled, he must have again sought readmission into the Anabaptist community, for in 1535 he was expelled once more from Augsburg. Bartholome's experience was typical; it illustrates the difficulties faced by ordinary Anabaptists seeking to be true to their religious convictions and family obligations. Bartholome was illiterate. His story illustrates not only his own vacillation but that of the authorities who increasingly shied away from the use of capital punishment against Anabaptists. Finally, Bartholome's case reveals that regular contacts existed between Anabaptists in Augsburg and the newly founded communities of Gabrielites and Philipites in Moravia.

It is against this background that the appearance of the anonymous pamphlet, *New Dialogue*, must be understood. But who in 1531/32 authored this Anabaptist pamphlet which clearly mirrored the religious milieu in Augsburg? Hans Kentner seems a plausible candidate. His recantation under duress did not last; he soon returned to the Anabaptist fold, resuming a leadership role among the Philipites. It is conceivable that the *New Dialogue*, a cathartic exercise, reflects prison conversations with Musculus and Wolfhart. But Kentner was not the only Anabaptist in Augsburg capable of composing the *New Dialogue*. Georg Probst Rotenfelder, also known as Jörg Maler, who later compiled and transcribed the *Kunstbuch*,[25] seems an even more likely candidate. True, his first appearance in historical records, dating from 1526, as an inebriated young man breaking into the house of a citizen late at night in pursuit of a young maiden gives little indication of the future Anabaptist leader in pursuit of holiness.[26] Nevertheless, by 1531/32 he had become a cantor at St Andrew's.[27] But if he aspired to a career in the evangelical church, his Anabaptist sympathies soon proved a liability. Sometime in March or April 1532 he permitted himself to be baptized by Sebold Feuchter, who had arrived in the city in late 1531. Son of a Nuremberg mint master and a goldsmith by trade, Feuchter

---

[25] About the contents of this 740-page codex see the *ME*, III, p. 259; or Heinold Fast, 'Pilgram Marbeck und das oberdeutsche Täufertum. Ein neuer Handschriftenfund,' *ARG*, 47 (1956), pp. 212–42.

[26] Described as curly-haired and good looking, Maler, even as an Anabaptist, came under suspicion of sexual impropriety, something he denied. Heinold Fast, 'Vom Amt des "Lesers" zum Kompilator des sogenannten Kunstbuches. Auf dem Spuren Jörg Malers' in Norbert Fischer and Marion Kobelt-Groch (eds), *Aussenseiter zwischen Mittelalter und Neuzeit. Festschrift für Hans-Jürgen Goertz zum 60. Geburtstag* (Leiden, 1997), pp. 189–90. Uhland, 'Täufertum und Obrigkeit', pp. 251–53.

[27] Maler is described as 'ein Vorsinger an der Predigt', and, according to one source, had such a reputation 'in the Word that he was almost chosen pastor'. Fast, 'Vom Amt des "Lesers"', pp. 191–2 ns. 17–19.

had been expelled from Kaufbeuren during the Peasants' Uprising because of the 'Word of God'. A similar fate overtook him in Esslingen, this time because of his Anabaptist views. These views are somewhat difficult to classify, since he distanced himself from the Swiss who were allegedly prepared to use violence [wollen drein schlagen]. He also distanced himself from those who refused to pay rents and taxes [steuern und zins].[28] Since his arrival Feuchter had baptized seven persons, including Maler, but answered questions as to whether he was an Anabaptist leader [Vorsteher] in the negative.[29] He saw himself merely as a divine instrument and contended further that small Anabaptist meetings of up to fourteen to seventeen persons in private homes did not constitute violation of city law against 'common gatherings'.

Without question Feuchter's most notable convert was Maler. Within a year of his baptism in early 1532 he too was in prison. His subsequent experience paralleled Kentner's. On 29 April 1533 Maler agreed to an ambivalently worded statement read to him by Wolfhart.[30] Like Kentner, he came to regret his 'recantation'.[31]

This is not the place to pursue Maler's subsequent career as an Anabaptist leader in St Gall and Appenzell or as Marpeck's emissary.[32] Suffice it to state that circumstantial evidence points to him as author of the New Dialogue. He was in Augsburg when the New Dialogue appeared in 1532 and a member of Marpeck's brotherhood when the second edition came off the press c. 1545.[33] The preamble of that second edition suggests that its author once had connections to

[28] It could be that this differentiation was based on existing divisions in Moravia. In this case the 'Swiss' were the followers of Hubmaier in Nicolsburg, the tax objectors the Austerlitzers, while Feuchter identified with the Gabrielites or Philipites.

[29] This was most likely true since the Anabaptists in Esslingen did not 'ordain' any leaders after 1530. I assume that Feuchter knew Kentner who came from the Kaufbeuren area. Perhaps both were associated with the Philipites. In the 1540s many Swabian Anabaptists from the Kaufbeuren area joined the Hutterites. The Chronicle of the Hutterian Brethren 1525–1665 (Rifton, NY, 1987), pp. 244, 246.

[30] Uhland, 'Täufertum und Obrigkeit', p. 263. Boyd, Marpeck, p. 141.

[31] Uhland, 'Täufertum und Obrigkeit', p. 253 n. 67; Fast, 'Vom Amt des "Lesers"', p. 197.

[32] Both Fast and Boyd have addressed this task sufficiently. It is noteworthy, however, that after his expulsion Maler, like so many others, made his way to Moravia. A letter from him reached Augsburg before 16 March 1534. Its carriers were most likely Hans Miller and Christoph Schaffdunn, a baker and tanner respectively, who were shopping in Augsburg for bibles. In the following year Maler learned the weaver's trade in Baden on Swiss soil. On his return to Augsburg he was beaten out of the city. Uhland, 'Täufertum und Obrigkeit', p. 253 n. 67. Fast, 'Vom Amt des "Lesers"', p. 197.

[33] I have sought to clarify the relationship between the two editions in an introduction to a translation of the New Dialogue which appears in a source book edited by Arnold Snyder. See n. 4.

Augsburg's clergy. Becoming disillusioned, his curiosity was aroused by all the criticisms he heard of the Anabaptists. He therefore attended some of their meetings, but was not yet baptized when he wrote the *Dialogue*. These autobiographical glimpses fit the known facts of Maler's life.[34] Moreover, the *Dialogue* makes a virtue of small meetings, which had become the order of the day after the abortive mass meeting on 5 March 1531. Maler was baptized by Feuchter in one of these small congregational house meetings.

And who was the sympathetic Predikant featured in the *New Dialogue*? As noted, Anabaptist recantations in the early 1530s consistently involved Bonifacius Wolfhart, whose conciliatory approach seemed irresistible. Years later Maler remembered private conversations with Wolfhart.[35] It seems conceivable, therefore, that Wolfhart served as the Predikant who agreed in private with the Baptist but wanted to stay at his magisterially appointed post in order to win more citizens for the evangelical cause.[36]

Turning to the *New Dialogue*, it is interesting to note that after some introductory haggling whether or not to address others as brothers, something the Preacher was prepared to do but the Baptist refused, addressing the Preacher instead as 'dear friend', the Preacher posed the question, as if longing to have the Anabaptists in his congregation: 'Why do you not attend my preaching nor celebrate the Lord's Supper with me and my congregation?' The answer came in the form of a rebuke: 'Because you and your parishioners are hearers only'. In contrast the Baptist saw himself and his little flock as obedient doers of Christ's commands. Obeying Christ's ordinances pertained above all to baptism as commanded in the Great Commission (Matthew 28:19–20): teach, confess, believe, receive baptism. The Preacher's feeble defence of pedobaptism as an 'ancient custom', and his rejection of adult baptism, simply because it had been forbidden by the authorities, struck the Baptist as spurious, an excuse to remain gainfully employed and avoid the cross. Any attempt at a scriptural defence of pedobaptism was rejected out of hand as 'unfounded, dishonest, twisted' and against the clear command of Christ.

Lack of discipline in the Preacher's church represented the second major stumbling block. 'Whores, avaricious persons, drunkards and foul mouths' attended and participated in the Lord's Supper against

---

[34] Since he was baptized in March or April of 1532, he could have written the *New Dialogue* in late 1531 or early 1532.

[35] Boyd, *Marpeck*, pp. 140–41. Uhland, 'Täufertum und Obrigkcit', p. 263.

[36] At one point in the *New Dialogue* the Preacher refers to his university education. Stayer has suggested Dr Sebastian Meyer as the other possible candidate. Cf. n. 14.

Christ's express command for an 'irreproachable Church'. Above all, the Baptist objected to the clerics' domination over the congregation which left no room for lay participation and congregational discernment. According to his reading of I Corinthians 14,[37] all members were to participate in discerning matters of faith and practice but instead the Preacher acted as if he possessed all the spiritual gifts. 'No one [else] was permitted to use his/her gifts for the edification of the congregation.'

Next the discussion turned to church–state relations and the use of the sword. The Baptist accused the Preacher of calling on the magistrates to decide and reinforce purely ecclesiastical matters. By soliciting the support of the temporal sword, the Preacher admitted to his lack of the spiritual sword, the Word of God. All who criticized or rejected the coupling of temporal and spiritual realms suffered persecution. As a result the sheep were scattered rather than gathered into the sheep fold. Thus the Preacher could not be considered a true shepherd. To know his sheep by name was an impossibility in a church with open doors. A flock of only twenty to thirty was more akin to Pauline congregational instructions.[38]

Put on the defensive throughout the dialogue, the Preacher agreed with the Baptist's criticism that his congregation did not yet conform to the church order prescribed by Paul, but evangelistic reasons prompted him to remain at his post for another year or two in order to entice [reizen] more citizens into the evangelical fold.[39] The Baptist responded that Luther had proposed the same strategy five or six years earlier but had since forgotten or given up on a church of committed believers with proper discipline. Little improvement of life had come from Luther's preaching and enticing, apart from the abolition of some rather elementary abuses.

When the Preacher inquired how best to establish a proper Christian congregation, the Baptist advised him to shun the friendship of this world, to keep Christ's and apostolic ordinances, and to accept persecution: 'for such is the school of Christ, into which he calls all who would

---

[37] I Corinthians 14 provided the main text on which the earliest Anabaptist congregational orders were based. Packull, *Hutterite Beginnings*, Appendix A, pp. 303–15.

[38] Noting that Feuchter and Maler in their interrogation made a virtue of small congregational meetings, Fast suggested a 'Traditionslinie' to the 'Common Congregational Order' attributed to Leopold Scharnschlager, which speaks of gatherings of twenty or so. 'Vom Amt des "Lesers"', p. 193 n. 25. Cf. Packull, *Hutterite Beginnings*, Appendix A, pp. 303–15.

[39] To what extent the *New Dialogue* reflected the real exchange that had taken place remains speculation. But this part sounds real. Since Wolfhart had only arrived in 1531 it seems reasonable that he pleaded for time until a more disciplined church could emerge.

become his disciples.' Only those spiritually transformed through the 'school of Christ' received the 'key of David' to unlock the meaning of the Scriptures. Applying an analogy from the building trade to the building of the house of God, he warned that the necessary personal transformation of individual members involved painful preparation. Trees of the forest needed to be felled, trimmed, hewn or planed before they could become useful building material. Similarly, would-be members of the house of God needed to suffer inner preparation and outer persecution in the 'school of Christ'.[40]

The pamphlet concludes with the Preacher's admission that he has not yet entered the school of Christ and is therefore not qualified to lead others. He gratefully accepts the Baptist's frank instructions and bids him farewell as a 'dear brother'.

Unfortunately Wolfhart's response to the *New Dialogue* remains unknown. As noted, his less sanguine colleague Musculus published his own *Peaceful and Christian Dialogue* with Anabaptists. Heinold Fast suggested that this pamphlet echoed Musculus' prison conversations with Maler, Feuchter and others. Whether this is true or not, Musculus' tract certainly indicates his familiarity with Anabaptist teachings and practices. The evidence suggests further that he knew of the *New Dialogue*. In an apparent allusion to the issue of fraternal greeting, Musculus remonstrated: 'He who believes in Christ Jesus, let him be your brother.'[41] This plea follows the assertion that it is not the 'sign of the covenant,' outer baptism, but faith in Christ that qualifies one for membership in the Christian community! A skilful debater, Musculus knew how to gain the attention and interest of his audience. Deploring coercion of consciences, the 'choking and shedding of blood', he preferred to restore the erring 'brethren' 'in a spirit of gentleness'.[42] To this end Musculus had chosen the genre of 'Christian dialogue'. His aim was to shore up 'troubled consciences', encourage the 'true hearted' but also to counter subversive literature clandestinely hawked by 'prowling brethren' in the 'corners' of the city. Thus he confirmed that in the early 1530s the Anabaptists remained a major concern in the religious tug-of-war for the hearts of Augsburg's citizens.

Musculus had chosen his topic all too well. Oath refusal highlighted Anabaptist sectarianism and lent itself to accusations that they

---

[40] The metaphor is an adaptation of Hans Hut's Gospel of all creatures found in a number of Anabaptist writers including Leonard Schiemer. The author was obviously familiar with the earlier literature which later appeared in the *Kunstbuch*.

[41] In another allusion to the *New Dialogue* in which the Baptist reminded the Preacher of the greater importance of the inner, Fridenrich reminded Adolf that outer things were of secondary importance and should not exclude from the community of faith.

[42] Fast, 'Vom Amt des "Lesers"', p. 194, n. 30.

undermined civic community. Not surprisingly, Musculus gave the evangelical argument to Fridenrich [rich in peace]; the defense of the Anabaptist cause was left to Adolf. Love of God and benefit to neighbour[43] were to be the guiding principles, Scripture the main court of appeal. Adolf was encouraged to make the case for Anabaptist oath refusal. He did so, citing the words of Jesus: 'Do not swear at all' (Matthew 5:33). These words were plain and needed no interpretation. Christ had forbidden his followers to swear!

In response Musculus insisted that a definition be agreed upon of what constituted an oath: an oath was simply a promise that invoked God as witness. Once Adolf agreed, Musculus proceeded systematically to cite the Law and Prophets, then Old Testament passages cited in the New Testament to demonstrate that oaths, properly given, brought honour to God and served the good of one's neighbour. Next, he turned to purely New Testament passages. He suggested that when Paul called on God as 'my witness' and Jesus used the formula 'truly, truly I say unto you', they were going beyond the 'yes, yes' and 'no, no' of Matthew 5 – indeed, uttered promissory oaths. It followed that Christ's prohibition, seen in the context of the Scriptures, Old as well as New Testament, had been directed against abuses, not against oaths in principle. It followed that Anabaptist oath refusal was not scriptural, serving neither God's honour nor the good of one's neighbour.

Adolf's contribution to the dialogue consisted primarily of objections, stubborn insistence on a literal, prohibitive interpretation of Christ's words and to distrustful utterances about the learned spin doctor who attempted to rob Christ's words of their unmistakable meaning. As Fridenrich developed his argument, Adolf fell increasingly silent, claiming repeatedly that God did not permit him to speak. The impression conveyed to the reader that Adolf had nothing to say in response to Musculus' persuasive arguments was, of course, precisely the impression intended by Musculus.[44]

---

[43] This was the standard criteria insisted upon by the Reformed theologians in all debates with Anabaptists, because Christ had summarized the meaning of the decalogue in love of God and neighbour. It will be recalled that Kentner and Riemer were inspired by the same motive on 5 March 1531.

[44] Musculus' persuasively argued treatise was not a solo effort. Evidence suggests that he used the published proceedings of the 1532 Disputation at Zofingen in which some of the same examples and arguments appear and the conclusion was reached that Jesus' prohibition referred to abuses of his day. The Bern clergy referred to Anabaptists as brothers, made love of God and neighbour the guiding principle, declared that the injunction referred to swearing in daily discourse and used the example of swearing by the temple or the gold of the temple. All this is found in Musculus' dialogue. Edmund Pries, 'Anabaptist Oath Refusal: Basel. Bern and Strasbourg 1525–1538' (PhD diss., University of Waterloo, 1995), pp. 140 ff. Pries did not examine Musculus' tract.

Curiously, the *New Dialogue* had made no mention of the oath. From the beginning 'Anabaptists in Augsburg had a history of divided opinions on the oath'.[45] It was certainly not a central issue but rather a by-product of Anabaptist political ethic. The author of the *New Dialogue* must have considered it as non-essential or avoided it deliberately. Or had he been persuaded by Reformed arguments? It is clear that by 1550, if not earlier, Jörg Maler had assumed a position on the oath similar to that advocated by Musculus. Yes, he agreed that the oath benefited the neighbour, 'maintained love and promoted justice'![46] By this point in time Maler was a member of Pilgram Marpeck's brotherhood. Marpeck himself seems to have taken a similarly benign view of the oath, at least during his Augsburg period.[47] James Stayer was one of the first scholars to document carefully that the political ethic of the Marpeck circle 'represented a less radical apoliticism' or a 'milder type than that of the Stäbler sects or the Swiss Brethren'.[48] But Stayer went further in detecting the influence of Hans Denck on Maler's and Marpeck's view on the oath and the sword.[49]

By way of summary, the following points deserve reiteration:

1. This study suggests that Anabaptism in Augsburg showed signs of reviving during the early 1530s. Charles V's attempt in 1530 to smother the Reformation in Augsburg only fuelled a more radical orientation. The Bucerians and Zwinglians, who arrived in 1531, were the beneficiaries, Lutherans the losers. Anabaptists, led by Kentner and Riemer, must have hoped for greater tolerance, perhaps even the possibility of dialogue with the Reformed party. The person who seems to have personified new conciliatory possibilities on the Reformed side was presumably Bonifacius Wolfhart and perhaps Hans Heinrich at St Ulrich, an ally of Wolfhart. Wolfhart certainly proved persuasive in extracting dubious recantations from imprisoned Anabaptists, including Maler.

---

[45] James M. Stayer's *Anabaptists and the Sword* (Lawrence, KS, 1972) remains the classic text.

[46] Boyd placed Dachser and Hans Schlaffer in Hut's camp, Maler initially in the Swiss camp. Unlike Hut's associates, the Swiss rejected both the oath and bearing weapons. This suggests that with time Maler changed his position. *Marpeck*, pp. 132–3, 142, 164.

[47] Martin Bucer had claimed in 1531 that Marpeck considered swearing and armed defence [*schweren und weren*] wrong. If true, Marpeck changed. Cf. *TQ Elsaß*, I, p. 350.

[48] Stayer, *Anabaptists and the Sword*, pp. 179, 180.

[49] Ibid., pp. 185–7. Here, too, as has so often been my experience, when my own research has intersected with Stayer's, I find my own conclusions preempted by his earlier findings. How fortunate to have had a scholar of this calibre as my 'doctor father'.

2. Circumstantial evidence suggests Jörg Maler as the most likely
    author of the *New Dialogue*. Maler later reminisced on conversa-
    tions with Wolfhart which had misled him to recant, an ambivalent
    recantation he came to regret. Hans Kentner and others went through
    a similar experience in 1531/32. I therefore suggest that Wolfhart
    served as the sympathetic Preacher featured in the *New Dialogue*.
    That Kentner, Maler and others returned to Anabaptism may sug-
    gest that Wolfhart and his supporters were unable to bring about
    the changes in Augsburg's church which they themselves had prom-
    ised and hoped for. The interaction between the Reformed clergy
    and the Anabaptists in Augsburg, although not fully documented,
    left a paper trail in the form of the two dialogues. These shed new
    light on a period of Anabaptist history in Augsburg which until
    now lay in the shadow of the founding years. Consequently the
    1530s assume greater significance in the Anabaptist story of
    Augsburg.
3. Musculus' *tour de force* of the Scriptures with its insistence on a
    holistic biblical approach to the oath constituted a public challenge
    to the Anabaptists. The issue as formulated by Musculus went
    beyond the oath to the hermeneutic question of the relationship of
    the two testaments to each other. No doubt this was not the first
    and certainly not the last time Anabaptists faced this issue. It was
    raised regularly by Reformed clergy in their disputations with
    Anabaptists. It can hardly be considered accidental that the pream-
    ble to the second edition of the *New Dialogue*, which appeared in
    the mid-1540s, explicitly addressed this issue. There the Anabaptist
    admonished his dialogue partner to remain in the heart of the
    Scriptures, the New Testament, not to deviate to the fringes: for the
    New Testament contained everything necessary for salvation.[50]

    The exchange of the 1530s was, of course, never one between
    equal conversation partners, since much of the exchange took place
    with the Anabaptists under duress. Yet, the public exchanges in
    print lacked the nastier polemics that were characteristic of so
    many Reformation pamphlets.
4. Finally we need to ask whether the recantations of Anabaptist
    leaders like Salminger, Dachser, Gross, Kentner, Maler and a host
    of others contributed to the development of a more moderate form

---

[50] 'Remain also in the Bible, totally in its centre, especially in the New Testament, in
which enough is written about that which leads to salvation, and do not flee to the
fringes.' *Flugschriften vom Bauernkrieg zum Täuferreich (1526–1535)*, ed. Adolf Laube
with the assistance of Annerose Schneider and Ulman Weiss, vol. II (Berlin, 1992),
p. 999.

of Anabaptism in Augsburg. In other words, is it possible that the moderate positions held by members of Marpeck's circle in the 1540s were influenced by experiences of the 1530s? Because of the mobility of Augsburg's Anabaptists, it is difficult to argue for the development of a linear tradition [*Traditionslinie*]. Nevertheless, Jörg Maler represents in his person a link between the 1530s and 1540s. If Maler and Marpeck can be seen as representing a developing tradition, then its direction on political ethic and the oath was clearly in a moderate direction.

CHAPTER THREE

Harmonizing the Scriptures: Swiss Brethren understandings of the relationship between the Old and New Testament during the last half of the sixteenth century

John D. Roth

Introduction

In the spring of 1532 Berthold Haller, city pastor and leading Protestant reformer of Bern, wrote to Heinrich Bullinger – his mentor and colleague in Zurich – seeking counsel about an upcoming disputation with a group of Anabaptists. According to Haller, a main article of faith for the Anabaptists was 'to reject the Old Testament and to distort the New Testament with unique cunning.'[1] In reply, Bullinger insisted that this point – the Anabaptist understanding of Scripture and specifically the relationship between Old and New Testament – was of paramount importance. 'What counts,' Bullinger wrote, 'is to define at the very beginning with what weapons the battle is to be waged, lest in the middle of the proceedings things which should have been taken care of and defined rise up to obscure and confuse completely what is being discussed.' It is crucial, he continued, that you not pursue any other point of discussion until the Anabaptists agree that whenever conflicts arise among Christians concerning matters of faith 'they should be decided and clarified with Holy Scripture of the Old Testament and New Testament.'[2] This way you can 'wring out of them if anywhere there lurks a negation of the Old Testament.' Then, Bullinger concluded, 'when you have dealt enough with this question ... show in your answers that you know more arguments than they do: this impresses the audience.'[3]

---

[1] Heinold Fast and John H. Yoder, 'How to Deal with Anabaptists: An Unpublished Letter of Heinrich Bullinger,' *MQR*, 33 (1959), p. 84.

[2] Ibid.

[3] Ibid., p. 86.

Bullinger's evident concern, elaborated in several more pages of detailed argumentation, went far deeper than merely a rhetorician's interest in impressing an audience. By seizing on this issue of the relationship of the Old Testament and the New Testament, Bullinger correctly identified one of the most foundational differences between the Reformers and the Anabaptist movement. At stake in the minds of the Reformers was not an abstract scholarly quibble over allegorical or tropological readings of Old Testament passages, but rather basic understandings of the sovereignty of God, the meaning of the Incarnation, the foundation of Christian ethics and the principles of order and authority essential to a stable society. Indeed, as subsequent debates would show, virtually every distinctive Anabaptist argument – on baptism, the sword, the oath, the Christian magistracy, and so on – hinged on their insistence that the New Testament was more authoritative than the Old in matters of Christian ethics.

In this paper I want to summarize briefly the narrative of the debate between the Swiss Brethren and the Reformers on the relationship of the two testaments as it crystallized and took shape in the course of the mid- to late sixteenth century. Though the Reformers came to view this question as the single most important point of contention with the Anabaptists, the Swiss Brethren themselves generally did not regard the issue as a theological priority and gave it very little attention apart from the formal disputations where they were forced to defend themselves on the matter. Nevertheless, by the end of the sixteenth century, one can identify at least three distinct attempts within the Swiss Brethren community to address the question of how the two testaments might be harmonized.

Zwingli and the early Swiss Brethren

In his study of Hutterite origins, Werner Packull has carefully detailed the process by which Ulrich Zwingli divided with his erstwhile disciples over the issue of scriptural interpretation.[4] From the time of his arrival in Zurich as the 'people's priest' in January 1519 through the end of 1523, Zwingli preached systematically – and almost exclusively – from the New Testament.[5] But as tensions began to emerge between Zwingli

---

[4] Werner O. Packull, *Hutterite Beginnings: Communitarian Experiments during the Reformation* (Baltimore, MD, 1995), pp. 15–32.

[5] In November of 1523, speaking before the City Council of Zurich, Zwingli identified a parallelism between Old Testament sacrifices and the Catholic mass – dismissing the Levitical sacrifices, and with it the mass – as only 'a figure of the coming of Christ'. Leland Harder (ed.), *The Sources of Swiss Anabaptism: The Grebel Letters and Selected Documents* (Scottdale, PA, 1985), p. 264.

and several of his supporters, especially over the issue of pedobaptism, Zwingli gradually shifted the focus of his study to the Old Testament where he found in the Jewish practice of circumcision a biblical precedent for the practice of infant baptism. The shift in Zwingli's orientation from New to Old Testament can be identified fairly precisely. In a fiery treatise of December of 1524 entitled *Those Who Give Cause for Rebellion* – his first major broadside against the incipient Anabaptist movement – Zwingli insisted that since the New Testament was silent on the question of infant baptism the Christian must therefore 'see whether there is anything in the Old Testament about it'.[6] He then developed the basis of an argument that would be refined and repeated frequently in Reformed circles over the next fifty years: namely, that infant baptism should be understood as the New Testament parallel to the Old Testament practice of circumcision. Both marked a sign of God's blessing and both signalled the entry of the infant into the covenanted community.

In the aftermath of the first adult baptisms in January of 1525, as the Swiss Brethren movement coalesced, Zwingli's defence of the authority of the Old Testament became more explicit. In his tract *Concerning the Office of Preaching*, published in June of 1525, Zwingli underscored the point that the apostles themselves had preached and taught exclusively from the 'Old' Testament. Though he readily accepted the standard Lutheran distinction between 'Law' and 'Grace', he insisted on a fundamental continuity between the Old Covenant and the New: God's nature, God's gift of grace, and God's will for His people were essentially the same in the Old Testament as they were in the New.[7]

Over the next two years, the hermeneutical divide between Zwingli and the Swiss Brethren dissenters over the relationship of Old and New Testaments became increasingly explicit. In June of 1527, for example, Swiss Brethren prisoners appealed to the Grüningen Diet, complaining that Zwingli had introduced a new hermeneutical principle: 'Note how the false prophet Zwingli, when he finds nothing on infant baptism in the New Testament, goes backward into the Old Testament which he should not do.'[8] A month later Zwingli responded in his *Elenchus* by explicitly accusing the Anabaptists of 'denying the whole Old Testament'. 'Since you reject the Old Testament for the reason that you cannot endure what is deduced from it with reference to infant baptism,' he thundered, 'you clearly show that you make of no account him who is God both of the Old Testament and the New.'[9]

---

[6] Ibid., p. 319.
[7] Ibid., p. 392, *passim*.
[8] Ibid., p. 516.
[9] Ibid., pp. 486–7.

Zwingli's hint – and Bullinger's later charge – that the Swiss Brethren bias in favour of the New Testament made them Marcionites, who explicitly rejected the authority of the Old Testament, is clearly untenable. In his famous letter to Thomas Müntzer of 5 September 1524, Conrad Grebel insisted that they preached the word 'according to the Old as well as the New Testament'.[10] Grebel's co-worker, Hans Krüsi, testified prior to his execution in July of 1525 that he had done nothing more than 'preach, read, teach in the Old Testament and New Testament'; and the famous collection of Scripture passages on faith and baptism which have been attributed to Krüsi include numerous references to Old Testament passages (especially on the theme of faith).[11] At the October 1523 disputation before the Zurich City Council, Balthasar Hubmaier – perhaps the most learned of the Swiss Brethren leaders – explicitly called for the proclamation of the 'clear Word of God as written in both Testaments'.[12] Zwingli himself complained in May of 1525 that the Anabaptists were presenting some 'strange interpretations from the Old Testament' though he did not elaborate on the nature of those interpretations.[13]

Nonetheless, the Christocentric approach to ethics advocated by the early Swiss Brethren and their attempts to model congregational life exclusively on the pattern of the apostolic church made it clear that the New Testament held greater authority in matters of faith and life than did the Old. But unlike Zwingli, Bullinger and the other Reformers, the Swiss Brethren did not regard this bias in favour of the New Testament – or the subsequent questions it raised about God's immutable nature – as a matter worthy of extended theological reflection. Even Balthasar Hubmaier, a man who cared about theological subtleties and whose systematic defence of voluntary baptism continued to echo among Swiss Brethren for more than a century, devoted surprisingly little attention to such questions. In his July 1525 treatise *On Christian Baptism*, for example, Hubmaier's defence of believers' baptism focused entirely on New Testament passages;[14] and a year later, when Hubmaier engaged Zwingli's argument more fully in his *Dialogue with Zwingli's Taufbüchlein*, he simply dismissed Zwingli's appeals to Old Testament

---

[10] Ibid., p. 28. Later in the letter Grebel did contrast the Old Testament tablets of stone with the New Testament law which 'is to be written on the fleshly tables of the heart'.

[11] Ibid., p. 423. Krüsi told his interrogators that had received his Old Testament on loan from a certain Aberli Schrumpf of St Gallen.

[12] H. Wayne Pipkin and John H. Yoder (trans. and eds), *Balthasar Hubmaier, Theologian of Anabaptism* (Scottdale, PA, 1989), p. 26.

[13] Harder, *Sources of Swiss Anabaptism* (Taufbüchlein, 27 May 1525), p. 366.

[14] Pipkin and Yoder, *Balthasar Hubmaier*, pp. 96–149.

examples out of hand, calling on Zwingli to 'drop your circuitous argument on circumcision out of the Old Testament. For you well know that circumcision is not a figure of water baptism.' Though he did not develop the point, Hubmaier claimed that the ark of Noah, not circumcision, 'is a figure of water baptism'.[15] Hubmaier was equally curt in his dismissal of the question as to 'whether the children of Christians and the children of the Old Testament are [both] children of God', saying that on this matter 'we want only to leave to him who knows all things and will not make any judgement'.[16]

The most explicit Swiss Brethren statement regarding their preference for the New Testament over the Old came from a letter by Leonhard Schiemer to the congregation at Rottenberg probably written shortly before his execution in 1528. Schiemer's main intent in the letter was to offer an interpretive gloss on the Apostles Creed, but in the preface he also instructed the congregation on some basic principles of worship and bible study. 'When you read,' Schiemer wrote, 'read mostly from the New Testament and the Psalms. You should know that God spoke in a very hidden manner to the Jews through Moses and the prophets, but since Christ himself came he and his apostles have illuminated everything with a much clearer understanding.' Moreover, Christ taught that all of the laws and prophets could be understood in the commandment to 'love God and love the neighbour'; thus, 'although it would be good to read in the prophets and the books of the kings and of Moses, it is indeed almost unnecessary. One can find everything in the New Testament.' Whatever is testified [angezaigt] in the Old Testament is brought more fully to light in the New Testament, concluded Schiemer in his introduction, 'and in the apostles is the fulfilment of all Judaism [der auszug aller israeliten]'.[17]

More typically, the Swiss Brethren articulated their understanding of the relationship of the two testaments indirectly or implicitly. In their hymnody, devotional writings, correspondence and debates they consistently argued that the New Testament call to follow Christ in life and death, and the model of Christian community offered by the apostolic church, relativized all other considerations. While many of the stories in the Old Testament could be adduced to support these emphases, in the

---

[15] Ibid., p. 180. In his *Theses Against Eck*, p. 54, Hubmaier made the standard argument that confusing or contradictory passages of Scripture were to be illuminated by texts whose meaning was clear: 'this is what Christ taught when he explained Scripture of Moses concerning Levirate marriages by reference to Scripture on the resurrection.'

[16] Ibid., p. 228.

[17] Leonard Schiemer, 'Ein Sendbrief, darrinen ist begiffen eine hübsche Erklärung der 12 Artikel unseres christlichen Glaubens,' in Lydia Müller, *GZI*, p. 45.

end Christ had come in order to fulfil the Law. Wherever there was any hint of contradiction or tension between the Old Testament and the New, Scripture must be read through the lens of the Incarnation and the fuller understanding of God's will in the life, death and resurrection of Christ.

The Reformed position crystallizes: 1531–71

By the beginning of the 1530s, as the separatist and pacifist themes in the Swiss Brethren movement began to crystallize, the question of the relationship of the Old Testament to the New became the primary focus of theological conflict with the Reformers, the very source – in their eyes – of Anabaptist radicalism. In April of 1531, setting the tone for virtually every disputation which followed over the next fifty years, the Reformed preachers of Bern insisted that this issue preface a public debate scheduled with the Swiss Brethren. Speaking on behalf of the Anabaptists, Hans Pfistermeyer argued that Christ had 'brought a higher and more perfect teaching' than that given in the Old Testament, and he stubbornly rejected the Reformers' arguments in favour of oath swearing, usury, infant baptism and Christian involvement in government by stubbornly returning to the words of Jesus in the Sermon on the Mount and Christ's own insistence that his teachings represented the fulfilment of the Old Testament law.[18]

As the Bernese preachers prepared for a second disputation – to be held at Zoffingen in July of 1532 – Heinrich Bullinger was convinced that the relationship between the two testaments was the fulcrum of the entire debate. 'Above all,' he admonished Haller in the letter cited above, 'do not waver on this point. Don't give an inch; press them and hold them bound to the spot.' To underscore his concern, Bullinger provided Haller with an elaborate set of arguments and scriptural proof texts for demonstrating the continuity between the Old and New Testaments. Condensed from lengthier arguments made in his *Von dem Unverschampten Fräfel* (January 1531), Bullinger insisted that the Brethren not be permitted to identify the Old Testament with the term 'law', thereby minimizing its relevance in light of Christ's saving gift of grace. Instead, he argued, the Old Testament provides a 'witness and confirmation' to the truth of the New Testament. Bullinger also introduced into the discussion the hermeneutical principle of 'the rule of faith and love' which he associated with Christ's summation of all the law under the principle of 'love of God and love of the neighbour'.[19] For Bullinger,

---

[18] *TQ Gespräche*, pp. 7, 8–13.
[19] Fast and Yoder, 'How to Deal with Anabaptists', p. 89.

of course, 'love of neighbour' included everything that promoted social order rather than lawlessness and anarchy. Only through this lens – not the naïve literalism of the Swiss Brethren – could the true meaning of the Sermon on the Mount be understood. If you use this principle, Bullinger concluded, 'you will always be able to hobble them'.[20]

In every subsequent public disputation between the Swiss Brethren and the Reformers – at Bern in 1538,[21] at Pfeddersheim in 1557, and at Frankenthal in 1571 – the Reformers insisted that the relationship between Old and New Testament be the very first point of debate.[22] Indeed, at the Frankenthal disputation, the question became the very lynchpin of the nineteen-day exchange, dominating the entire proceedings.[23] The very first item of debate – framed, of course, by the Reformed theologians – asked the question:

> Whether the Old Testament Scripture is as valid to the Christian as the New; that is, whether the principal doctrines of faith and life can and must be proved from the Old Testament as well as the New.

The issue also re-emerged as the central theme in Article V of the debate which asked 'Whether the Believers in the Old Testament are one community and people of God with those in the New Testament'. All told, more than one-third of the 710 pages of the published transcript of the debate addressed this question in some way.[24]

In brief, the Reformers argued that Jesus and the apostles all accepted the authority of the Old Testament in matters pertaining to faith and ethics [Wandel]; that the central doctrines of faith and ethics taught in the New Testament were the same as those taught by Moses and the prophets in the Old Testament; and that the salvific work of Christ, the

---

[20] Ibid., p. 90.

[21] Cf. Walter Klaassen, 'The Bern Debate of 1538: Christ the Center of Scripture', MQR (1966), pp. 148–56 for an analysis of the key points.

[22] These disputations can be found in Haas, TQ Gespräche. John H. Yoder provides important commentary on these debates in his Täufertum und Reformation in der Schweiz. I: Die Gespräche zwischen Täufern und Reformatoren, 1523–1538 (Karlsruhe, 1962) and in his Täufertum und Reformation im Gespräch (Zürich, 1968), pp. 36–42. John Oyer provides the full text and a helpful overview of the Pfeddersheim debate in 'The Pfeddersheim Disputation, 1557', MQR, 60 (1986), pp. 304–51.

[23] Heinold Fast has argued that the central theme of the entire disputation at Frankenthal was 'die Frage nach der christologischen Deutung des Alten Testamentes' – Die Täuferbewegung im Lichte des Frankenthaler Gespräches, 1571', MGBl 23 (1971), p. 15.

[24] For a very good summary and rhetorical analysis of the Frankenthal disputation, see Jess Yoder, 'A Critical Study of the Debate between the Reformed and the Anabaptists Held at Frankenthal, Germany in 1571' (PhD diss., Northwestern University, 1962).

presence of the Holy Spirit and the principles of Christian doctrine were efficacious in the Old Testament just as much as they were in the New Testament since God – who is eternal and unchanging – was the author of both.

The Swiss Brethren were ill-equipped to engage the sophisticated theological subtleties of the Reformers and, more importantly, they regarded such intellectual exercises as strained efforts on the part of state-salaried theologians to avoid the clear and simple teachings of Christ. Nowhere is the difference in theological world-view more apparent than in the lengthy – at times tedious – exchange between Peter Dathenus, the chief spokesperson for the Reformed and the responses of Rauf Bisch of Odenheim who spoke most frequently on behalf of the Swiss Brethren. Repeatedly, Dathenus demanded a simple answer of 'yes' or 'no' to such questions as 'were the children of Israel one and the same people of God as the church of the New Testament' or 'is the Old Testament of equal authority as the New Testament in matters of faith and ethics [Glauben und Wandel]?'

Much to his evident exasperation, the Swiss Brethren would invariably equivocate, wanting to know exactly what all was implied by such a statement of affirmation. Dathenus did finally wring out from the Swiss Brethren that 'the main articles of Christian faith can and may be proved from the Old Testament' but they then immediately added the proviso 'but only in so far as the teaching of Christ and his Apostles permit'; and they consciously distinguished between matters of faith and matters of ethics. In terms of the latter, Bisch stubbornly insisted that 'there is a difference between the teaching of Moses and the prophets and Christ and his apostles'. In language familiar to the Swiss Brethren repertoire from earlier disputations, they also argued that the New Testament was the fulfilment and the perfection of the Old Testament law and that any attempt to read the testaments on an equal plane denied the significance of the Incarnation and the efficacy of Christ's teachings. Their primary concerns were with ethics and ecclesiology, not with theological abstractions or the interests of political and social stability. Not surprisingly, the exchange on the question concluded with a kind of stalemate, although the Reformed theologians were quick to claim victory.

The Swiss Brethren response

In tracing the rough outlines of the debate between the Swiss Brethren and the Reformers over the relationship of the Old and New Testaments it is striking how persistently the Swiss Brethren simply deflected questions regarding the immutability or sovereignty of God which so troubled the Reformers, refusing to acknowledge it as a matter of primary theological concern. Nevertheless, over time the Swiss Brethren did develop a number of arguments to explain how the Old Testament could be harmonized with the New Testament while retaining a high view of the transformative, unique work of Christ. It is doubtful whether Bullinger or Dathenus would have found any of these arguments convincing, since none proceeded in a systematic manner or addressed theological nuances with any amount of precision. For the most part, the responses emerged in the course of defending or explicating other theological principles which were seemingly more central to the Swiss Brethren cause; and, with one possible exception, the arguments seem to have been clearly borrowed, imported ad hoc from other Anabaptist traditions to fill a theological void. Seen together, however, these efforts point toward a creative theological *bricolage* emerging within Swiss Brethren circles which sought to defend the basic principles of adult baptism, pacifism, a separatist ecclesiology and a disciplined congregation, while also responding to charges such as that of Calvin that they regarded 'the Israelites as nothing but a herd of swine'.[25]

The Marpeck influence: a recently discovered commentary on the Frankenthal Disputation

The first, and most explicit, of these efforts to respond creatively to the question was almost certainly borrowed from the Marpeck circle. In contrast to the Swiss Brethren, Pilgram Marpeck took the hermeneutical question of the Old Testament very seriously and devoted one of his longest books, the *Testamenterleutterung* (published *c.* 1550), to an extended comparison of Old Testament and New Testament scriptures. Until very recently, little has been known about the ongoing influence of the Marpeck circle since they disappear from the historical record as a distinct group sometime in the 1560s. But in a remarkable bit of historical detective-work, Arnold Snyder has recently untangled a web of interdependent Swiss Brethren manuscripts and developed a line of argument suggesting that several key theological themes of the Marpeck circle were adopted by the Swiss Brethren during the waning decades of the sixteenth century.[26]

---

[25] Jean Calvin, *Institutes of the Christian Religion*, trans. Henry Beveridge (London, 1957), vol. 1, p. 369 (II.x.1). For a more detailed account of Calvin's denunciation of the Anabaptists on this point, see Susan E. Schreiner, *The Theater of His Glory: Nature and Natural Order in the Thought of John Calvin* (Durham, NC, 1991), pp. 107 ff.

[26] Arnold Snyder, 'The (not-so) "Simple Confession" of the later Swiss Brethren. Part I: Manuscript Communication in an Age of Print' [forthcoming, *MQR*].

Specifically for our story, Snyder has transcribed a lengthy codex from the Bern Burgerbibliothek in which an anonymous Anabaptist author penned a detailed response to all of the points debated in the Frankenthal disputation, offering along the way a more systematic, theologically sophisticated Anabaptist perspective on each of these issues.[27] Since the relationship between the Old and New Testament figured so prominently in the Frankenthal debate, the author naturally devoted considerable attention to this issue. According to Snyder, the author introduces to the Swiss Brethren a 'figurative' reading of the Old Testament in which the people, events and rituals of the Old Testament are to be understood symbolically, as 'prefigurements' of their essential truths which were only revealed in the New Testament.[28] The examples noted and the logic developed in this codex, claims Snyder, are fully consistent with the language and reasoning developed in Marpeck's *Testamenterleutterung*.[29]

The author of the commentary further developed a tripartite division of the Old Testament: (1) Law, such as the Ten Commandments, which teaches us 'how one should behave toward God and humankind'; (2) the priestly, levitical and civil authorities who sought to enforce the Law through coercion; and (3) specific rituals and ceremonies. According to the commentator, Jesus fulfilled the first part of these Old Testament elements; he explicitly amended and corrected the second part; and he annulled virtually all of the third part. Throughout, the author assumes that the Old Testament is 'essentially provisional and progressive [rather than an essentially eternal and unchanging expression of God's will], pointing figuratively and prophetically beyond itself to the future Christ and His church.'[30] The Old Testament thus gives witness to that which is to come. Contrary to the charges of the Reformers, the Anabaptists do indeed grant authority to the Old Testament, but 'only a spiritual, God-learned person knows how to seek the witness of Christ and His Kingdom in the Old Testament, and to extract the truth from the figures by means of a spiritual judgement, and have it correspond to Christ.'[31]

---

[27] 'Ein kurtze einfaltgie erkanntnuss uff die dryzehen artickell so verlouffens 1572 [*sic*] Jars zu Franckenthal in der Pfaltz disputiert worden' (microfilm of the original and the transcription in the Mennonite Historical Library, Goshen, IN).

[28] Arnold Snyder, 'The (not-so) "Simple Confession" of the later Swiss Brethren. Part II: The Evolution of Separatist Anabaptism' [forthcoming, *MQR*].

[29] In that work, Marpeck described the Old Testament as 'yesterday' (which he associated with 'law' and 'promise') and the New Testament as 'today' (which he associated with the present age of grace in Christ and the fulfilment of the promise).

[30] Snyder, 'The (not-so) "Simple Confession" of the later Swiss Brethren. Part II', p. 14.

[31] Quoted in ibid.

Whether this argument had a deep or lasting impact on Swiss Brethren thinking is not altogether clear. Large portions of the manuscript do turn up in another document, allegedly written by Andreas Gut entitled 'A Simple Confession' which he presented to Zurich authorities in 1588. But the original commentary apparently never appeared in print form and seems to exist intact only in a single manuscript. Nevertheless, at the very least, this argument within Swiss Brethren circles did provide the elements of a more spiritualist reading of the Old Testament which could have tempered the sharp dualism characteristic of Swiss Brethren theology.

Thomas von Imbroich's Confession: *the influence of Dirk Philips*

Pilgrim Marpeck, of course, was not the only Anabaptist thinker to address the question of the Old Testament. Among the Dutch Anabaptists, Melchoir Hoffman, Menno Simons, Dirk Philips and Bernhard Rothmann all developed hermeneutical principles which informed their readings of Old Testament scriptures. The lines of influence emanating from these writers is exceedingly complicated to trace with any certainty. But the writings of Thomas von Imbroich suggest one significant way in which the thought of Dirk Philips – including Dirk's use of the Old Testament – made its way into Swiss Brethren circles.

Thomas von Imbroich (also known as Thomas Drucker), was an Anabaptist leader in the Cologne area who had extensive contacts with both Dutch and North German Anabaptist congregations. Shortly after his imprisonment in December 1557, von Imbroich wrote a confession of faith in defence of believers' baptism that was smuggled out of prison, printed and widely circulated among various Anabaptist groups during the decades which followed.[32] Although von Imbroich's *Confession* was really a lengthy defence of adult baptism and a separatist ecclesiology, assumptions regarding Old Testament scriptures are closely woven into the development of the argument. Unlike Hubmaier, who had avoided reference to the Old Testament in his own classic defence of voluntary baptism, von Imbroich began his treatise with a reference to Adam, thereby introducing from the very outset a symbolic approach to the Old Testament which would pervade the entire text: by clothing himself with the skin of animals, Adam 'prefigured the sign of grace' by

---

[32] In 1562, four years after von Imbroich's martyrdom in Cologne, Heinrich Bullinger noted that an edict against Anabaptist books published by the Duke of Jülich in 1560 was directed specifically against the von Imbroich confession. Dutch Anabaptists translated the work already in 1579, a shortened version of which appeared in the 1660 *Martyr's Mirror*.

which Christians – who 'put on Christ' – make invisible their sins. Then followed a lengthy exegesis of the story of Noah's ark: just as the ark preserved Noah's physical family, so does Christ's church preserve his spiritual family from destruction. The waters which saved Noah and the waters through which the Children of Israel passed in their exodus from Egypt are analogous, claimed von Imbroich, to the waters of Christian baptism.

Von Imbroich's *Confession* explicitly refuted the claim that circumcision in the Old Testament justifies the practice of infant baptism: after all, women were not circumcised in the Old Testament; are they then not to be baptized? Are they not part of the covenant? Instead, 'circumcision was given to Abraham as a sign, as a prefigurement of the newborn children of God who, through the living rock Christ are circumcised in their heart.' The difference between circumcision and baptism, argued von Imbroich, is 'as letter to spirit, as between symbol and actuality. All was done symbolically; they were promised an earthly land, but in the New Covenant it became the spiritual Canaan of salvation.'

'In short,' he concluded, 'in everything they had a foreshadow, of which Christians have the reality ... such as circumcision, Passover lamb, priests, sacrifices, tabernacles, temples, feast days, Sabbath, king and nation, etc. All of this points to what was to come in the New Covenant.' 'But the symbols of the New Covenant, like baptism and the Lord's Supper, are not foreshadows or prefigurements of the future, but indicate what is present, which has taken place.'

According to Dirk Philips's biographer, Jacobus ten Doornkaat Koolman, von Imbroich's *Confession* drew heavily on a similar confession in Philips's *Enchirdion* that had circulated widely among Dutch Mennonites in the middle of the sixteenth century.[33] So the confession probably cannot be understood as an original piece of Swiss Brethren theologizing. But von Imbroich was widely read by Swiss Brethren in the late sixteenth century; and his status within the Swiss Brethren theological canon was assured a century later when his *Confession* – along with a collection of seven letters written in prison prior to his martyrdom – was included in an influential Swiss Brethren compilation of devotional literature entitled *Golden Apples in Silver Bowls* (1702).[34]

---

[33] Jacobus ten Doornkaat Koolman, *Dirk Philips: Friend and Colleague of Menno Simons, 1504–1568*, William Keeney (trans.), (Kitchener, Ont., 1998), pp. 70–72. Koolman describes von Imbroich's dependency on Philips as 'indisputable' but my initial effort to confirm this suggests that the nature of the dependency is not as self-evident as he implies.

[34] Eventually a condensed version of his *Confession* appeared as well in Swiss Brethren/Amish hymnal, the *Ausbund*, beginning with the 1742 Germantown edition.

Interestingly, the anonymous Swiss Brethren editor of the *Golden Apples*, who introduced von Imbroich's *Confession*, made a point to remind his readers of the biblical context of persecution. Though the editor made no specific argument about the place of the Old Testament in Christian theology, the evidence he cited that the righteous would inevitably suffer at the hands of the world began with a long list of people in the Old Testament who had suffered or died for their faith. By the end of the seventeenth century the Swiss Brethren clearly regarded their own history in continuity with the biblical story that reached back beyond the example of Christ to the stories of God's people in the Old Testament.

Hans Schnell: an original voice from within the Swiss Brethren tradition?

By far the most interesting and original attempt to address the relationship of the two testaments came from the pen of Hans Schnell, a shadowy figure from Hohenstauffen who was active as a Swiss Brethren itinerant preacher and baptizer in the region of Göppingen.[35] Around 1575 Schnell, who sometimes went by the name Hans Beck, wrote a lengthy, at times repetitive, commentary on Article VI of the Schleitheim Confession in which the Swiss Brethren asserted that the sword was ordained by God to punish the evil and protect the good, yet simultaneously 'outside the perfection of Christ'. The sub-text of the argument is a response to a question that recurred persistently in interrogations and debates with the Anabaptists: namely, could a magistrate who used the sword against evildoers still be regarded as a Christian?

Schnell's approach to the question placed the treatise unmistakably within the Swiss Brethren tradition. In classic Swiss Brethren fashion, he began with a ringing re-affirmation of the absolute, uncompromising dualism between the kingdom of this world – a kingdom associated with 'carnal weapons' used to fight for a 'perishable crown' – and Christ's kingdom which is armed only with spiritual weapons. 'Neither [kingdom],' Schnell asserted, echoing Article IV of the Schleitheim

---

[35] The full title of the pamphlet is: *Thorough Account from God's Word, How to Distinguish Between the Temporal and Spiritual Regimes, Each with its Order; and Concerning the Power of the Temporal Sword* ... . A manuscript of the treatise is extant as part of the Codex Geiser, but a slightly abridged print version of Schnell's text also appeared in 1710 and was included in a least one Swiss Brethren eighteenth-century *Sammelband* of devotional materials. A translation of the treatise can be found in Leonard Gross, 'H. Schnell, Second-Generation Anabaptist,' *MQR*, 68 (1994), pp. 358–77.

Confession, 'can participate in or have communion with the other.'[36] But whereas earlier Swiss Brethren writings frequently collapsed the relationship of the Old Testament to the New Testament in this dualism,[37] Schnell went on to develop a much more subtle and creative argument.[38] Throughout the entire text, he sought to establish lines of continuity between the Old and New Testament while simultaneously underscoring the distinctive character of the new spiritual kingdom inaugurated by Christ.

Thus, according to Schnell, the dualism between Christ's kingdom and the kingdom of the world is written into the Old Testament as well as the New. The children of Israel, for example, lived in darkness in Egypt before they were called out into the light as a holy people. So, too, the story of Daniel in the lions' den, or the three young men who refused to bow before Nebuchadnezzar, or the story told in the Apocryphal book of II Macabees of Eleazar and his seven sons who suffered martyrdom for their refusal to eat pork, all gave evidence of God's consistent desire for a holy people, called out and separated from a fallen world. This dualism took on an enduring symbolic form in the two lineages of Abraham: Ishmael, 'born of the flesh to an Egyptian maidservant', and Isaac, 'born of the promise' to Abraham's wife. The offspring of Hagar and Sarah thus 'signify the two testaments and also two different peoples ... and two kingdoms'.[39] Ishmael must 'serve within the confines of a servant's marriage' meaning that the task of his offspring was 'to rule and govern lands and peoples'. His children were the twelve princes who had 'courts and fortresses'. The children of Isaac, on the other hand – the twelve patriarchs – were itinerant, poor

---

[36] Gross, 'H. Schnell', p. 359.

[37] As in tract entitled *On Two Kinds of Obedience* – it could serve as the foil for series of dualisms which contrasted the servile/filial; Moses/Christ; ceremonies/love of God and neighbour; death/life; Old Covenant/New Covenant.

[38] By presenting these two kingdoms in symbolic language, Schnell argues, 'God wanted to encourage the world to be reasonable, to be circumspect and truly and certainly to be aware of such matters which were figuratively indicated, presented and sketched by these two examples.'

[39] Gross, 'H. Schnell', pp. 366–7, 369, 377. It should be noted that Pilgram Marpeck also expounded on the contrast between Sarah and Hagar in his 'The Churches of Christ and of Hagar' which he addressed to members of his group in Württemberg in 1544. But Marpeck interweaves his commentary with imagery from the Song of Songs and identifies the descendants of Hagar with those people (presumably the Swiss Brethren) who are only concerned with the letter of Scripture and who have not feasted from the living sustenance which comes from the breast of Sarah (via Christ and the Holy Spirit). While Schnell may indeed have known of this letter, his use of the Sarah/Hagar imagery is elaborated here in much greater detail and Hagar is identified with those who live according to vengeance and the law of Moses.

'herders of cattle'. The true covenant was clearly given to Isaac. But even though Ishmael was banished and forsaken, he nevertheless also received a promise from God. His rewards, however, are here on earth, so he cannot inherit with Isaac the eternal life which God offers to the children of the covenant. Ishmael's descendants are not without hope. But if Ishmael's son wants to become with Isaac an heir to the family 'he must be born anew through the Holy Spirit ... and must conform to the teaching of Christ and his example. ... He must not resist evil and may no longer execute vengeance with the sword but must love his enemy, and in suffering with Christ must pray for his enemy, must follow the poor, rejected, crucified Christ and help him bear his cross.'[40]

These same oppositions can be found elsewhere in the Old Testament as in the two sons of Isaac, Esau and Jacob. Thus, throughout all of Scripture, 'God has figuratively represented to us these two peoples – namely the people in the kingdom of this world that are born of the flesh and the people of Christendom that are born of the Spirit.'[41]

Elsewhere Schnell refers to the Old Testament in symbolic terms. The outward worship and the literal law of Israel, for example, 'foreshadowed the true essence in Christ and his kingdom: namely a spiritual king, a spiritual power, sword, rule and order, a spiritual kingdom that is not of this world ... For just as the shadow on the wall reveals a man, so the law shows Christ and the new inward nature of his kingdom and its essence his power, spirit and truth.'[42] More specifically, Christ inherited the eternal high priesthood from the tribe of Levi and the royal throne from the tribe of Judah, both of which were foreshadowed in the union of these two offices under Melchizedek.[43] Or again, 'the figurative royal throne [of David], was transformed into the spiritual and eternal kingdom of Christ'.[44]

At the same time, however, Schnell is equally clear that the Incarnation of Christ has ushered in a new aeon which marks a decisive break with the old covenant. Nowhere is this break seen more clearly than in the new law of love which replaces the law of vengeance and the sword. 'Although God in the figurative law gave and commanded to Moses the vengeance and power of the sword to punish evil,' writes Schnell, 'this does not apply to Christians in the New Testament. For Christ, who is the fulfilment of the law, has cancelled it.'[45] 'The Christian church has

---

[40] Ibid., p. 377.
[41] Ibid., p. 367.
[42] Ibid., p. 370.
[43] Ibid., p. 371.
[44] Ibid., p. 369.
[45] Ibid., p. 374, 372.

never exercised vengeance or resisted evil. It has always suffered violence, drunk the cup of suffering and stood under the cross and persecution to be conformed to its Lord and Master. For the servant is not above his master, and a Christian should be minded as Jesus Christ was minded.'[46]

Specifically, for the magistrate, Christ has replaced vengeance with 'kind mercy'. The office of government executes vengeance, 'but whoever wants to be a Christian, according to Christ's teaching, shall not take revenge nor resist evil'. Christ's coming did not abolish the law of vengeance, but it is the function of government to rule and the calling of the Christian to drink the cup and to suffer. 'If then a magistrate wants to be a Christian he must be obedient to Christ's teaching and follow his example [which means that] he then may punish nobody according to the law or give vengeance but must love the enemy, suffer blows, drink the cup of suffering and also turn the other cheek, as Christ teaches.' 'Therefore,' Schnell argued, 'ruling and being a Christian are two different things. Those who do not remain in the teaching of Christ have no God.'

In the end, it remains an open question as to whether the rapprochement Schnell tried to construct between the Old and New Testament actually succeeded, especially in light of his conclusion that 'it has been sufficiently shown that in the New Testament Christ has annulled vengeance in the law of Moses and made it powerless and transformed everything into love and mercy.' But his 'Thorough Account from God's Word' – and the other documents we have noted – make it clear that, by the end of the sixteenth century, the Swiss Brethren had developed at least an implicit understanding of the relationship between the Old and New Testaments. Though they rarely considered the nature of this relationship as a theological problem to be resolved, they did recognize the need to incorporate the Old Testament into their theological worldview.[47]

---

[46] Ibid., p. 374.

[47] Interestingly, the debate over this issue seems to fade in significance by the end of the seventeenth century; the issue of the Old Testament is not raised as a major problem in the lengthy polemics of Wolleb, Thormann, Ottius, Salchi, all Reformed theologians writing against the Swiss Brethren in the second half of the seventeenth century. Instead, disputations and court records in the seventeenth and eighteenth century seem to focus much more consistently on specific questions of church discipline and the ban, on simplicity in speech, on the moral integrity of the Swiss Brethren *vis-à-vis* their Reformed neighbours.

Conclusions

Given the fact that the Swiss Brethren approach to this question tended to be ad hoc and unsystematic – more frequently woven into their apologies for adult baptism, separation from the world, and a rejection of violence than isolated as a distinct theological issue in the manner of the Reformed theologians – what general conclusions can we make about their understanding of the Old Testament?

1. At a fairly simple level, the Old Testament provided a rich store-house of proof texts which could be cited in concordances, hymnody and devotional literature as evidence to defend or to illustrate general arguments. Thus, for example, Hans Schnell could cite a list of Psalms wherein God destroys the weapons of the godless as a defence of his argument regarding non-resistance; and a Swiss Brethren concordance lists numerous Old Testament references under such varied headings as 'separation', 'the church', or 'love'. Despite a clear bias in favour of New Testament texts, the Swiss Brethren clearly regarded the Old Testament as an authoritative source to be cited in a deductive fashion if it suited one's purposes.

2. A number of Swiss Brethren writers went beyond mere proof texts to identify several fundamental themes of theological continuity between the Old Testament and New Testament which could explain or legitimate their own convictions. They were aware, for example, that righteous people suffered for their faith in the Old Testament as well as the New Testament; they argued that God had called out a holy people in the Old Testament just as the body of believers in the New Testament was called out from the world; and some Swiss Brethren saw in the story of Noah's Ark a reminder of God's saving grace to the small group of the redeemed as well as God's coming judgement on those who were 'given over' to the world.

3. At yet a third level, the Swiss Brethren were clearly sympathetic to a line of biblical interpretation that understood the Old Testament primarily in a symbolic or figurative sense. This, of course, was not an original approach to Scripture, and was certainly not unique to the Swiss Brethren or the Anabaptists; after all, anyone who had heard a Catholic homily on the allegorical meaning of an Old Testament text had already been primed to read the Old Testament through a symbolic or figurative lens. But such a reading – influenced likely by the Marpeck circle and Dutch Anabaptism – provided the Swiss Brethren with a reasonable method of taking the Old Testament seriously without denying the fundamental

discontinuity in human history which was marked by the Incarnation of Jesus Christ.

4. Most commonly, however, the Swiss Brethren fell back into an implicit progressive understanding of Scripture which regarded the Old Testament as belonging to a time in which the fullness of God's intention for humanity had not yet been revealed. Though it failed to respond to the Reformers' charges that such a view did violence to the immutable character of God, the Swiss Brethren found this progressive reading of Scripture to conform neatly with their dualistic view of the cosmos, their emphasis on orthopraxis over orthodoxy, and their Christocentric approach to theology. Such a view was articulated clearly in a letter of 1529 written by Wolfgang Brandhuber to the Swiss Brethren congregation at Rattenberg in which he admonished them 'not to let Christ be made into Moses, retaining the word according to the law of Moses'. 'Moses was in the shadows,' he explained, echoing the sentiment more often implied than stated in dozens of other Swiss Brethren treatises, 'for the veil had not yet been torn to the light which has appeared to us ... which is Christ Jesus.'[48]

During the past fifty years, scholars of the Radical Reformation have debated vigorously over the shape and essence of the Anabaptist movement. As a result of that productive debate we now have dozens of essays and monographs on Anabaptist views of the sword, the visible church, baptism and the ban. But it is noteworthy that the Reformers themselves regarded all these issues as derivative of a prior, more fundamental, question regarding the place of the Old Testament in biblical hermeneutics. At the very least, the intensity of their concern suggests that this is a topic worthy of more attention than has hitherto been accorded it.

---

[48] *GZI*, pp. 137–43.

CHAPTER FOUR

The 'Perfection of Christ' reconsidered: the later Swiss Brethren and the sword

C. Arnold Snyder

In the 'General Introduction' to his seminal *Anabaptists and the Sword*, James Stayer described good historical writing as 'putting what seems to the historian to be the most reasonable interpretation on as comprehensive a body of evidence as possible'.[1] It was precisely because Stayer's own work on the sword carried out this prescription so well that it led to a fundamental redefinition of Anabaptist studies. But more than that, *Anabaptists and the Sword* continues to be an essential point of reference for its topic, filled to the brim with helpful references and surprising insights – a testimony both to the reasonableness of its interpretation and the comprehensive scope of its documentation. As a consequence, those of us who have followed in Stayer's wake find ourselves essentially adding footnotes to his earlier work.

This present chapter is one such footnote. It is based on evidence that was not available at the time of Stayer's writing *Anabaptists and the Sword*. Furthermore, the documentation dealt with here dates from the 1570s and 1580s, hence falling outside the time frame covered by his study of the sword, which he described as spanning 'from the 1520s through the 1560s'. Nevertheless, this footnote will propose a modification to one of James Stayer's conclusions concerning the Swiss Brethren and their view of the sword.

Stayer's work on the early Swiss Brethren was a master stroke. By a meticulous sifting of the sources, he demonstrated that it had been a mistake to judge all early Swiss Anabaptists by the measure of Conrad Grebel and Felix Mantz. Early Swiss Anabaptism was full of great uncertainty and considerable variety on the question of the sword. The decisive change came in 1527 with the Schleitheim Articles, whose fourth and sixth articles defined an apolitical, separatist understanding of the sword. The 'radical apoliticism' of Schleitheim gained quick

---

[1] James Stayer, 'General Introduction', *Anabaptists and the Sword* (Lawrence, KS, 1972), p. 6.

acceptance among the Swiss and soon replaced alternative views. Evidence drawn from the disputations held with Reformed ministers in the 1520s and 1530s in Zoffingen and Bern[2] led Stayer to the conclusion that 'later, more extensive statements of the Swiss Brethren on nonresistance ... were essentially glosses on the Schleitheim Confession'.[3]

Recent evidence both confirms and modifies Stayer's conclusion concerning Schleitheim's influence on the early Swiss Brethren, as we will see below. Evidence from the Frankenthal Disputation of 1571 confirms that even a decade beyond the period covered by *Anabaptists and the Sword*, the radical apoliticism of Schleitheim still remained the standard Swiss Brethren position. Nevertheless, manuscripts circulating and being copied by Swiss Brethren later in the 1570s and 80s contain formulations on separation from the world and the sword of government that can in no way be called 'glosses on the Schleitheim Confession'. Some surprising alternatives to radical apoliticism were being considered among the Swiss Brethren in the last quarter of the sixteenth century – the long-term effects of which on the Swiss Brethren are yet to be studied.

Reformed and Swiss Brethren debate the sword at Frankenthal

The Frankenthal Disputation was an extended debate between Reformed (Calvinist) theologians and Swiss Brethren, sponsored by the Palatine elector, Frederick III. Swiss Brethren representatives to the disputation were given safe conduct and were lodged and fed at state expense for the twenty-three days of debate (28 May to 19 June 1571). At the conclusion of the debate, the minutes recorded by three official scribes were collated, reviewed, and then corrected and approved by Reformed and Anabaptist participants. The results were published in an official Protocol document in that same year in Heidelberg.[4] This

---

[2] Ibid., p. 125.

[3] Ibid., p. 93. For further analysis of Schleitheim's influence on the descendants of the early Anabaptists, see Arnold Snyder, 'The Influence of the Schleitheim Articles on the Anabaptist Movement: An Historical Evaluation', *MQR*, 63 (1989), pp. 323–44.

[4] The official publication was titled: *Protocoll. Das ist/Alle handlung dess gesprechs zu Franckenthal inn der Churfürstlichen Pfaltz/mit denen so man Widertäuffer nennet ...* (Heidelberg, 1571) (hereafter *P*). The best study of the Disputation in English is the dissertation by Jess Yoder, 'A Critical Study of the Debate Between the Reformed and the Anabaptists, Held at Frankenthal, Germany in 1571' (PhD diss., Northwestern University, 1962). See also the two-part article by Jess Yoder, 'The Frankenthal Debate with the Anabaptists in 1571: Purpose, Procedure, Participants', *MQR*, 36 (1962), pp. 14–35; 'The Frankenthal Disputation: Part II. Outcome, Issues, Debating Methods', *MQR*, 36 (1962), pp. 116–46. See also Heinold Fast, 'Die Täuferbewegung im Lichte des Frankenthaler Gespräches, 1571', *MGBl*, N.F. 23 (1971), pp. 7–23. See also the *ME*, II, pp. 373–5.

document thus provides unusually detailed and accurate documentation of how the Swiss Brethren at Frankenthal presented and defended their theological views generally, and more particularly, provides insights into their view of the sword of government.

The official Protocol of the Frankenthal disputation reveals that the views on the sword of the Swiss Brethren who participated could well be described as 'glosses on the Schleitheim Confession', or a reworking of arguments already presented in previous disputations. There was, first of all, a particular hermeneutic in evidence at Frankenthal that allowed the Swiss Brethren to draw separatist and apolitical conclusions. The Swiss Brethren emphatically insisted that the New Testament superseded the Old, and that Jesus had taught a new and more perfect ethic in the New than had Moses in the Old. This distinction provided the essential underpinning for the Swiss interpretation of Matthew 5:39 and related verses. The Swiss Brethren at Frankenthal interpreted the words and the deeds of Jesus as having provided the norms of conduct for all Christians of all times and places. This literalistic, Christocentric reading of biblical ethics cemented Swiss Brethren apolitical separatism. All Christians, magistrates included, are called to take up their cross of suffering, follow in Christ's footsteps, separate from an evil and fallen world, and enter the 'perfection of Christ'.

This approach, these arguments, and the separatist conclusion were all well known to the Reformed disputants at Frankenthal, and they had counter-arguments prepared. The Reformed argued for the unity of teaching (both doctrinal and ethical) in the Bible as a whole. The God of the Old Testament was the same God as that of the New, and God did not change His mind. As far as the words and the example of Jesus were concerned, the Reformed argued that they should not be read as being applicable to all people at all times and places. Concerning the central Anabaptist text on the sword, in which Jesus commands His followers to 'resist not evil', the Reformed at Frankenthal contended that with that verse Jesus was correcting the Pharisees, who did not understand the 'proper use of vengeance'. In the second place, God has only one, eternal will and Law. The Anabaptist position would mean that 'the eternal Son of God contradicts the Law of Moses and himself' which must be false.[5]

The Reformed maintained that there were parallel and harmonious teachings concerning vengeance in both the Old and the New Testaments. Believers should never avenge themselves, but rather leave vengeance to God. This teaching is found in both Testaments and

---

[5] Yoder, 'Critical Study', pp. 155–6.

applies to individual believers and the church. But on the other hand, civil authority was instituted to enforce justice. This teaching is also found in both testaments, but it applies to the civil authority, not to individual believers or the church. Therefore, concluded the Reformed, 'While both Testaments say that vengeance does not belong to the church, they not only permit it for the rulers, but command it.' The Swiss Brethren, said the Reformed, had not distinguished between churchly and civil offices,[6] nor had they recognized the fact that the distinction of offices was present in both testaments in the same way.

The Swiss Brethren at Frankenthal responded in the manner already outlined at Schleitheim: there is only one God, but in Jesus Christ, God made clear that He had ordained two opposed kingdoms. The New Testament perfects the partial revelation of the Old. The brethren agreed that in Matthew 5 Christ was speaking specifically to His church, and they also agreed that Christians should obey civil authority. Nevertheless they concluded that the Christian 'cannot be a ruler and punish evil with the sword'.[7] The Reformed, said the brethren, could not demonstrate that the New Testament church had ever allowed believers to be rulers and to use the sword. Christ had decreed that all his followers were to love enemies, forego vengeance and violence, and leave the world behind. This divine decree included rulers who wished to be Christians, for New Testament teaching made no allowances of different behaviour according to 'office'.[8]

The Reformed, however, continued to press the brethren at a sensitive point: if the brethren would not allow that a Christian might serve as a magistrate, were they saying that the office of a civil ruler was 'of God or the Devil, right or wrong, sin or not sin?'[9] The difficulty for the brethren was that since Schleitheim their position had held that the civil authority was 'ordained of God outside the perfection of Christ'. The logic of the case thus led to the conclusion that the God-ordained civil authority was necessary, perhaps, but nevertheless essentially evil – just as Satan was allowed by God to hold sway in the world, but was evil. When the brethren answered by insisting upon scriptural proof that a Christian could serve in government office, the Reformed refused to budge and asked in return: 'Did God ordain something that is evil?'[10]

To this pointed query the Reformed never got a satisfactory reply. The brethren repeated again that there were two kingdoms, and that the

---

[6] Ibid., pp. 156, 157.
[7] Ibid.
[8] *P*, p. 437.
[9] Yoder, 'Critical Study', p. 157.
[10] Ibid., p. 158.

sword belongs in the hands of government, in the kingdom of the world, but the kingdom of Christ is not of this world. One cannot serve two masters. The Reformed insisted that the 'ruler is not serving two masters, but rather, only one', and concluded: 'It is terrible for a Christian to say that government is necessary, wanting its protection, yet not granting it the power to enforce evil and protect the right.'[11]

Having thus been pushed to the limits of this difficult paradox, the brethren at Frankenthal made some surprising (even if brief and temporary) concessions. Rauf Bisch, speaking for the Swiss Brethren, continued to maintain that the civil authority was not to use the sword in the church. Nevertheless, he said that 'magistrates are able to be Christians'. Bisch clearly was allowing more latitude here than had Schleitheim, but Bisch did not go on to explain how magistrates might be 'Christian' while yet standing 'outside the perfection of Christ'.[12]

In the end Rauf Bisch and the Swiss Brethren backed away from the idea that a 'Christian magistrate' might be possible, and reiterated the same basic point that Schleitheim had maintained: all Christians are to follow Christ, which means that they will not punish with the sword, but rather will love enemies. All Christians, including Christian rulers, suffer rather than inflict suffering.[13] Given the hermeneutical presuppositions the Swiss Brethren assumed, they were pushed to affirm the existence of two kingdoms, one of Christ and one of Satan, with no real intercourse between them. This was, in all essential ways, a repetition of the radical apoliticism of Schleitheim, argued with the same language and categories.

A Marpeckite responds to the Frankenthal Protocol

If the published Protocol of the Frankenthal Disputation was the last word on sixteenth-century Swiss Brethren views of the sword, we could well conclude that the Swiss Brethren had not moved very far beyond the Schleitheim Confession. But the Frankenthal Protocol was not the last word, and in fact provoked a thoughtful and thorough response from an anonymous Anabaptist. An analysis of this writing leads to the conclusion that its author had been strongly influenced by Pilgram Marpeck's ideas. The Marpeckite reply to the Frankenthal Protocol, which we have described elsewhere and called *Q1*, was never printed,

---

[11] Ibid., pp. 159–60.

[12] 'Dann wir glauben wol / dass Ampt unnd Hauptleut Christen werden können ... ', *P*, p. 468.

[13] Ibid., p. 470.

as far as is known at present, but circulated in manuscript form.[14] The
discussion on the sword in this manuscript marks a significant departure from Schleitheim. In fact, it repeats and elaborates upon Pilgram
Marpeck's 'less radical apoliticism' which, as Stayer's original work
noted, was 'a more radical apoliticism than Luther's but a milder type
than that of the *Stäbler* sects or the Swiss Brethren'.[15]

The finding of a Marpeckite manuscript that differs from Schleitheim
on the sword would not be of particular relevance to the Swiss Brethren, except for the fact that there is ample archival evidence that in the
1570s and 1580s Swiss Brethren leaders were interested enough in this
Marpeckian, non-Schleitheimian reply to the Frankethal Protocol to
copy it repeatedly and to circulate it in their communities. This fact
suggests that the later Swiss Brethren were actually not content simply
to gloss Schleitheim. In point of fact, they seem to have been interested
in more moderate alternatives.

Figurative hermeneutics

The *Q1* response to Frankenthal begins by outlining a more flexible
hermeneutic than the Swiss Brethren were accustomed to utilizing. Although the Marpeckite author agrees with the Swiss Brethren that the
New Testament takes precedence over the Old Testament, *Q1* arrives at
that conclusion by utilizing a figurative hermeneutic. A figurative reading of Scripture was commonly used in early Melchiorite Anabaptism,
by Menno Simons and especially Dirk Philips, as well as by Pilgram
Marpeck and his circle. This approach assumed that persons, places,
and events in the Old Testament were to be read as physical 'figures' of
spiritual things to come in the latter days.[16]

---

[14] See the two-part article, to be published in *MQR*: 'The (not so) "Simple Confession" of the later Swiss Brethren. Part A: Manuscripts and Marpeckites in an age of
Print', and 'The (not so) "Simple Confession" of the later Swiss Brethren. Part B: The
Evolution of Separatist Anabaptism'. The manuscript in which the *Q1* document is
found is codex 628, located in the Berner Burgerbibliothek, Berne, Switzerland; microfilm copy #203, Mennonite Historical Library, Goshen, IN.

[15] Stayer, *Sword*, pp. 179–81, *passim*.

[16] For more on the use of the 'figurative' method in Anabaptism, see C. Arnold Snyder,
Anabaptist History and Theology: An Introduction (Kitchener, Ont., 1995), pp. 166–9;
206; 212–13; 369–71. The Münsterites held that Old Testament 'figures' needed to have
both a literal and a physical manifestation in church of the Last Days. This provided
them with the rationale for the literal 'restitution' of Old Testament practices. Obbe
Philips (followed by Joris, Menno and Dirk Philips) argued strenuously against this view,
and held that the Old Testament figures would have spiritual manifestations only.
Nevertheless, they were agreed on the use of the figurative method of Old Testament
interpretation. See ibid., pp. 211–12.

The pattern of figurative exegesis in *Q1* is most reminiscent of similar exegetical exercises of the Marpeck circle. Not only did the Marpeck circle edit and republish Bernard Rothmann's *Bekenntnisse*, including a section where a figurative reading of the Old Testament is expressly outlined and expanded upon,[17] the Marpeck circle also published a huge concordance, the *Testamenterleutterung*, in which the same approach to the two Testaments was argued.[18] This 800–page printed concordance (published *c.* 1550) was intended to explicate a correct 'spiritual' reading of the Old and New Testaments. Old Testament Scripture ('yesterday') provides concrete instances whose deeper meaning consists in their figurative pointing to the spiritual realities of the present and future church of Christ ('today' and 'tomorrow').

The direct application of this exegetical approach to the matter of the sword was addressed already in the *Q1* preface, which begins by interpreting the exodus of the children of Israel out of Egypt as the Old Testament 'figure' for the Christians who left the papal church. Behind them are those who persecute with 'sword, spear, bow, water and fire,' and before them is the glassy sea mixed with fire (Revelation 15). What are these Christians of the Last Days to do? Following Moses' lead, their natural response would be to attempt to slay their human enemies. But this would be to respond in a physical way, when what Christ calls for is a spiritual response; Christians must follow the spiritual law of Christ, not the physical law of Moses.

Isaiah and Micah both prophesy that in the Last Days, God will raise up the mountain of the house of the Lord and that 'from now on a people will not raise weapons against another'. This, then, is what the church of the Last Days is to be like. Likewise the temple of the Last Days is not a physical temple on earth built by human hands such as was done in the Old Testament (which temples have continually been defiled by kings and nobles), but rather is a spiritual temple in heaven and built by God. Likewise, Christ entered not a physical temple, but heaven itself, and is the high priest for all Christians. *Q1* concludes:

---

[17] ' ... in the Old Testament nearly everything was done in a figurative way ... ' William Klassen and Walter Klaassen (trans. and eds), *The Writings of Pilgram Marpeck* (Scottdale, PA, 1978), p. 222. The words are Rothmann's in this case. Later in the tract the Marpeck circle expands the point: 'In summary, the ancients had a sketchy, figurative, yet symbolic faith which focused on hope. ... Just as a shadow points forward to the light and the figure to the essence, the faith of the ancients pointed forward to Christ and His true believers.' Ibid., p. 233.

[18] Cited hereafter as *TE*. See the 'Preface to the "Explanation of the Testaments"', in Klassen and Klaassen, *Writings*, pp. 555–66 and 586, nn. 1, 2. A microfilm of the Zurich copy of this rare print can be found in the Mennonite Historical Library, Goshen, Indiana. My thanks to the MHL for making their copy available to me.

'Since we in these last days have another temple and another high priest, therefore we also have another law.'[19]

In short, *Q1* did far more than simply affirm the ethical priority of literal New Testament 'commandments' over the Old. It provided a sophisticated exegetical tool with which the Swiss Brethren could mine Old Testament Scripture in search of physical 'figures' that were to be 'spiritually' fulfilled in their church, according to the more perfect pattern of New Testament revelation. Furthermore, *Q1* introduced the importance of the spiritual dimension in assessing matters of the sword. The point was not only that Jesus laid down an external 'law' concerning non-violence, but, rather more profoundly, that there was a new *spiritual law of love* that needed to be fulfilled for those who now were under the new, spiritual covenant. In fact, a characteristic of the New covenant is that it is a spiritual covenant, not an external one. The author of *Q1* wrote:

> The Old has an outer, fleshly mediator, namely Moses; it had an outer priesthood, outer unction, an outer kingdom, sword, law and judgment. The New has an inner, spiritual mediator, namely the person Jesus Christ. It has an inner kingdom and priesthood, the kingdom of our Lord Jesus Christ which he establishes in the newly reborn person, in justice, peace and joy in the Holy Spirit, (Romans 14).

Likewise the Old Testament established a physical authority with a physical sword; in the New a spiritual authority is given, namely Jesus Christ.[20] Readers of the Marpeck circle's *Testamenterleutterung* recognize immediately the Marpeckian nature of this approach and argument. The distinctive Marpeckian spiritualist foundation of a thoroughly Christocentric ethic grows out of this exegetical approach, and stands in contrast to the more separatist, literalist ethic of Schleitheim and the earlier Swiss Brethren.

Concerning the Reformed contention at Frankenthal that Moses also commanded the love of enemies in Exodus 23, which was introduced as a key 'proof' at Frankenthal that the Old Testament and the New Testament were equivalent, *Q1* answers 'in this way they mix Moses and Christ together, so that the true spiritual sense and understanding remains hidden under cover and curtain, so that the Mosaic power and sword might be kept and defended in the church and community of God.' The author of *Q1* notes that no one can prevent people distorting Scripture 'according to their own sense', but that no one who 'allows the Holy Scripture to remain in its clear meaning' will come to the

---

[19] *Cod. 628*, p. 86.
[20] Both examples in *Cod. 628*, p. 101.

conclusion that Matthew 5 and Exodus 23 'are the same teaching'.[21] It is the spiritual law of love in the hearts of the reborn that constitutes an advance beyond the Mosaic law.

The copying and circulation of a figurative exegesis with a strong spiritualist undercurrent among the Swiss Brethren of the later sixteenth century is a noteworthy event. The more spiritualist viewpoint of the Marpeck circle not only provided the Swiss with a new exegetical tool for interpreting all of Scripture in a 'progressive' manner, it also provided a strong rationale for religious toleration (based on spiritual freedom) and provided a tool for tempering Schleitheim's separatist finality, as will be noted below.

The sword

Having already established a figurative, spiritualistic underpinning for understanding matters of the sword, the author of *Q1* took on the matter of the sword of government as the third article under discussion: 'Whether a Christian may be a Magistrate and punish those who are evil with the sword.'[22] The author of *Q1* joined the Frankenthal discussion on this topic by stating that one must first distinguish what a Christian is, and in the second place, understand what it means to be a magistrate. The argument is taken forward with biblical examples.

Certainly the Apostle Peter was rightly called a Christian, when he declared Jesus to be the Son of the living God. Peter also was a Christian even when he told Jesus that he wished to accompany Him even unto death, but nevertheless then denied Jesus three times, for which failing he was profoundly sorry and wept from the heart. But Peter 'really became a true Christian only when ... he stood before the authorities and rejoiced, because he was accounted worthy to suffer for the sake of the name of Christ.'[23]

Likewise the disciples of the Lord were Christians when they still had their own possessions, lived with their families in their own houses, and pursued their various professions. 'But they were far better [Christians] when they left everything behind for the sake of Christ's name, and followed the Lord's footsteps into suffering.'[24] Therefore, when Jesus

---

[21] *Cod. 628*, p. 103. The argument continues, 'for the loving of enemies commanded by Moses was to be observed only among the Israelites ... and not ... the Gentiles, their enemies.'

[22] Ibid., p. 112.

[23] Ibid., p. 113.

[24] Ibid., pp. 113–14.

praised the disciples and promised that his followers would sit on thrones and judge the twelve tribes of Israel (Matthew 19:28–30) he promised this not on the basis of the life the disciples were then leading, but rather based on the life they would lead after the Holy Spirit was sent upon them, and they were spiritually reborn.

In order to answer the question if a Christian may be a magistrate and punish evil people with the sword, *Q1* argues that one must understand what one means by 'Christian' for, the point is made, there are many kinds (or degrees) of Christians. As the case of the Apostles demonstrates, some people may do something today that appears to be good and Christian, but yet be thoroughly ashamed of the same thing tomorrow, when they come to a better understanding.

A *true* Christian, said the author of *Q1*, 'is already a citizen of the kingdom of heaven and a member of the saints'. The true Christian 'forges his earthly weapons into hoes, pruning knives, sickles and saws' and 'does not oppose evil by wreaking vengeance on his enemies'. Such a Christian 'walks according to the law that has come out of Zion, and according to the Lord's Word which comes from Jerusalem, written in his heart through the Holy Spirit;[25] he punishes the godless and the sinners with the sword which proceeds from the mouth of the Lord.' By contrast a magistrate is 'an earthly lord who, just as a Christian is rooted above, is rooted here below. He must pass judgment and make demands according to the law that was given on Mount Sinai and which also grows in human hearts, namely an eye for an eye and a hand for a hand, ... and this not only with words, but also with earthly power and might.'[26]

What is to be concluded, therefore? In contrast to the unequivocal 'two kingdoms' pronouncement of Schleitheim, the writer of *Q1* says

> Therefore to be a true Christian ... and to be a ruler and to wield the sword of the world are so opposed to each other, that *it is very difficult for one person to manage both at one and the same time.* But this is not to say that a ruler is of the devil, as we are accused of saying by our detractors; they [magistrates] should remain in their office as is ordained and commanded by God.[27]

---

[25] For the exact argument concerning the 'outer' and the 'inner' law, elaborated at length, see *TE*, ch. 48, pp. CXXXVIII, a to CLI, b. Concerning the Old Testament law, *TE* cites numerous passages and then comments that it is clear that 'yesterday the law and the commandments still were written only outside the heart, namely written on stone tablets by God ... and with ink in a book by Moses.' *TE*, p. CXLIII, b. After citing many more passages, *TE* comments that it is clear how 'yesterday's' external law was 'changed, yes annulled and ended, namely today through the writing of God's law in human hearts ... '. *TE*, p. CXLIX, a.

[26] *Cod. 628*, pp. 114–15.

[27] Ibid., p. 115. Emphasis mine.

This argument, with its statement that 'it is very difficult for one person to manage both', immediately brings Pilgram Marpeck and his circle to mind. Unlike Schleitheim's unequivocal consignment of all political magistrates to the kingdom of the world, Marpeck had allowed for the faint possibility of rulers also being Christian, insisting all the while that such rulers would no longer coerce, but would be governed by the Spirit of Christ. In fact, we read what is essentially the *Q1* argument in the writings of Hans Denck and Pilgram Marpeck, pointing again to a Marpeckite origin for the *Q1* reply to Frankenthal.[28]

The *Q1* reply, however, does add further elaborations not read in Marpeck's writings. As noted, *Q1* began the discussion of the sword of government by suggesting that there had been different degrees of 'being Christian' among the disciples. *Q1* continues to make the same point by putting a figurative exegesis to work, pointing to the Old Testament examples of Noah's ark, the Tents of the Presence, and Solomon's Temple.

Noah's ark is interpreted by *Q1* as an Old Testament figure for the church of Christ. This reading itself was not novel; the ark was generally considered to be a figure for the church because it saved Noah and his family from death in the flood. *Q1* interpreted the ark figuratively as follows: 'But the ark had three separate floors: one for the impure beasts, the second for the pure beasts, the third for the people, all of whom, with no distinction, were to be saved from the flood.'[29] In other words, all within the ark of the church will be saved; they are 'Christian' to this extent. Nevertheless, there are degrees or levels of purity among Christians.

In the same way the Tents of the Presence and the Temple of Solomon, which the writer of *Q1* also takes to be Old Testament figures for the church, had different chambers for the Israelites depending upon their various and different roles and degrees of purity.

> The tents of the presence were distinguished according to rooms: one for the children of Korah who were commanded to look after

---

[28] See Snyder, *Anabaptist History and Theology*, pp. 189–91 and p. 199 n.19. The parallels are clearly seen in the following citations from Denck and Marpeck. Denck wrote: 'Insofar as it were possible for a government to act in this way [i.e. with love] it could well be Christian in its office. Since however the world will not tolerate it, a friend of God should not be in the government but out of it, that is if he desires to keep Christ as a Lord and master.' Walter Klaassen, *Anabaptism in Outline* (Scottdale, PA, 1982), p. 250. Marpeck wrote: 'It is difficult for a Christian to be a worldly ruler. ... if everything concerning the kingdom of this world was done properly according to the true human and divine order ... how long would his conscience allow him to be a magistrate ... '. Ibid., p. 263.

[29] *Cod. 628*, p. 115.

external things, but not to enter inside or they would die; one below the door of the tent that was called holy, in which the priests sacrificed daily; and one further inside called the holy of holies, in which no one dared go but the high priest once a year. And the temple was made according to this same plan, and had the same customs and rights. But the children of Korah wished to be pure, and were not satisfied that they were the servants of the Lord to render external service, and they were swallowed up and consumed by the wrath of the Lord. Saul was cast out of the kingdom for the same offence. Usa, who thoughtlessly laid his hands on the treasures of God was struck dead by the Lord; when Nadab and Abihu, the sons of Aaron brought foreign fire into the sanctuary of the Lord, which he had not commanded them to do, they were consumed by fire from the Lord.[30]

The lesson to be drawn from this figurative reading of the Old Testament, according to the author of *Q1*, is that there are people and practices that do not belong to the proper, or 'inner' church of Christ, but rather are preliminary to it. The church of Christ, which is the spiritual essence indicated by the above Old Testament figures, also has different 'rooms' into which each one enters 'according to his walk and life, as is fitting. [But] when one goes further than is appropriate, he is an abomination to the Lord in the holy city, rather than a welcomed servant.' When such people overstep their place, their calling, and their appointed tasks (it is clear that the magistrates are meant here) they will inherit the wrath of God.[31]

There are, then, different levels or degrees of being Christian in *Q1*'s conception of the church. The highest level of obedience and purity is the best, of course, but salvation is not therefore denied outright to those at the lower (or outer) levels – all within the ark were saved, and those in the outer reaches of the temple were still God's people. This is a more inclusive, catholic understanding of the church than Schleitheim or the Swiss Brethren had heretofore considered to be biblical.

Magistrates and the Church

Following the lead of such Anabaptists as Hans Denck and Pilgram Marpeck, the author of *Q1* made the borders of the church considerably more permeable than had the Swiss Brethren after Schleitheim. Nevertheless, the church as described by *Q1* was not 'known to God alone', but rather continued to be marked by very visible boundaries.

---

[30] Ibid., pp. 115–16.
[31] Ibid., pp. 116–17.

This was especially true for the boundaries pertaining to magistrates, which *Q1* took pains to explain carefully.

Those who overstep their proper bounds and transgress in the Temple of the Lord are truly an abomination before God, says *Q1*, 'But when we say all this we do not mean to depreciate a ruler of the people one calls Christian, or to give cause for the removal of the same, may our Lord and God protect us from this.' The crucial distinction concerning rulers and their sphere of legitimate activity is activity that is proper to the world, and that which is proper to the church. 'We recognize and maintain that [magistrates] are necessary among the children of men (who do not wish to allow themselves to be ruled by the illumination of the Holy Spirit) so that they be maintained in decency and fear.'[32] Clearly rulers are needed in the 'world of men' outside the church, but just as clearly, insofar as they are to be considered Christian, rulers are commanded to lay down their powers of coercion in the communion of saints, inside the church, among those now ruled by the Holy Spirit.

The point is cemented with further figurative exegesis of Old Testament examples.

> The Holy Spirit of God lamented and cried through the prophet Ezekiel, chapters 43 and 44 to the children of Israel and said, You from the house of Israel have gone too far with your abominations. You bring a person with an uncircumcised heart and body into my sanctuary, through which you desecrate my house, etc. There should be no stranger in my sanctuary whose heart and body is uncircumcised. Likewise, in addition your kings set their thresholds and my threshold, their doorposts and my doorposts next to one another, with only a wall between them.[33]

The figurative application to the church of the 1570s was quickly and easily drawn.

> For we also bring people with uncircumcised hearts and bodies into his sanctuary when we recognize as good Christians, people stuck in open sin and vice, such as the proud, grasping, puffed up, clever, fornicators, adulterers, greedy, usurers, guzzlers, gluttons, etc., on whom Paul already proclaimed judgement (unless such people convert with true repentance), 1 Cor. 6, Gal. 5, Eph. 5. ... Likewise, we set the Lord's threshold, and the kings' threshold too close to one another when we bring a ruler with his worldly sword into the sanctuary of the Lord, and admonish and urge him that anyone that we punish with the Word of God and the sword of the spirit, he ought to punish with the same worldly sword that he may wield and use (outside the church) against murderers, thieves and other wrongdoers ... For the use of such power in the church or

---

[32] Ibid., p. 117.
[33] Ibid., p. 118.

> sanctuary of the Lord is as much of an abomination to the Lord as when the priests in the Old Testament brought foreign fire in, and lit their offering with it, when it was on account of their uncleanliness that the holy fire did not wish to burn.[34]

The lesson to be learned from Old Testament examples is that the sanctuary of the Lord is not the place for those who are 'uncircumcised' spiritually or who wish to use unspiritual weapons there.

But in fact, the *Q1* document tends to waver in the course that it had been navigating. Contrary to the more inclusive, optimistic foregoing examples of 'degrees of being Christian', the *Q1* manuscript now seems taken with the opposite conclusion:

> To be a true Christian and also to be a ruler is impossible for human beings; but it is possible for God, for He can give grace. According to the words of the prophet Isaiah, bears, lions and leopards will live with the lambs and will eat their food. That is, the higher and lower authorities lay down their sword and staff, which they have to punish the above-mentioned vice, before the Lord's threshold, and go to the place where one treats and ought to treat Christian teaching, behaviour, and discipline, not as a ruler, but exactly like a child, and like a child allow themselves to be shown and taught. For one must receive the kingdom of God in the condition of a child, and not in the form of a great lord, according to the Word of the Lord, and in his holy mountain, that is in the Christian church, no one will any longer be wounded or offended, Isaiah 2, Micah 4.[35]

Magistrates who exercise 'earthly power' inside the church, or who try to coerce religious belief, give evidence that they have not received God's grace which would have enabled them to enter His kingdom 'as children'. The worldly sword belongs in the world, to punish evil persons; only the spiritual sword belongs in the church of Christ.[36]

A strong separatist sentiment is also evident in the *Q1* manuscript, perhaps inserted in the midst of the Marpeckian argument by Swiss Brethren copyists. In any case, the argument moves into more familiar Swiss Brethren exegetical territory with pages of examples and citations drawn directly from the New Testament, with the literal conclusion that 'Christians should do likewise, and reject the worldly sword'. But what then of the beginnings of the argument? Are magistrates who leave their swords at the church door, so to speak, free to exercise coercion in the world outside, as Christian magistrates? Will magistrates be *saved* if they stop interfering inside the church, but nevertheless continue to

---

[34] Ibid., pp. 118–19.
[35] Ibid., p. 120.
[36] Ibid., pp. 123–4.

wield the civil sword outside the church? The answer is not clear or unequivocal in *Q1*, but several conceptual shades of grey are introduced which occupy the space between the stark black and white poles of Schleitheim's two kingdoms. The answer to the question of whether 'pious' or 'godly' authorities would be saved, following Schleitheim, would have been a definite 'No'. Following *Q1*, in what appears to have been a further elaboration of the Marpeckian position, the answer would be better framed as 'God knows'.

The *Q1* manuscript continues to insist throughout that true Christians are 'sheep' and not 'wolves', whose weapons are spiritual, not physical. There is no doubt that magistrates are admonished to lay aside their swords altogether as their 'highest' call. But just when the separatist, apolitical duality of the case is becoming clear, the *Q1* manuscript includes a remarkable passage like the following:

> When a magistrate possesses the virtues that should belong to a reborn Christian, as noted above, we believe that a magistrate can certainly be a Christian, and that a Christian may be a magistrate, insofar as he truly lives and walks according to the Gospel. Without any doubt the Christians of the New Testament who held offices, such as the Centurion, Cornelius, Paul, Sergius, Erastus, the jailer of all the emperor's people, and others besides, lived and walked according to the Gospel. Whenever that happens certainly the Spirit, who is the ruler of consciences, teaches one how one is to act, and how one is to be ruled much more by love than by any lesser standard. Such a person will not tolerate or wish to continue any improper government action, such as twisting the law for some powerful person, and oppressing the poor, but rather will flee far from such things. But where there is no such [evidence of love], we will let those who have been anointed by the Holy Spirit judge whether such people are actually Christian rulers, or rather worldly [un-Christian] magistrates. In brief, according to Gospel teaching we cannot consider a fleshly, un-regenerated person to be a Christian even if such a person is a king or an emperor. For the office makes no one a Christian, but rather the Holy Spirit who brings new birth to the heart is the one who creates Christians.[37]

There can in fact be 'Christian rulers', concludes *Q1*, but this possibility depends upon a proper understanding of both 'Christian' and 'ruler'. In contrast to the Schleitheimian position, which would deny that rulers can be Christian, *Q1* holds that insofar as a ruler does not have to violate the spiritual law of love, a ruler can indeed be a Christian. In contrast to the Reformed argument, which would have automatically qualified rulers as Christians by virtue of their God-ordained office (Romans 13), *Q1* insists that the status of rulers as Christians depends

---

[37] Ibid., pp. 152–3.

on their spiritual rebirth. This rebirth will be evidenced by the loving way in which rulers rule.

Conclusion

It should not be surprising if by the last quarter of the sixteenth century the Swiss Brethren were interested in formulations that were less emphatically separatist than was Schleitheim. It is useful to recall that the Schleitheim Confession was an apocalyptic document. In the apocalyptic context of 1527, the prevailing Anabaptist mood was the maintenance of purity for the Bride of Christ and separation from an abominable world that was soon to be punished for its sins. But fifty years later Jesus had not yet returned. The Swiss Brethren found themselves attempting to create living spaces, looking not just to community purity in the short term, but also to the future survival of their communities. It is certainly no accident that several of the surviving Swiss Brethren manuscripts that copy the *Q1* material were writings directed to the governments of Zurich and Berne, and were essentially appeals for toleration. In the context of the 1570s and 80s, 'Pure Bride' separatism was certainly a less-than-useful apologetic paradigm.

The Marpeckite manuscripts that circulated and were copied by the Swiss Brethren provided some new and potentially useful ideas for the Swiss Brethren. This was evident in hermeneutics, where the Marpeck circle had expended much energy already by 1550 in elaborating a comprehensive figurative and spiritualist reading of the Bible as a whole. The earlier literal measures of obedience (for example, Christ was not a judge, therefore Christians cannot be judges) had virtually predetermined black and white boundaries of faithful church membership. By contrast, when the measure of obedience was defined rather as the love of Christ planted in the hearts of believers by the Holy Spirit, the boundaries of the church could expand accordingly.

Likewise concerning questions of church, government and the status of government officials, the more flexible Marpeckite understanding was tailor made for appeals to government toleration of Anabaptists – in large part because it was itself a more tolerant spiritualist position that allowed more 'world' inside the church. *Q1* introduced more permeable boundaries in its concept of the church, resulting in less certainty about the damnation of those 'outside the perfection'.

Taken as a whole, and bracketing what appear to be separatist interpolations, *Q1*'s argument implies much more than Schleitheim's either/or choice: human beings are either Christians who are 'in the perfection of Christ', or rulers who are necessarily 'outside the perfection of Christ', but never both at once. In *Q1*'s conceptual universe, by contrast, there are degrees of perfection among Christians. One of the degrees of perfection may include a magistrate who manages to balance being both a Christian (spiritually reborn) and a magistrate, who manages to restrain evil in the world while yet leaving the sword at the church door.

How far – or even if – this more flexible Marpeckian understanding of the sword penetrated and modified subsequent Swiss Brethren views concerning the sword of government is a subject for further study. Looking at internal evidence from the manuscripts suggests some real resistance to Marpeckite ideas. The flow of *Q1*'s arguments moderating church boundaries appears to have been interrupted by more literalist and separatist arguments that actually paraphrase Schleitheim here and there. Internal evidence thus suggests that the older and more direct separatist Swiss Brethren answers were not immediately vanquished by Marpeckian moderation – even at the same time that the Swiss Brethren were busily copying Marpeckian materials. The separatist and the moderate positions on the sword coexist uneasily in the manuscripts under consideration.

Nevertheless, the manuscripts in circulation in Switzerland at the end of the sixteenth century teach us that alternatives to Schleitheim's stark polarity were being considered, copied and circulated among the Swiss Brethren. This finding points to considerably more cross-fertilization between the Marpeckian and Swiss Brethren camps than we had suspected before. Marpeck's views did not mysteriously disappear without a trace, but rather appear to have percolated into Swiss Brethren writings and consciousness as the sixteenth century drew to a close. Whether this fact helps explain perceived Swiss Brethren laxity in the next century, thus leading to the backlash of the Amish schism, remains an open question inviting a definitive answer.

PART TWO
Anabaptists, witches and Reformation radicalism

'A common future conversation': a revisionist interpretation of the September 1524 Grebel Letters to Thomas Müntzer

Hans-Jürgen Goertz, translated by Werner O. Packull

The consultations at the Second Zurich Disputation in October 1523 on what to do with images and the eucharist ended in disagreement. Conrad Grebel and Simon Stumpf turned against Ulrich Zwingli's intention to leave the timing of the removal of images and mass to the city council. Grebel and Stumpf, who were among Zwingli's earliest supporters, saw in Zwingli's decision to leave the timing to the council a compromise between Christian community and the authority's policy, which in its subject territory [*Landschaft*] was directed against the communal reform aspirations of the 'commoners'. The authority thereby demonstrated its true, anti-Christian face. Under no circumstances were Grebel and Stumpf prepared to tolerate this blending of Christian with anti-Christian endeavours: the Reformation in Zurich had not begun under such a motto. Zwingli, however, thought otherwise. As early as January 1523 he had entrusted the power to enforce decisions reached during the Disputation to the city council. At that time, the followers who were now protesting had not complained. Indeed, the council's power of decision had been clearly articulated in the official call for the Second Disputation, hence Zwingli found it difficult to understand his former supporters' change of mind. He misunderstood the criticism of the council's temporary failure in the subject territories as a fundamental rejection of all participation by the temporal authority in church matters. He was therefore perplexed when Grebel and Stumpf approached him shortly after the Second Disputation with the suggestion for the election of a new, truly Christian council by the reform-minded citizens of Zurich, a council that would engage itself with all its might for the advancement of the Reformation.

In order to keep disagreements to a minimum the suggestion by the Comptur of Küssnacht, Konrad Schmid, had been adopted during the Second Disputation. Accordingly, the clergy and laity in the subject territory [*Landschaft*] were to be thoroughly instructed. Only then could there be any thought of translating the decisions on reform into practice.[1] This approach should have been agreeable to everyone, but the radicals were not satisfied with it. Again and again quarrels broke out concerning payment of the tithe and the removal of images. Warnings were issued, consultations held and actions taken, all in order to seek ways that would enable Zurich's authority to translate the agreed-upon reforms into action. Finally, in June 1524, shortly after the deaths of the mayors of Zurich, Felix Schmied and Max Roist, the orderly cleansing of the churches began, first in the city, then in the villages. Noteworthy is the concession made by council to rural communities: every community was permitted to undertake the cleansing of its own church, if a majority decided to do so.[2] The stubborn persistence of the radicals and the unrest they spread had borne fruit.

The attempt to abolish the mass proved more difficult than the issue of images. Not until Maundy Thursday, 1525, did it take place. As early as December 1523 Zwingli had expressed his intention to celebrate, if possible, the Lord's Supper at Christmas in both kinds, but the council had urged him not to pursue this plan. In the final analysis Zwingli's insight that he need not lose hope for change while yielding to the pragmatic considerations of the political leadership came to him in a sudden 'revelation'.[3] But for the radicals this was only a further sign of the questionable compromises which Zwingli was prepared to make, since the controversy regarding the tithe had begun in rural communities. Annoyed and angered, Grebel wrote to Vadian: 'Whoever thinks, believes and says Zwingli acts according to the obligation of a shepherd, thinks, believes and speaks godlessly.'[4] Incidentally, one of Zwingli's sermon topics, with which he hoped to strengthen the resolve of the clergy to support the Reformation during the days of the Disputation, had been 'the shepherd'. In this sermon he distinguished clearly between true shepherds desiring reform and 'false' shepherds. This sermon must have been on Grebel's mind when he wrote those damning words. In his eyes Zwingli had decidedly joined the false shepherds and forsaken the road of the Reformation.

---

[1] Emil Egli, Georg Finsler, Walther Köhler et al. (eds), *Huldreich Zwinglis sämtliche Werke. Unter Mitwirkung des Zwingli-Vereins* (Zurich, 1905), II, pp. 794–6.

[2] Lee Palmer Wandel, *Voracious Idols and Violent Hands. Iconoclasm in Reformation Zurich, Strasbourg and Basel* (Cambridge, 1995), pp. 96 ff.

[3] *Zwinglis sämtliche Werke*, IX, p. 281. Cf. John H. Yoder, *Täufertum und Reformation in der Schweiz*, vol. I: *Gespräche zwischen Täufern und Reformatoren* (Zurich, 1968), pp. 27 ff; Robert Walton, *Zwingli's Theocracy* (Toronto, 1967), p. 207; also 'Was There a Turning Point of the Zwinglian Reformation?' *MQR*, 42 (1965), p. 45.

[4] *TQ Zürich*, p. 8.

Little is heard from the radicals during the first half of 1524; only two insignificant letters from Grebel to Vadian have survived. In a letter dated 3 September 1524, in which he paraphrased the first speech of Elihu [Job 32], he confided to his brother-in-law that he had deliberately held back: 'I have waited and they did not speak, they stood there and have not answered.'[5] Apparently the radicals still hoped that Zwingli would give the decisive word and continue the Reformation in the direction they assumed had been agreed upon. At any rate, they used the time after the October Disputation to reflect on the situation and to prepare for further action. Grebel held Bible studies on the Gospel of Matthew in the circle that formed around the book pedlar Andreas Castelberger.[6] Just as Zwingli, after coming to Zurich, had begun with an exegesis of the Gospel of Matthew, so Grebel apparently hoped to make a new beginning with an exegesis of the same gospel. In order to help his followers argue more convincingly about baptism, he prepared at the same time a biblical concordance on passages dealing with the theme of faith and baptism. This concordance appeared belatedly in April 1525 under the name Hans Krüsi from St Gall.[7] Grebel informed Vadian further that he was in the process of answering a letter by Andreas Bodenstein von Karlstadt and that he planned to make contact with Thomas Müntzer and Martin Luther – an intention that signalled his coming to self-consciousness as a Reformer. Nothing is known about a letter to Karlstadt, but in two letters to Müntzer he sought contact with a like-minded person whose writings on faith and baptism he had read. At the same time he entertained the thought of 'cornering Luther'. A letter with that intent is said to have arrived in Wittenberg, but Luther did not respond to it, sending instead friendly greetings through the student Erhart Hegenwald.[8] Grebel gave no indication of resignation during this time period. On the contrary, he emanated self-confidence and a desire for action: 'For I am full of sermons, and my

---

[5] Grebel to Vadian on 18 December 1523. *Vadianische Briefsammlung der Stadtbibliothek St Gall*, Emil Arbenz and Hermann Wartmann (eds), vols I–VII (St Gall, 1888–1905), no. 374; *TQ Zürich*, p. 8; German translation in Mira Baumgartner, *Die Täufer und Zwingli. Eine Dokumentation* (Zurich, 1993), p. 205; English translation in Leland Harder (ed.), *The Sources of Swiss Anabaptism. The Grebel Letters and Related Documents* (Scottdale, PA and Kitchener, Ont., 1985), p. 29.

[6] Cf. Werner O. Packull, 'The Origins of Swiss Anabaptism in the Context of the Reformation of the Common Man', *Journal of Mennonite Studies*, 3 (1985), pp. 38 ff.

[7] Cf. Heinold Fast, 'Hans Krüsis Büchlein über Glaube und Taufe. Ein Täuferdruck von 1525', *Zwingliana*, 2 (1962), pp. 456–75.

[8] Grebel to Vadian on 3 September 1524, *Vadianische Briefsammlung*, III, no. 404; *TQ Zürich*, pp. 11 ff; Baumgartner, *Täufer und Zwingli*, p. 206; Harder, *Sources of Swiss Anabaptism*, p. 276; regarding Erhart Hegenwald see ibid., pp. 322–31.

inner spirit stirs me. Behold, my belly feels like it is filled with young wine that, without an air escape, bursts new bottles. I have to speak to get some air; I will open my lips and answer.'[9] Here too he borrowed the words of Elihu. As long as he had belonged to Zwingli's inner circle, he did not need to articulate his own theology; the master did it for him. But now the student had taken time to educate himself theologically and to find his own language – totally on his own and without consideration of others. The rationale he gave was remarkable: 'since I do not know how long I will remain or whether my creator will soon take me away.'[10] He had not only a premonition regarding his own demise but knew that the general state of Christendom was catastrophic. He cited a passage from the Prophet Daniel which was circulating in the militantly, anti-clerical milieu of those days: 'And the abomination of devastation will be in the temple and will remain until the end' [Daniel 9:27].[11] But Grebel went beyond this general anti-clerical, apocalyptic diagnosis. What he wanted to communicate was the experience of the past months, that even in the Great Minster of Zurich the powers of devastation were at work. As proof he pointed to certain persons, especially Zwingli, who knew better but refused to move ahead: 'they themselves drink the purest water, but muddy the rest with their feet. This they give to the sheep who have to drink that which they muddied with their feet' [Ezra 34:18 ff]. Grebel continued forcefully:

> They begin with a plan but not from the Spirit of God; they consult but not with God, so that sin is added to sin and they move down to Egypt without asking for God's counsel. And they place their hope in the help and strength of Pharaoh and their trust in the shadow of Egypt. But the strength of Pharaoh will turn to their shame.[12]

This too was a biblical citation [Isaiah 30:1–3], a borrowed word. Clearly Grebel had in the meantime immersed himself in the study of the Holy Scriptures; he was beginning to make biblical commentaries on his own time period. Zwingli was not the true shepherd. Because he relied on the strength of God's enemies, his appeal to the Holy Spirit was rejected. He led the Church not into freedom but deeper and deeper

---

[9] Baumgartner, *Täufer und Zwingli*, p. 206; Harder, *Sources of Swiss Anabaptism*, p. 276.

[10] Baumgartner, *Täufer und Zwingli*, p. 206; Harder, *Sources of Swiss Anabaptism*, p. 276.

[11] Baumgartner, *Täufer und Zwingli*, p. 206; Harder, *Sources of Swiss Anabaptism*, p. 276.

[12] Baumgartner, *Täufer und Zwingli*, p. 206; Harder, *Sources of Swiss Anabaptism*, p. 276.

into its ruin; he refused to permit God to speak directly. Here Grebel sounded notes similar to those already heard from Müntzer.[13]

The two documents that permit the deepest insight into Grebel's theological perception of the tense and as yet undecided situation of reform in Zurich are the two letters which he and his friends wrote to Müntzer in the early days of September 1524. They are candid letters that engage the self-willed radical reformer of Allstedt in Electoral Saxony with sympathy but also criticism. These letters indicate that the group around Grebel had formed out of the reservoir of early activists – the fast-breakers, tithe-refusers, iconoclasts and Bible readers – who had in the meantime become disillusioned with the Reformer of Zurich. Missing from this group was Simon Stumpf, who had been its leader.[14] Stumpf had to leave Zurich's territory several months earlier because he had contravened the orders of council on the matter of images and stirred up an iconoclastic riot in Höngg.[15] Thus the radicals now looked to Grebel who convinced them with his learnedness, religious competence and who had taken the reins of leadership into his hands. It was he who authored the two letters.

The Grebel circle had over time developed its own theological position and deliberately approached those who found themselves in a similar situation, in particular Karlstadt and Müntzer. What initially united them all was the rejection they had experienced from the main Reformers: here from Zwingli, there from Luther. Grebel complained bitterly about Zwingli: 'For our shepherds are so angry with us; they deride us publicly from the pulpit as evil doers, devils disguised as angels of light.'[16] This must have already occurred in the summer of 1524. Meanwhile, Luther had published *A Letter to the Elector of Saxony Concerning the Rebellious Spirit*, a letter Grebel felt was no one's business to write.[17] In it Luther wrote that the vagrant spirit [Müntzer] had invaded Electoral Saxony and 'made himself a nest in Allstedt'.[18]

---

[13] Thomas Müntzer, *Schriften und Briefe. Kritische Gesamtausgabe*, Günther Franz (ed.), (Gütersloh, 1968), p. 505.

[14] Cf. James M. Stayer, 'Die Anfänge des schweizerischen Täufertums im reformierten Kongregationalismus', in Hans-Jürgen Goertz (ed.), *Umstrittenes Täufertum 1525–1975. Neue Forschungen* (2nd edn, Göttingen, 1977), p. 35.

[15] Cf. Wandel, *Voracious Idols*, pp. 83–6; Emil Egli (ed.), *Actensammlung zur Geschichte der Züricher Reformation in den Jahren 1519–1533* (Zurich, 1879), p. 190.

[16] Heinold Fast (ed.), *Der linke Flügel der Reformation. Glaubenszeugnisse der Täufer, Spiritualisten, Schwärmer und Antitrinitarier* (Bremen, 1962), p. 25.

[17] Ibid., p. 24.

[18] Martin Luther, 'Eyn brieff an die Fürsten zu Sachsen, von dem auffrurischen geyst, Wittenberg 1524', in Ludwig Fischer (ed.), *Die lutherischen Pamphlete gegen Thomas Müntzer* (Tübingen, 1976), p. 3.

The commonalities between Grebel's and Müntzer's circles were not only to be found in battles against Zwingli and Luther. They had not only their adversaries but also the 'Word' and their trials and tribulations in common.[19] Both groups thought of themselves as on the right path in their interpretation of the sacred Scriptures, while accusing the Reformers of perverting the same: 'You [Müntzer, Karlstadt, Strauss and Stiefel] are much purer [in your treatment of the Scriptures] than ours here and those at Wittenberg who daily fall from one perversion of the Scripture and from one blindness into another greater one.'[20] The radicals in Zurich used only one measuring stick with which they also measured Müntzer's liturgical reforms, inasmuch as they had knowledge of them: 'What we are not taught with clear Scriptural examples shall be to us as if it were forbidden, as if it were written not to do.'[21] This was also Müntzer's measuring stick. Furthermore, both preached not the 'sweet' but the 'bitter' Christ, whom they followed in tribulation and suffering. Both understood themselves as 'poor in spirit', that is, as relying not on their own but only on God's Spirit. Finally, the Zurich radicals welcomed Müntzer's criticism of child baptism. 'We like your writing well in regards to baptism and would like to be further instructed by you.'[22] Most likely they had already discussed the practice of baptism in their own circle; perhaps they knew of the yet unpublished booklet on baptism by Karlstadt. But even if that were the case, they did not arrive at their view or practice of baptism by this information from Karlstadt.[23] Wilhelm Reublin had called for the refusal of pedobaptism in Witikon as early as the spring of 1524. And, as may be seen from a letter by the peoples' priest in St Gall, Benedict Burgauer, the practice of child baptism – if one ignores its earlier criticisms by Zwingli – had become an issue as early as 1523.[24] On Easter Sunday of 1524 some parents at Witikon refused to carry their children to baptism. Refusals were also reported from Zollikon where Johannes Brötli was active as 'helper'. Thus the problem of child baptism was already a

---

[19] Fast, Der linke Flügel, p. 27.

[20] Ibid., p. 26.

[21] Ibid., p. 15.

[22] Ibid., p. 20. Regarding baptism by Müntzer cf. Hans-Jürgen Goertz, Innere und äussere Ordnung in der Theologie Thomas Müntzers (Leiden, 1967), pp. 109–14. Ernst Koch, 'Das Sakramentsverständnis Thomas Müntzers', in Siegfried Bräuer and Helmar Junghans (eds), Der Theologe Thomas Müntzer: Untersuchungen zu seiner Entwicklung und Lehre (Göttingen, 1989), pp. 129–55.

[23] Cf. Calvin A. Pater, Karlstadt as the Father of the Baptist Movements. The Emergence of Lay Protestantism (Toronto, 1984), p. 144.

[24] Vadianische Briefsammlung, II, no. 137; Harder, Sources of Swiss Anabaptism, pp. 222 ff.

subject of public debate, and the Grebel letter, which Brötli also signed, does not give the impression that the signatories were only just beginning to have their own doubts about it.[25]

What attracted the Zurichers especially to Müntzer was his view of false faith, a criticism which bound all the above-mentioned commonalities together. In his *Counterfeit Faith* and *Protestation and Proposition* (1524), 'which extraordinarily enriched and strengthened us who are spiritually poor',[26] Müntzer had criticized the 'invented' faith: a faith which was only accepted outwardly and did not fundamentally change the human being, for example, did not lead to moral improvement. Similarly, the Zurichers did not want everyone to run after the 'outer' while neglecting the 'inner'.[27] Müntzer spoke of the 'inner essence' of baptism, while Grebel spoke of 'inner' baptism that brings about 'the washing away of sins through faith and the blood of Christ'.[28] For both this was apparently a perceivable process. Müntzer developed the concept of the 'experienced' faith from late medieval mystical sources. The Zurichers were influenced by Erasmian and Zwinglian spirituality. Both shared the emphasis on emotional inner spiritual genuineness as well as the moralistic pragmatic emphasis on purity and the practical application of the Word of God. Understood spiritually, the Word lifts the whole life of the believer into an order which has, individually and collectively, far-reaching consequences in this world. This view explains why Karlstadt, Müntzer and the Zurichers could not understand that the Reformers did not immediately seek to convert their theological insights into practice but instead sought to protect the consciences of those who were weak in the faith. It is possible that Grebel already knew of Karlstadt's *On Offending the Weak* (Basel, 1524). He and the radicals were of the opinion that only Scriptural ordinances could advance true faith, put consciences at ease, bring about true active piety and destroy the various forms of illusionary self-righteousness with its 'hypocritical works'.[29] Only so could true piety come to full fruition.

This fundamental position reflected the situation in which the sacred Scriptures were read, understood and appropriated: in the rural territory, church and temporal authority had to be created entirely new, against existing ordinances. The notion that experienced faith changes

---

[25] Cf. Walter Klaassen, 'Die Taufe im Schweizer Täufertum,' *MGBl*, 46 (1989), pp. 75–89.

[26] Fast, *Der linke Flügel*, p. 18.

[27] Ibid., p. 16.

[28] Ibid., p. 20; Müntzer, *Schriften und Briefe*, p. 227.

[29] Müntzer, *Schriften und Briefe*, pp. 226, 231.

the person and creates new relationships fits this perception. Such changed persons were believed capable of creating or reinstituting the scriptural, apostolic reality of life. The blending of radical ideas of reform with the desire of rural communities to free themselves from inherited lordships in their struggle for the autonomy of their own community was similar to the engagement which Müntzer was to manifest on behalf of the commoners. Müntzer sought to change outward circumstances in order to make room for the 'arrival of true faith'; at the same time he expected true faith to bring about changes in circumstances.[30]

Because of the above commonalities the Zurichers believed that they should give their 'beloved brother' and 'genuinely faithful proclaimer of the Gospel' some advice. They were not criticizing the above-mentioned writings of Müntzer but rather some news relayed by Hans Huiuff after the latter's visit with Müntzer in Allstedt; they were also responding to information received through a letter from Huiuff's brother. Hans Huiuff, a goldsmith from Halle on the Saale, had moved to Zurich where he had obtained citizenship in 1520.[31] Whether he had joined Grebel's circle before or only after the visit to his homeland is no longer clear. The point is that Grebel and his friends criticized only peripheral rather than fundamental matters of Müntzer's thought; for example, they criticized the continued use of 'altar pieces' in his worship services, the use of German songs, the use of 'clerical and liturgical vestments' (perhaps the Zurichers already knew Müntzer's first liturgical writings) and that he, like Karlstadt, had not broken with the system of benefices. The Zurichers were apparently unaware that Müntzer had given up his altar benefices in Braunschweig as early as 1522 and was supported by the congregation of Allstedt. Grebel counselled Müntzer to adhere strictly to the Scriptures and to put an end to the above-mentioned abuses. Above all, he was to abolish the mass, root and branch. Furthermore, Grebel let it be known 'that the Gospel and its adherents should not seek the protection of the sword'.[32] Perhaps the Zurichers had heard rumours about Müntzer's propensity towards the use of force. It is interesting to note how carefully they raised this issue in their first letter: surely this did not apply to Müntzer at all; they were merely mentioning it. Only in the second letter, which as a postscript reacted to

---

[30] Cf. Hans-Jürgen Goertz, 'Zu Thomas Müntzers Geistverständnis', in Bräuer and Junghans, Der Theologe Müntzer, p. 96.

[31] Cf. Siegfried Bräuer, 'Sind beyde dise Briefe an Müntzer abgeschickt worden? Zur Ueberlieferung der Briefe des Grebelkreises an Thomas Müntzer vom 5. September 1524', MGBl, 55 (1998), pp. 7–24.

[32] Fast, Der linke Flügel, p. 20.

news just received from the pen of Huiuff's brother, do they offer direct criticism. This criticism was surely a reaction to Müntzer's *Sermon before the Princes* of July 1524. In it Müntzer threatened that power would be taken from the princes and given back to the common people if the princes refused to protect the god-fearing from the godless.

> If that is true, or if you intend to war, the tablets, chanting, or other things for which you do not find a clear word (as you do not find for any of these aforementioned points), I admonish you by the salvation common to all of us that if you will desist from them and all opinions of your own now and henceforth, you will become completely pure, for you satisfy us on all other points better than anyone else in this German and other lands.[33]

But this criticism is not so harsh and brusque as to permit the conclusion that an unbridgeable gap existed between the Zurichers and Müntzer. The commonalities were stronger than the differences. Only so is it explicable that the Zurichers signed the second letter as 'seven new young Müntzers for Luther'.[34]

The Grebel circle had declared its solidarity with Müntzer but had also criticized him. In the past, false conclusions have often been drawn from the letters. Either the commonalities have been played up into a dependency of one on the other, such as, for example, considering Müntzer to be the violent one who drew all radicals into his orbit and infected them with his destructive spirit. This is how Karl Holl described the relationship and how Heinrich Bullinger, Zwingli's successor at the Great Minster in Zurich, already saw it very early on.[35] Or the rejection of the sword and the preparedness to suffer as followers of Christ became the evidence for claiming a fundamental antithesis between the Zurichers and Müntzer: 'Grebel is concerned not with leading a social revolution but with establishing the church of Christ on earth according to the Gospel.'[36] That was Harold S. Bender's view. He saw Müntzer's 'revelatory spiritualism' as being in fundamental opposition to Grebel's plain scriptural faith.[37] This view of Bender's did neither Müntzer nor Grebel justice. Müntzer used the Scriptures exactly as

---

[33] Ibid., pp. 24 f; Harder, *Sources of Swiss Anabaptism*, p. 293.

[34] Fast, *Der linke Flügel*, p. 26.

[35] Karl Holl, *Luther und die Schwärmer. Gesammelte Aufsätze* (2nd and 3rd edns, Tübingen, 1923), p. 425; Heinold Fast, *Heinrich Bullinger und die Täufer* (Weierhof, 1959).

[36] Harold S. Bender, *Conrad Grebel, c. 1498–1526. The Founder of the Swiss Brethren, Sometimes Called Anabaptists* (Goshen, IN, 1950), p. 174.

[37] Harold S. Bender, 'Die Zwickauer Propheten, Thomas Müntzer und die Täufer', *Theologische Zeitschrift*, 8 (1952), pp. 262–78. Cf. dagegen Hans-Jürgen Goertz, *Innere und äussere Ordnung* (Leiden, 1967), pp. 79–84.

Grebel did, to support his views, and Grebel appealed to the Holy Spirit just as Müntzer did, in order to prove the correctness of his scriptural exegesis.[38] Christoph Wiebe recently dissolved the either-or approach through a careful reconstruction of the steps in the argument on baptism found in Grebel's letter. Grebel did not intend to set forth his own systematic position nor to emphasize the spiritual origins of baptism; instead he wanted to engage Müntzer with what he had read and heard about him. In the final analysis he wanted to strengthen Müntzer's principal position and to advance greater clarity where this seemed necessary. But Grebel did not take over Müntzer's views in order to construct his own theology. Perceived similarities suggest that Grebel argued with Müntzer on the assumption that they were of a 'common Christian opinion', and that together they needed to achieve greater clarity regarding the true road of renewal for Christendom. That was not a mere reception of ideas but real communication.[39]

Thus the letters become outstanding examples of fraternal conversation of praise and admonition. Just as the Zurichers had been better instructed and made even more certain by Müntzer, so they also felt they could be of help to him.

> Therefore we ask and admonish you as a brother in the name, power, Word, Spirit, and salvation which comes to all Christians through Jesus Christ our Master and Saviour, to seek earnestly only God's Word unflinchingly, to establish and defend only divine practices, to esteem as good and right only what can be found in definite clear Scripture, and to reject, hate, and curse all the schemes, words, practices, and opinions of all men, even your own.[40]

The Zurichers did not intend to pursue the correction of Müntzer, who had grounded the fraternal relationship of believers similarly and spoken of the 'revelatory biblical text' or the 'clear text'.[41] They wanted to support the strongest leader of the kind of reformation they themselves envisioned.

At the beginning of their first letter they had described the decay of Christendom and lamented the failure of the Reformers. Luther and Zwingli had uncovered the error of the papal church but not prevented the rise of a 'hypocritical faith without fruit' through which everyone

---

[38] Cf. Rolf Dismer, 'Geschichte, Glaube, Revolution. Zur Schriftauslegung Thomas Müntzers' (theological dissertation, Hamburg, 1974); Goertz, *Innere und äussere Ordnung*, p. 83.

[39] Fast, *Der linke Flügel*, p. 14; Christoph Wiebe, 'Konrad Grebels Ausführungen über Glaube und Taufe,' *MGBl*, 46 (1989), pp. 43–74; Wiebe speaks of 'kommunikativen Signalen', pp. 60 ff.

[40] Fast, *Der linke Flügel*, p. 14; Harder, *Sources of Swiss Anabaptism*, p. 286.

[41] Müntzer, *Schriften und Briefe*, pp. 233, 234.

now wanted to be saved. Essentially, the Reformers found themselves in the most 'shameful error that had ever existed since the beginning of the world'.[42] Here they spoke with deep disappointment of those to whom they had initially entrusted themselves. Then follows a surprising turning point. They too had been in such error as long as they listened only to the evangelical preachers and read only their writings. But when they took the Scriptures into their own hands they were taught something better. They discovered 'the great shameful failings of the shepherds and of ourselves, namely that we did not daily and earnestly pray with continuous sighing to be led out of this destruction of the godly life and out of this human abomination to proper faith and true service of God.'[43] This self-recrimination is less a gesture of humility than an attempt to build a measure of trust. Grebel wanted to signal to his conversation partner that a person does not believe simply because 'he has heard it from someone else'; he wanted him to understand that his critics knew the experience of painful self-correction that expected no praise in return. They were prepared to be corrected should they be found in error, as well as to be comforted and strengthened.[44]

Grebel did engage the arguments of Müntzer, but, as might be expected in a conversation, drew them also into his own conceptual frame of reference. He had made them not only his own but also strengthened and changed them where they seemed to be weak. Grebel confessed his adherence to the principle of *sola scriptura* as early as the poem for the *Apologeticus Archeteles* of Zwingli. He welcomed enthusiastically Zwingli's express support for the laity's right to read and interpret the Bible. No one individual has the mandate to interpret the Scriptures, but all who believe in Christ. To be poor in spirit was seen as a special disposition, enabling the laity to understand the Scriptures.[45] It was not clerical ordination, not philosophical learnedness, but faith, a work of the Holy Spirit, that unlocked the Scriptures. Grebel and his friends inherited this understanding of the Scriptures from Zwingli; broadly considered, it also agreed with Müntzer's view. According to Müntzer only the poor in spirit were in a position to understand the Word of God and to await the 'arrival of faith'.[46] And if Müntzer looked to the Scriptures as a source of concrete instructions concerning the way to faith and the scriptural construction of life, then the Zurichers were similarly convinced that the Scriptures contained 'more than enough wisdom and counsel' as to 'how

---

[42] Fast, *Der linke Flügel*, p. 13.
[43] Ibid.
[44] Müntzer, *Schriften und Briefe*, p. 237.
[45] Fast, *Der linke Flügel*, p. 18; Müntzer, *Schriften und Briefe*, pp. 219, 224.
[46] Müntzer, *Schriften und Briefe*, pp. 219, 224.

one should teach all estates and all people, rule, direct them and make them holy'.[47] Apparently they were here speaking about the significance of the Scriptures in the context of a peoples' church [all estates]. A separatist-free church was not yet in view. Grebel emphasized in particular that the spiritual origin of the Word presses to take on concrete form. Inwardly it leads to repentance and conversion, outwardly to clear distinctions: divine Word and human word, believers and unbelievers, customs of the apostles and customs of Antichrist. Müntzer's writings contain a similar message. Renewal moves from the inner to the outer.[48] The radicals emphasized these distinctions more strongly and consistently than Zwingli. Yes, they particularly criticized the compromises which Zwingli had allegedly made. The puritan tendency in Grebel's letter is unmistakable and corresponds with Müntzer's distinctions inasmuch as these were at the time discernible to the radicals: 'invented' and true faith, weeds and wheat, elect and damned.

If the *sola scriptura* principle led to the demise of clerical ordinances, because these were founded on human wisdom rather than the Word of God, then it was in the nature of things that the radicals in Zurich showed a special interest in church ordinances and developed proposals for their renewal. They felt themselves returned to the time of early Christendom and endeavoured to revive the apostolic church with its simplicity, obedience, sense of community and its 'customs'. They did not want to reform the church but to reinstitute it; not to rid it of its failings but to restore it from the bottom up. Here Grebel merely reinforced Zwingli's desire to purify the church and its worship service.[49] Since the *Prague Manifesto* [1521], Müntzer wanted something similar: 'The new apostolic church will begin in your country and thereafter spread everywhere.'[50]

Central to the church as envisioned by Grebel's circle was the fellowship of the Lord's Supper, a fellowship in which brothers and sisters encounter each other in love and collectively remember Christ's death on the cross, which takes away the sin of the world. Grebel named the Lord's Supper a 'sign of fellowship'.[51] 'False brothers' were to be excluded from this meal, while true brothers grew into one body. Here too Grebel essentially followed Zwingli, who intended to replace the mass

---

[47] Fast, *Der linke Flügel*, p. 19.

[48] Goertz, *Innere und äussere Ordnung*, pp. 133–49.

[49] Walton, *Zwingli's Theocracy*, pp. 127, 141.

[50] Müntzer, *Schriften und Briefe*, p. 504; cf. p. 255: 'For is Christendom not to become apostolic, Acts 27, where Joel is cited/ why should one then preach?' Cf. Bräuer, Junghans, *Der Theologe Müntzer*, pp. 109 ff., 118 ff.

[51] Fast, *Der linke Flügel*, p. 16.

with a memorial meal. But the radicals transferred the puritan tendency, which excluded sinners and the unclean from participation in the Lord's Supper, to the church as a whole. Not only the core fellowship must be purified and kept pure, but the whole church. The church cannot consist of believers and unbelievers, or of a mixture of wheat and weeds as Müntzer put it in an allusion to one of Jesus's parables.[52] Those who unite in the Lord's Supper bring not only their faith but also the fruits of faith with them. Here faith and love are at work. When the Zurichers read that Müntzer criticized Luther's writings because they allegedly failed to connect faith with its confirmation through works ('The goal is missed by far if one preaches that faith must justify us and not works') and that he, Müntzer, intended to improve 'the evangelical doctrine',[53] they found reaffirmation of their own general criticism of Zwingli. True, Müntzer meant the inner work or cleansing process of the person experienced in suffering; what the Zurichers heard was the concern about a faith that would change the whole person in both its inner constitution and outer relationships.

For the Zurichers the 'rule of Christ' – admonishing and disciplining the stumbling brother as prescribed in Matthew 18:15–18 – was the special instrument for cleansing the church. This was especially important to Grebel. During this early stage church discipline was still considered to be an instrument to cleanse and not yet an institution of a withdrawn community alienated from the world. Initially, the 'rule of Christ' was intended to replace the power of the ban abused by the traditional clergy; it was not to be used in a dictatorial but in a fraternal manner. But for the time being the primary concern was to cleanse the existing church, not to protect a newly founded, separated one from its quarrelling members (or the black sheep).[54]

To this puritan endeavour was later added believers' or confessional baptism. The person who desired this baptism gave witness and confessed that his/her sins were washed away by the blood of Christ, freely submitted to the 'rule of Christ' and was committed to walk in the 'new life of the Spirit' and in purity of mind.[55] Not only inner baptism cleanses but because of its consequences outer baptism cleanses as well.

According to Müntzer, 'the entrance into Christendom, baptism, had become a stupid monkey business', a game played by priests who from

---

[52] Müntzer, *Schriften und Briefe*, pp. 227, 233, 237; also 222, 226.

[53] Ibid., p. 240. Müntzer did not mean the works which up until then were necessary for earning salvation, but God's work inside the person which had to be suffered.

[54] 'Zur Stossrichtung des frühen Schweizer Täufertums'; Stayer, 'Anfänge des schweizerischen Täufertums', esp. pp. 39–46.

[55] Fast, *Der linke Flügel*, p. 20.

generation to generation aped liturgical formulas and ritualistic gestures without meaning and understanding, misleading and deceiving the laity with hope of the promised, heavenly kingdom. Baptism, properly understood, was implemented in order to cleanse the church's foundation: 'where mud and slimy sludge squishes and fumes'.[56] The Zurichers saw it similarly. In their eyes, child baptism in effect declared the laity spiritually immature and made their salvation dependent on priestly mediation. Confessional baptism, in contrast, derived its spiritual strength from the person's 'inner' baptism and therefore implied lay maturity and emancipation. It served as a symbol of anticlerical resistance, although not yet as an initiation rite into a free church.[57] Müntzer had not yet progressed to the more radical practice of believers' baptism, and the Zurichers at this stage were also as yet only critics of pedobaptism and not yet Anabaptists. But the argument of emancipation played an important role in the thinking of the proto-Anabaptists as well as Müntzer's.[58]

Finally, the radicals knew that they would meet with further resistance. They consciously relinquished the use of strong-arm tactics in imposing their views and refused to enlist the temporal sword for their cause. Gospel and worldly power, as they had come to understand them, constituted an ungodly mixture, a pollution of the church to the highest degree. By way of contrast, martyrdom, which awaits those who confess the crucified and resurrected Son of God in their baptism, is pure. For the very meaning of the word 'confessing' is rooted in martyrdom.

In this context Grebel wrote the words which in modern times have often been read as the founding text of Christian pacifism:

> True believing Christians are sheep among wolves, sheep for the slaughter. They must be baptized in anguish and tribulation, persecution, suffering and death, tried in fire, and must reach the fatherland of eternal rest not by slaying the physical but the spiritual. They use neither worldly sword nor war, since killing has ceased with them entirely, unless indeed we are still under the old law ... .[59]

Here were sketched the first contours of a small fellowship prepared to suffer, a fellowship which, separated and defenceless, tries to follow Christ in suffering. The question arises whether we are here dealing

---

[56] Müntzer, *Schriften und Briefe*, p. 229.

[57] Cf. Klaassen, 'Taufe im Schweizer Täufertum', pp. 82, 87.

[58] Ibid., p. 87 (Baptism: 'Zeichen religiöser Mündigkeit'); Goertz, *Innere und äussere Ordnung*, p. 109.

[59] Fast, *Der linke Flügel*, p. 20; Harder, *Sources of Swiss Anabaptism*, p. 290.

with the conception of a pacifist, free church being intentionally called into life, or merely with an attempt to process inwardly the circumstances that existed in Zurich. Pushed aside by Zwingli, powerless against the decisions of the council, Grebel and his friends were drawn to Müntzer, believing that he thought about suffering in the same way that they did: whoever seeks to avoid suffering does not follow Christ. 'If you do not join head and members, how could you follow in his footsteps?'[60] The question of interpretation is difficult to answer. It is possible that the motif of suffering aided the proto-Baptists to extract a positive meaning from the situation of powerlessness and thus to continue with their reform intentions without a change of direction. In painful experiences they recognized that the blessing of God rests on the little flock which in defencelessness and peacefulness differentiates itself intentionally from the behaviour of this 'world'. It was an insight that would strengthen many in martyrdom.

Grebel's letters did not reach Müntzer and no one knows how they ended up in Vadian's collection of letters. Walter Elliger wrote:

> According to his own account Grebel had 'not kept a copy'; and yet the manuscript in Grebel's hand remains to this day in the letter collection of his brother-in-law Vadian in St Gall so that we must have the original before us in the St Gall letters. Either they had not been sent at all or they were given back undelivered by the messenger who 'came again to us; because at the time of their composition Müntzer was no longer in Allstedt.'[61]

Whatever the case, the letters failed to open a 'future common conversation' between the radicals in the north and south.[62] Müntzer's answers, objections and admonitions remained unexpressed, so we are not dealing with an actual exchange. All the more valuable therefore seems the possibility of interpreting the Grebel letters in the way the Zurichers may have conceived a conversation with Müntzer; a conversation, not a settlement of accounts, a conversation that does not confront one side with the other's own programme and practically hoists it on him, but instead engages the other, takes up his problems, proposes solutions and with him seeks clarity in the adverse, desolate situation of the individual's task of reform. For the Grebel letters were not, as John C. Wenger called them, 'programmatic letters'.[63] A passage from the end

---

[60] Müntzer, *Schriften und Briefe*, p. 234; cf. also Fast, *Der linke Flügel*, p. 25.

[61] Walter Elliger, *Thomas Müntzer. Leben und Werk* (3rd edn, Göttingen, 1976), p. 630.

[62] Fast, *Der linke Flügel*, cited in *TQ*, 1, p. 13.

[63] John H. Wenger (ed.), *Conrad Grebel's Programmatic Letters of 1524* (Scottdale, PA, 1970). Fritz Blanke also spoke of a 'new programme', *Brüder in Christo. Die Geschichte der ältesten Täufergemeinde* (Zurich, 1955), p. 13.

of the first letter clearly points to their conversational character: 'Consider us your brothers and understand this letter from us as a sign of great joy and hope in the name of God towards you. Admonish, comfort and strengthen us, as you are well able to do.'[64] Thus the Zurichers placed themselves under the discipline of brotherly conversation.

The special emphasis on the 'rule of Christ' found in Grebel's first letter inspired John H. Yoder to see conversation as a 'structure of the congregation'. Here was something new when compared to the reformed use of the ban. Here admonition was conversation aimed at winning and reconciling the erring brother with the congregation. Thus conversation developed into a medium (a hermeneutic tool) through which one arrived at understanding and judgement concerning doctrine.[65] But did the idea of brotherly conversation with Müntzer originate and come from Grebel's circle? Could it not have been the other way around, that Müntzer sought and opened a conversation when he published the above-mentioned *Protestation*? It certainly seems striking that he did not send an academically formulated, doctrinal tract out into the world but a personal composition that addressed 'most beloved brethren', that is, those who had been made 'his brothers' in Christ.[66] He criticized them, taught them, admonished and comforted them. In short, he drew them into conversation while declaring his own willingness to be corrected by them should he be found in error.[67] True, Müntzer was prepared to give an account only before a 'non-threatening congregation', not before Luther in 'a corner' of Wittenberg. But in principle he admitted to fallibility and declared his readiness to participate in conversation. Is it not possible that the Zurichers felt themselves addressed by Müntzer, and that with their two letters they sought to continue what he had begun? They mentioned at the beginning that his publications had 'prompted' their letter.[68] It is possible that they had come to the insight 'that obligatory conversations with the brother leads to understanding',[69] as Yoder thought; that is, if it is permissible at

---

[64] Fast, *Der linke Flügel*, p. 22.

[65] John H. Yoder, *Täufertum und Reformation im Gespräch. Dogmengeschichtliche Untersuchungen der frühen Gespräche zwischen schweizerischen Täufern und Reformatoren* (Zurich, 1968), pp. 111 ff.

[66] Müntzer, *Schriften und Briefe*, pp. 231, 236; p. 233 (dear Christians, dear friend); 232 (most beloved brother); 224 (chosen brother); 226 (chosen friends of God); 227 (you dear person); 220 (dearly beloved Christian); 228 (dear friend). Peter Matheson recently referred to the communicative intentions of Karlstadt's pamphlets. *The Rhetoric of the Reformation* (Edinburgh, 1998), p. 66. See also Matheson's chapter on Reformation dialogues in general, ibid., pp. 81–110.

[67] Ibid., p. 239.

[68] Fast, *Der linke Flügel*, p. 12. cited in *TQ*, 1; Müntzer, *Schriften und Briefe*, p. 240.

[69] Yoder, *Täufertum und Reformation im Gespräch*, p. 112.

all to make the stumbling brother into a prototype of one concerned with theological understanding. Whatever the case, conversation can only have a provisional character – to search for truth that is still forthcoming. Conversation is not, as its designation as 'structure of the congregation' implies, the non-negotiable result of reformatory insight from which one proceeds. Instead, it emphasizes the incomplete character of proto-Anabaptist reflections.

James Stayer's investigations of early Anabaptist history have shown the tentative and ambivalent nature of proto-Anabaptists' perceptions. These still fluctuated between a people's and a separatist-free church conception of Anabaptist reformation. During the fall of 1524, for example, with all hope for a reformation of the entire society in Zurich dashed, the only possibility seemed, for some people at least, to be renewed through willing suffering as a separated fellowship of believers. Yet, after the first faith baptisms in January 1525 and the withdrawal from Zurich to Schaffhausen, St Gall and the Grüningen district, the Anabaptists made an all-out effort to support the local insurrectionists and to further a communal reformation in the spirit of local political-ecclesiastical unity. Even Conrad Grebel and Johannes Brötli, who had admonished Müntzer to peaceableness and warned against any attempt to protect the Gospel with the sword, supported the insurrectionists, strengthened them in their negative opinion of Zwingli and Zurich's council and accepted their protection when they were being pursued by the authorities.[70]

Stayer's observations have helped me to read the Grebel letters as exploratory and provisional, in search of conversation rather than as the 'oldest documents of a Protestant free church', the normative manifesto of the 'Anabaptist vision' or the explication of 'congregational structure'.[71]

To this day I am grateful that more than thirty years ago James Stayer reviewed my first book in his historiographical essay on Thomas Müntzer[72] and in a friendly, critical fashion sought conversation with me. At that time began a 'scholarly fellowship' [*Arbeitsgemeinschaft*] which convinced me of the revisionist view of Anabaptism and saved me from despairing with the 'normative Anabaptist vision'. For I find it

---

[70] Stayer, 'Anfänge des schweizerischen Täufertums,' pp. 39–46; Matthias Hui, 'Vom Bauernaufstand zur Täuferbewegung. Entwicklungen in der ländlichen Reformation am Beispiel des Züricherischen Grüninger Amts', *MGBl*, 46 (1989), pp. 131–5.

[71] Blanke, *Brüder in Christo*, p. 15; Harold S. Bender, 'The Anabaptist Vision', *Church History*, 13 (1944), pp. 3–24; Yoder, *Täufertum und Reformation*, p. 111.

[72] James M. Stayer, 'Thomas Müntzer's Theology and Revolution in Recent Non-Marxist Interpretation', *MQR*, 43 (1969).

more stimulating and promising to interact with searching, imperfect, yes, even contradictory and inconsistent 'fathers in the faith' than to be frustrated by an unattainable ideal. When we first met in 1974 to consider the conception and collection of essays for the *Umstrittenes Täufertum* (1975), we did not yet realize that we would succeed in having 'a common future conversation'. Over the many years this conversation helped us to clarify research problems, while leaving us free to publicly present common as well as diverging opinions. Our conversation concerning the radicals of the Reformation has continued uninterrupted and will hopefully continue to keep us in good spirits.

CHAPTER SIX

Sebastian Franck and the Münster Anabaptist kingdom

Geoffrey L. Dipple

It may seem odd, if not downright perverse, to suggest a connection between the irenic, bookish Sebastian Franck and the fanaticism of the Münster Anabaptist kingdom. In many ways these two aspects of the Reformation appear as antitheses. Franck's frequently noted tolerance, pacifism and scepticism about all group claims to a monopoly on religious truth stand in sharp contrast to the strict dogmatism, missionary zeal and apocalyptic crusading ideals of Münster. Yet the connections between them do exist. It is possible that Bernhard Rothmann, the chief idealogue and propagandist for the Münster kingdom, met Franck while both were in Strasbourg in the spring of 1531.[1] More certain is the fact that Rothmann knew at least some of Franck's writings. In his *Confession of Two Sacraments* Rothmann cites Franck's massive chronicle, the *Chronica* or *Geschichtsbibel*, and its reference to the Pseudo-Clementine Epistle IV, in support of his claim that the early church practised community of goods.[2] This has led some historians to conclude that Franck influenced Münsterite thinking on community of goods.[3] George Williams has argued in addition that Franck may have also influenced Münsterite

---

[1] Robert Stupperich, 'Sebastian Franck und das münsterische Täufertum', in Rudolf Vierhaus and Manfred Botzenhart (eds), *Dauer und Wandel der Geschichte. Festgabe für Kurt von Raumer zum 15 Dezember 1965* (Münster, 1966), p. 149.

[2] Cf. Robert Stupperich (ed.), *Die Schriften Bernhard Rothmanns* (Münster, 1970), pp. 184–5 (hereafter *SBR*), Sebastian Franck, *Chronica, Zeitbuch unnd Geschichtsbibel* (Ulm, 1536; photoreprint edn, Darmstadt, 1969), ccxliiii. Unless otherwise noted, citations are from the 1536 edition of the *Chronica*, but these have been checked against the original edition printed in Strasbourg in 1531 and the cross-references included in parentheses after the citation (=1531, ccccxcv).

[3] George Huntston Williams, *The Radical Reformation*, 3rd edn (Kirksville, MO, 1992), pp. 566, 569 n. 28; Martin Brecht, 'Die Theologie Bernhard Rothmanns', *Jahrbuch für Westfälische Kirchengeschichte*, 78 (1985), p. 71; Taira Kuratsuka, 'Gesamtgilde und Täufer: Der Radikalisierungsprozess in der Reformation Münsters: Von der reformatorischen Bewegung zum Täuferreich 1533/34', *ARG*, 76 (1985), p. 251; James M. Stayer, *The German Peasants' War and Anabaptist Community of Goods* (Montreal, 1991), p. 132. An exception to this line of interpretation is the opinion of John Toews, 'Sebastian Franck: Friend and Critic of Early Anabaptism' (PhD diss., Minnesota, 1964), p. 249.

thinking on polygamy.[4] More recently, James Stayer has suggested an even greater impact of Franck on Münster and the Melchiorite Anabaptist tradition of North Germany and the Netherlands, arguing that '[h]is anti-authoritarian reflections on sacred and profane history conveyed among northerners the radicalism of the south German Reformation'.[5]

The present chapter investigates Stayer's suggestion. In particular it focuses on Franck's possible influence on Münsterite perceptions of the sword, another theme for which Stayer is well known. It is especially concerned with Franck's impact on Rothmann's justifications for the Anabaptist kingdom and its apocalyptic mission. As will become evident, this theme involves as well an investigation of Rothmann's historical theology, and it is at this point that Franck had his greatest impact on Rothmann's thought, largely through the medium of the *Chronica*. This is, then, primarily a study of Franck's impact on the process of radicalization of Münsterite political thought. Within this context, some explanation for the focus on Rothmann may be in order. Initially the moving force behind Münster's reformation, Rothmann's role is usually perceived to have been reduced to that of essentially a propagandist for the Anabaptist regime with the arrival of Jan Matthijs in Münster in January 1534.[6] As a result, his writings are often seen as primarily *ex post facto* rationalizations for decisions already made and actions already undertaken. Nonetheless, they do provide interesting insights into the self-understanding of the Münsterite mission.[7]

In the minds of many interpreters, the key distinguishing feature of Münsterite Anabaptism is the willingness of its members to employ force in their own defence and in the cause of the Gospel.[8] Traditionally

---

[4] Williams, *Radical Reformation*, pp. 568–9.

[5] James M. Stayer, 'Christianity in One City: Anabaptist Münster, 1534–35', in Hans Hillerbrand (ed.), *Radical Tendencies in the Reformation: Divergent Perspectives* (Kirksville, MO, 1988), p. 127; *Anabaptist Community of Goods*, p. 132.

[6] James M. Stayer, 'The Münsterite Rationalization of Bernhard Rothmann', *Journal of the History of Ideas*, 28 (1967), pp. 180, 192; Willem de Bakker, 'Bernhard Rothmann: The Dialectics of Radicalization in Münster', in Hans-Jürgen Goertz (ed.), *Profiles of Radical Reformers: Biographical Sketches from Thomas Müntzer to Paracelsus* (Scottdale, PA and Kitchener, Ont., 1982), pp. 191–9; Williams, *Radical Reformation*, p. 574; Arnold Snyder, *Anabaptist History and Theology: An Introduction* (Kitchener, Ont., 1995), p. 148.

[7] Cf. Ralf Klötzer, *Die Täufferherrschaft von Münster: Stadtreformation und Welterneurung* (Münster, 1992) and W.J. de Bakker, 'Bernhard Rothmann: A Civic Reformer in Münster' in Irvin B. Horst (ed.), *The Dutch Dissenters: A Critical Companion to Their History and Ideas* (Leiden, 1986), pp. 105–16.

[8] See Williams, *Radical Reformation*, pp. 553–4, 567 and Franck J. Wray, 'Bernhard Rothmann's Views on the Early Church', in Franklin Littell (ed.), *Reformation Studies* (Richmond, VA, 1962), pp. 237–8.

this aberration was seen as inherent in the movement, at least from the time of the arrival of Jan Matthijs in Münster.[9] One of the more significant revisions in our understanding of Münster Anabaptism is the realization that the decision to employ the sword was a gradual process in response to external conditions and internal power struggles. Initially the Münster Anabaptists were ambivalent or undecided about the use of the sword and only gradually did they come to espouse its employment.[10]

This evolution in thinking on the sword among the Münster Anabaptists is reflected in the writings of Rothmann, especially in his statements justifying its use and, with them, his evaluations of the origins and nature of secular authority. Indications are that Rothmann's rationalization for the employment of the sword, and with it his thinking about political authority, was an ongoing process from the beginning of the Münster Anabaptist kingdom until its demise. At the beginning of this process, Rothmann's political ethic can probably best be characterized by what James Stayer has labelled the Christian Realpolitik of Ulrich Zwingli.[11] His writings from the period prior to his rebaptism by the emissaries of Jan Matthijs in January 1534 suggest that his political ethic, like many of his theological positions, owed a strong debt to the Reformed tradition of southwest Germany and Switzerland. Notable is the latitude Rothmann gives to the secular authorities in matters broadly defined as ecclesiastical. While he adopts the common Reformation position that secular authorities should be obeyed in all things that do not contravene divine commandments, he also stresses the complementary roles of spiritual and secular authority. He argues for the possibility of, and desire for, the establishment of godly rulers, and he calls on the authorities to suppress false teaching.[12]

This faith in secular authorities appears to have been eroded somewhat after Rothmann's break with the Münster city council in the summer of

---

[9] This interpretation has been espoused most recently by Brecht, pp. 72–3.

[10] Of crucial importance in this revision has been the work of Karl-Heinz Kirchhoff, 'Was There a Peaceful Anabaptist Congregation in Münster in 1534', *MQR*, 44 (1970), pp. 357–70. See also Williams, *Radical Reformation*, pp. 553–4, 562–4; James M. Stayer, *Anabaptists and the Sword* (Lawrence, KS, 1972), pp. 228, 230–33 and 'The Radical Reformation', in Thomas A. Brady Jr, Heiko A. Oberman and James D. Tracy (eds), *Handbook of European History, 1400–1600*, vol. 2: *Visions, Programs and Outcomes* (Leiden, 1995), p. 269; Richard van Dülmen, *Reformation als Revolution: Soziale Bwegung und religiöser Radikalismus in der deutschen Reformation* (Munich, 1977), pp. 288–98; de Bakker, 'Civic Reformer', pp. 107–11.

[11] On Zwingli's political thought, see Stayer, *Anabaptists and the Sword*, pp. 49–69.

[12] Brecht, pp. 52–8, 64–5; de Bakker, 'Dialectics of Radicalization', pp. 194–5; Klötzer, pp. 139–40.

1533. Thereafter Rothmann was much less willing to allow interference from the secular arm in matters of religion, although he continued to hope for the establishment of godly authorities.[13] Of note, though, is his continued respect for, and calls for obedience to, established temporal authority. And this respect for secular authority continued to influence his thinking and statements on the relationship of the Münster Anabaptists to the sword. On 23 February 1534 a new city council dominated by the Anabaptists was elected in Münster. In other words, the Anabaptists came to power there by legal means.[14] This event likely reinforced Rothmann's respect for secular authority. It certainly aided him in justifying the activities in Münster. In the spring of 1534, after the bishop's armies were already investing the city, Rothmann completed his *Confession of the Belief and Life of the Community of Christ at Münster.* In this work, he characterizes the Anabaptists' decision to resort to arms as the justifiable activity of a legally constituted government in response to the tyrannical activities of the bishop of Münster.[15] As numerous interpreters of Rothmann's writings have noted, this legitimation of a legal defensive war continues in Rothmann's writings throughout the seige.[16]

Behind these arguments lie continued references to the legitimacy of temporal authority, at least insofar as it has been established by divine ordinance. In Rothmann's later works the origins of temporal power continue to be described in 'quasi-Lutheran' terms as the divine remedy for human wickedness. In his *Restitution of True Christian Teaching,* printed in October 1534, Rothmann makes this point clearly. He argues that temporal authority has resulted from the human fall from obedience to God and righteousness to disobedience and unrighteousness. The resulting conflicts between humans led God to establish the sword, in the form of temporal authority [*Obrigkeit*], to protect the righteous and exact vengeance on the unrighteous.[17] And even in *On Earthly and Temporal Power,* Rothmann's extended exposé on the origins, nature and history of temporal authority, left behind as an unfinished fragment after the fall of Münster, secular authority is described as divinely instituted and derived from human wisdom and the law of nature.[18]

---

[13] Cf. Brecht, pp. 66–7 and Kuratsuka, p. 249.

[14] Stayer, *Anabaptists and the Sword*, p. 234.

[15] *SBR*, pp. 206–8. See also Brecht, p. 73 and on the question of dating this work, *SBR*, p. 195, de Bakker, 'Civic Reformer', p. 111 n. 13 and Klötzer, p. 204.

[16] Stayer, *Anabaptists and the Sword*, pp. 235, 238–9; de Bakker, 'Civic Reformer', p. 112.

[17] *SBR*, pp. 276–7. On the characterization of Rothmann's thought about the origins of temporal authority as 'quasi-Lutheran', see Stayer, *Anabaptists and the Sword*, pp. 241, 243.

[18] *SBR*, pp. 376–7, 380–82, 387. See also Stayer, *Anabaptists and the Sword*, p. 243.

Yet, as Stayer notes, these claims are increasingly overshadowed by Rothmann's denunciations of existent temporal authority in his later writings.[19] Parallel to his continued claims that the office of the temporal sword has been instituted by divine decree, Rothmann argues that the exercise of that authority throughout history has departed from its divine origins and become heathen and tyrannical. In the *Restitution* Rothmann charges that early in its history secular authority had been perverted by human pride and self-interest. He claims that for a long time secular authorities have not only forgotten and abused the divine commands for their offices, but also they have turned their authority against God Himself and His Word. This, Rothmann asserts, is clear today, especially among rulers who call themselves 'Christian'.[20] Shortly thereafter, in *A Report on Vengeance*, printed in December 1534, he contrasted the need for obedience to divinely established authority in the form of the revived Davidic kingship of Jan of Leyden with the need to resist the tyranny of the 'Babylonian rulers'.[21] This process comes to full fruition in *On Earthly and Temporal Power*, in which Rothmann develops a detailed historical argument to justify his claims that existing secular authority derives from heathen, godless roots. He traces the origins of temporal authority to Nimrod, the son of Ham, and the cursed line among Noah's descendants. Although instituted by divine decree, this authority was perverted by Nimrod's pride and transformed into tyranny, which is the chief characteristic among Nimrod's successors to the present day.[22]

It is interesting to note that Rothmann's critique of existing temporal authority begins in the *Restitution of True Christian Teaching*, and this raises the question of why he first turned to this tactic in the autumn of 1534. The answer to this question likely lies in the constitutional history of Anabaptist Münster. As has been noted, with the elections to the city council of 23 February 1534 the Anabaptists were able to assume authority by legitimate means. Although this seizure of power amounted to a significant change in the practical locus of authority, largely through the extra-institutional role of the prophet exercised by Jan Matthijs, the institutional structure of the city government remained largely untouched. Indeed, the transfer of power from the old to the new city council occurred according to the usual forms.[23] All of this changed, however,

---

[19] Stayer, *Anabaptists and the Sword*, pp. 235–6.

[20] *SBR*, p. 277.

[21] Ibid., pp. 287, 296.

[22] Ibid., pp. 376–7, 382–7, 392, 399.

[23] Eike Wolgast, 'Herrschaftsorganization und Herrschaftskrisen im Täuferreich von Münster 1534/35', *ARG*, 67 (1976), pp. 180–81.

at Easter 1534 with Matthijs's suicidal sortee against the besieging army. Jan of Leyden's attempt to 'institutionalize charisma' was accompanied by a thoroughgoing constitutional change. The established city council was replaced by an Elders' Constitution, supposedly derived from biblical models.[24] After a failed attempt to storm the city on 31 August, the Elders' Constitution was supplanted by the kingship of Jan of Leyden, again a political form purportedly with biblical precedent. Both of these new constitutions were seen as marking a sharp break with all existing political forms and traditions. They were of divine, not human, origin. Unlike existing power structures, they synthesized both temporal and spiritual authority in one institution. And their appearance was integral to the establishment of a new age of world history.[25] The novelty of Münsterite political forms, then, provided the opportunity, even the necessity, for Rothmann's criticism of all existing political structures.

In addition to providing a justification for Münster's constitutional experiments, Rothmann's reflections on the origins and nature of political authority also helped to explain Münsterite relations with the world beyond the city walls. Parallel to his developing denunciations of governments outside Münster, there emerged detailed arguments for the Anabaptists to take up the sword and assume an active role in the great apocalyptic crusade of the dawning new age. This theme appears first in the *Restitution* and is expanded in subsequent writings. It is especially well developed in *On Vengeance* when Rothmann calls on the righteous to lay aside the spiritual weapons of the apostles and take up the physical weapons of the restored Davidic kingdom. And later in *On the Obscurity of Scripture* he calls on the saints to put an end to 'Babylonian authority' and to do away with all unrighteous rulers.[26]

Rothmann's developing views on the sword were intimately tied to his understanding of history and his speculations about the Apocalypse.[27] The latter connection is obvious. The rationalization for the

---

[24] Ibid., pp. 182–3 n. 14. Wolgast surmises that the model for Münster's government of twelve elders was an amalgam of the description of the Israelite tribal leadership contained in Numbers 1 and the title elder from the New Testament.

[25] Ibid., pp. 181–9. Further on the novelty of these political forms and their union of temporal and spiritual authority, see Gerhard Brendler, *Das Täuferreich zu Münster 1534/35* (Berlin, 1966), pp. 128–9 and Klötzer, pp. 89–93, 103–5. The fact that Rothmann's rationalization for Münster's constitutional experimentation first appeared after the Davidic monarchy had replaced the Elders' Constitution is explained by the time lag involved in the writing and printing of Rothmann's justifications. As James Stayer has noted, Rothmann's justifications for activities of the Anabaptists in Münster were often out of synch with events, see 'Christianity in One City', pp. 133–4.

[26] *SBR*, pp. 281–2, 287, 290, 292–5, 297, 307, 350–56, 365–6.

[27] Stayer, *Anabaptists and the Sword*, p. 240.

righteous to take up arms is rooted in the idea of an apocalyptic crusade emanating from Münster and then filling the entire world. In the works written after the establishment of the Davidic kingdom of Jan of Leyden, Rothmann calls on the faithful to cleanse the world of the wicked in preparation for the return of Christ. This theme is implicit in the *Restitution* and then appears with increasing frequency and takes on added significance in *On Vengeance* and *On the Obscurity of Scripture*.[28] But for Rothmann, a proper understanding of the apocalyptic timetable, and of the scriptural references to it, required a careful reading of history and understanding of one's own place in it. And he frequently advises his readers to pay careful attention to these matters.[29] Rothmann saw the flow of human history as a pattern of falls from divine ordinances and their subsequent restitution, all in the greater context of three great 'world ages'. His own time he regarded as that of the final restitution which would usher in the last, third age of the world. One's place in history determined, among other things, how one read the scriptures and the proper ethic for the righteous.[30] This lies at the basis of Rothmann's statements in *On Vengeance* that the time has come for the righteous to lay aside the weapons of the apostles and take up those of the Davidic kingdom. The age of suffering was giving away to the age of vengeance.

Rothmann's political thought, then, is inseparably tied to his hermeneutics, his reading of the apocalyptic timetable and his theology of history. Historians have long noted that in all these areas he owed a profound debt to the thought of Melchior Hoffman. Yet, they have also noted that Rothmann's debt to Hoffman was anything but slavish. Rothmann adapted crucial elements of Hoffman's thought to suit his own purposes and agenda. It is generally agreed that Rothmann's most important departure from Hoffman's thought centres on his advocacy of the use of force and the role he assigns the righteous in the apocalyptic showdown.[31] Like Rothmann, Hoffman began from an essentially conservative Lutheran understanding of the origins and nature of temporal authority. However, unlike Rothmann, Hoffman never lost his

---

[28] *SBR*, pp. 278, 287, 290, 292, 295, 297, 346, 350–52, 355, 357, 364–7. See also Stayer, *Anabaptists and the Sword*, p. 249 and Klaus Deppermann, *Melchior Hoffman: Social Unrest and Apocalyptic Visions in the Age of Reformation* Malcolm Wren (trans.), Benjamin Drewry (ed.), (Edinburgh, 1987), p. 347.

[29] *SBR*, pp. 281, 288, 332, 335. On the importance of history for Rothmann's hermeneutics, see Stayer, 'Rothmann's Rationalization', p. 181, Deppermann, p. 344, Snyder, p. 205.

[30] *SBR*, pp. 212–19, 239–43, 255–6, 332–5, 349, 382–99.

[31] For a concise summary of Rothmann's adoption and adaptation of Hoffman's central theological tenets, see Deppermann, pp. 342–8.

respect for, or commitment to obedience to, that authority. To the end of his life he refused to take up arms in defiance of established authority or to encourage his followers to do so. Instead, he argued at different times that force in the coming apocalypse was to be employed by the Turks, whom Hoffman identified with Gog and Magog, two pious kings of the empire, or a defensive alliance of the imperial cities.[32] This distinction led James Stayer at one time to posit a fundamental gulf between the thought of Hoffman and Rothmann – Münster Anabaptism he described as the bastard line of the Melchiorite movement.[33] Subsequently, however, this judgement has been qualified somewhat, largely as a result of the research of Klaus Deppermann. Deppermann argues that in his late work, *On the Pure Fear of God*, Hoffman anticipated certain crucial elements of the Münsterite agenda. Of particular importance is the fact that he predicted the establishment of a theocratic interim kingdom as preparatory to the second coming. Nonetheless, even in this work Hoffman continued to insist that force be exercised only by legitimately established secular authorities and not by the righteous.[34] While the early history of Anabaptist Münster seemed to confirm Hoffman's prescriptions, changing circumstances soon began to undermine them. During the initial phase of Anabaptist ascendancy at Münster, until April 1534, the city council appeared to fulfill the apocalyptic role assigned by Hoffman to legitimate authorities.[35] However, with Jan of Leyden's assumption of power, and the constitutional experimentation that accompanied it, Hoffman's speculations began to lose their applicability and Rothmann's political ethic assumed an independent course.

As we have seen, questions on the use of the sword and perceptions of the legitimacy of temporal authority are closely intertwined in Rothmann's thought. Furthermore, Rothmann's arguments against the legitimacy of established temporal authority rested on arguments derived primarily from the historical record. It is, then, to these themes that we must look to establish the roots of Rothmann's independence from Hoffman and to identify other potentially important influences on his developing political ethic.

To fully assess such influences, we need to review some of the central elements of Rothmann's historical vision, both in its general outlines and as it applied specifically to the development of political authority.

---

[32] Stayer, *Anabaptists and the Sword*, pp. 219–26, Deppermann, pp. 254–6.

[33] Stayer, *Anabaptists and the Sword*, pp. 222–3.

[34] Deppermann, pp. 257–64. Stayer has subsequently acknowledged the significance of Deppermann's argument, see 'Christianity in One City', p. 118, *Anabaptist Community of Goods*, p. 124.

[35] Wolgast, p. 180.

As noted above, Rothmann viewed history as a series of falls and restitutions culminating in an imminent final restitution which would establish the earthly kingdom of Christ. This pattern was established in the first age of the world, but continued through the subsequent two ages.[36] The first age of the world lasted from Adam's fall to the Flood. The second age lasted from Noah to the Restitution, which Rothmann thought was at hand, and the third age would witness the physical and temporal reign of Christ and the saints.[37] Within the context of this pattern, Rothmann saw a divergence of secular and sacred history. At the time that temporal authority was established and divine rulership usurped, God had singled out His chosen people in the person of Abraham. Thereafter history developed in two parallel but independent streams.[38] These two streams of history would be reunited in the impending restitution, which would develop out of the flow of sacred history and would witness the end of all secular, human authority.[39]

The source of Rothmann's theology of history is usually thought to be Hoffman. And certainly, especially in terms of the general outlines of Rothmann's vision, the influence of Hoffman appears to have been significant. Hoffman, too, read the flow of history through apocalyptic glasses and understood historical events in the context of their apocalyptic significance. In particular, he relied heavily on the book of Revelation in his understanding of history from the age of the New Testament to the contemporary world.[40] Klaus Deppermann has argued as well that Rothmann was indebted to Hoffman for his vision of history as a series of falls and restitutions.[41] Again, this theme is particularly prominent in Hoffman's understanding of history from the incarnation to his own age, which he perceived as a series of spiritual awakenings and falls.[42] Furthermore, Hoffman, like Rothmann, divided human history into three periods. But here the symmetry between the schemes of Hoffman and Rothmann breaks down. Hoffman's three ages are organized according to a strictly trinitarian pattern. The first

---

[36] SBR, pp. 213–15, Stayer, *Anabaptists and the Sword*, pp. 241, 245.

[37] SBR, pp. 332–3, 346. See also Stayer, *Anabaptists and the Sword*, pp. 240–41.

[38] SBR, pp. 388–9. See also, Stayer, *Anabaptists and the Sword*, p. 245, Deppermann, p. 345.

[39] SBR, pp. 388, 394–7. See also Stayer, *Anabaptists and the Sword*, pp. 242, 244, 248.

[40] Stayer, *Anabaptists and the Sword*, p. 216.

[41] Deppermann, pp. 342–3. There has been some debate on whether or not Rothmann was also influenced in his restitutionist or restorationist thought by John Campanus' *Restitution of Godly Scripture*, see Williams, *Radical Reformation*, p. 576, Brecht, pp. 53–4, 63, Klötzer, p.167.

[42] Stayer, *Anabaptists and the Sword*, pp. 216–17.

age, identified with God the Father, corresponds to the age of the Old Testament. The second, the age of the Son, refers to the period from the New Testament to Hoffman's own age. And the third age of the Spirit Hoffman saw as imminent.[43] It is likely, then, that Rothmann had adapted Hoffman's tripartite periodization to suit his own needs.

James Stayer has argued as well that Rothmann's perception of the divergence of secular and sacred history, too, derived from Hoffman's thought. Parallel to the series of spiritual awakenings and falls he identified as central to the sacred history of the world, Hoffman saw profane history developing through eight kingdoms of the Antichrist.[44] If in fact Rothmann was indebted to Hoffman on this point, he was likely strongly reinforced in this belief by his reading of Franck's *Chronica*. The basic organization of this work posits a fundamental distinction between sacred and profane history. The first two chronicles contained in it cover secular matters from the beginnings of temporal authority to Franck's own age. The remaining chronicles deal with so-called spiritual matters. In the introduction to this second group of chronicles, Franck is quite explicit that this division is intentional and significant:

> To this point, faithful reader, we have heard about the activities, histories and tragedy of the external world and movements, which are nothing other than warring, strife, shedding of blood, hewing, stabbing, ruling, compulsion, and every manner of external misfortune, sword, kingdom and everything. Now we want [to turn] with God to the spiritual double world, to the Devil who stalks at midday, to the epidemic and illness which destroys the day, to the lost multitude who think themselves clean and pure and who nonetheless have not been washed clean of their filth, among whom the Christians circulate like grains in a mass of chaff, like Lot in Sodom, Daniel in Babylon, Moses in Egypt and a rose among thorns.[45]

Beyond a clear divergence of secular and sacred history, Franck's statements anticipate Rothmann's vision in his characterization of the nature

---

[43] Deppermann, pp. 245–6.

[44] Stayer, *Anabaptists and the Sword*, p. 242.

[45] Franck, *Chronica*, ii(b): 'Bis hieher haben wir/ gott gleübiger leser/ die händel/ historien und Tragedi der eüsserlichen welt und bewegnissen gehört/ da ist nichts gewesen dann kriegen/ zancken/ blütvergiessen/ hawen stechen/ regieren/ nöten und allerley eüsserlich unglück/ schwert reich und alles. Nun wöllen wir mit Gott an die geistliche doppel welt hin/ an den Teüfel der im mittag schleicht/ and die seücht unnd pfeil/ die des tags fliegen und verderben/ ja an den verlornen hauffen/ der sich reyn und sauber dunckt/ und doch nit von seimunflat geweschen ist/ darunder die Christen eyngemengt umbfaren/ wie etlich körner under eim hauffen sprewer/ wie Loth in Sodoma/ Daniel in Babilone/ Moses in Egypten/ und ein ross under den dornen.' (=1531, ccliiii(b)).

of secular authority and his depiction of much of sacred history prior to the restitution.

According to Rothmann, the calling of Abraham, and with it the disjunction between sacred and profane history, occurred at the same time as temporal authority was established.[46] Franck does not make this point explicitly, but he does link closely the calling of Abraham to the theme of the rejection of divine overlordship by other peoples, and the close proximity between the description of Nimrod's monarchy in Genesis 10 and the calling of Abraham in Genesis 12 likely would have encouraged this identification among his readers.[47] When we turn to Rothmann's statements specifically about secular authority, his debt to Franck's *Chronica* becomes much clearer. Rothmann saw the origins of temporal authority in the first, antediluvian age of the world. In response to the wickedness of fallen man, God ordained temporal authority through the medium of human reason and the law of nature.[48] However, secular authority was not truly developed until the second age of the world, that is after the Flood.[49] A survey of Rothmann's statements on the history of secular authority suggests that he was gradually working toward a full elucidation of an historical argument to undermine the legitimacy of established temporal authority. At first his references to the history of temporal authority are scattered. But gradually they come together into a comprehensive vision of its origins and history down to the contemporary age. This, I believe, should provide us with some insight into the importance Rothmann placed on arguments from history.

In his *Restitution*, Rothmann claims that the tyrannical nature of temporal authority is clear from its contemporary abuses which surpass even those of some of the most notorious tyrants among the Roman emperors at the time of the apostles. To illustrate this point he draws on the examples of Nero and Maximus Thrax (Maxine, CE 235–38?).[50] In *On Vengeance*, Rothmann reaches back to the history of the Old Testament when he identifies secular authority as 'Babylonian tyranny' and describes its dominance over the faithful as the Babylonian Captivity.[51] But his historical arguments are first fully developed in *On Earthly and*

---

[46] *SBR*, pp. 388–9.
[47] Franck, *Chronica* (1531), xiii(b), xlii–xlii(b). Interestingly, in the 1536 edition Franck is much more explicit about the connection between the calling of Abraham and the founding of secular authority by Nimrod, see *Chronica* (1536), xii.
[48] *SBR*, p. 387.
[49] Stayer, *Anabaptists and the Sword*, p. 242, Deppermann, p. 345.
[50] *SBR*, p. 277.
[51] Ibid., p. 287.

Temporal Power. This work includes a comprehensive vision of the tyranny of temporal authority from its institution to the present day. As has been noted, Rothmann traces the roots of secular authority to Nimrod, the alleged founder of Babylon. This attribution was not unusual in the medieval and early modern world. But in its characterization of Nimrod's activity as tyrannical and a usurpation of divine authority, Rothmann's description of the founding of Babylon goes well beyond the accounts contained in Genesis, Augustine's *City of God* or Josephus' *Antiquities of the Jews.*[52] According to Rothmann, Nimrod's tyranny was carried on by his successors, in Rothmann's eyes all subsequent rulers, in a process marked by continual deterioration. This process Rothmann understood in terms of the visions contained in Daniel 2 and 7.[53] Such a reliance on Daniel to chart the history of temporal authority is reminiscent of Thomas Müntzer's better known exposition of Daniel 2 in the *Sermon to the Princes.* However, as James Stayer notes, in the exegesis of Rothmann the Holy Roman Empire is regarded as part of the fourth monarchy described in Daniel 2 rather than as an independent entity as in the thought of Müntzer.[54] To reinforce his point about the godlessness of Nimrod's usurpation of divine authority, Rothmann ties it closely to the origins of idolatry, which he attributes to Ninus or Nini, the grandson of Nimrod and founder of the Assyrian empire. Nini, Rothmann claims, set up a statue of his father, Bel or Belus, and encouraged its adulation among the populace. We have here the roots of the cult of Baal. Shortly thereafter, while reiterating the origins of temporal authority and its connections to the birth of idolatry, Rothmann claims that Nimrod has been identified with Saturn by some and Bel with Jupiter by others. And, Rothmann continues, subsequent tyrants have employed this idolatry to bolster their own authority, claiming that they, too, were gods.[55]

In his discussion of the origins of temporal authority the extent of Rothmann's debt to Franck becomes clear. In fact it appears that Franck's *Chronica* laid out the interpretive structure for Rothmann's thinking on this issue. Franck claims that there was no settled government before the Flood and quotes Cain's claim that all had the right to punish him as evidence of this fact. Nonetheless, the roots of temporal authority

---

[52] Cf. ibid., pp. 382–5, Genesis 10:8–12, Augustine, *City of God*, Henry Bettenson (trans.), David Knowles (ed.) (Harmondsworth, 1972), pp. 653, 657–8 and Flavius Josephus, *Works*, vol. 1: *Antiquities of the Jews*, William Whiston (trans.) (London, 1820), pp. 82–3.

[53] *SBR*, pp. 385, 392, 395–404.

[54] See Stayer, *Anabaptists and the Sword*, p. 243, Deppermann, pp. 345–6.

[55] *SBR*, pp. 385–6.

were laid at this time by divine mandate through the agency of human reason and the law of nature:

> And although rulership comes from the heathens, whom the Jews then copied, nonetheless all power comes from above as Christ said to Pilate, and it is a divine ordinance as Paul teaches. [It is] implanted by nature and [human] reason for the protection of the righteous and the punishment of the evil ...[56]

We may not go too far wrong in seeing the antediluvian world according to Franck as a Lockean state of nature. Furthermore, Franck, too, attributes the establishment of organized temporal authority to the activities of Nimrod, which, like Rothmann, he regards as tyrannical and a usurpation of divine rulership.[57] Again, like Rothmann, Franck describes subsequent authority as a continuation of this tyrannical tradition. He argues that almost all rulers are descended from Nimrod, as is evidenced daily by their activities:

> It is also important to note here that all lordship comes from the left godless side of Noah's progeny and his descendants who were inclined to evil, not from the line of Christ or the ranks of the righteous. Therefore, princes and lords quickly began to boast of their pedigrees; also there was no prince, emperor or lord pleasing to God until God's people, driven by envy, begged [God] to provide them with a king and leader. Then they were provided, and out of grace rather than the justness [of their request], and only infrequently, with a godly, devout king like David or Hezekiah. Therefore, I say that the origin of the lords is hardly honourable, and they receive all too often very little praise in Scripture, and almost all have conducted themselves evilly. As one still sees, a devout prince is indeed scarce game in heaven ...[58]

---

[56] Franck, *Chronica*, x(b) (=1531, x), ccx(b): 'Und wiewol die herrschaft von Heyden kumpt/ denen es die Juden nachtheten/ so ist doch aller gwalt von oben herab geben/ wie Christus zü Pilato sagt/ und ist ein göttliche ordnung/ wie Paulus leret/ der natur und vernunft eyngepflantzt/ dem frummen züschutz/ dem bösen zür straff/ ... ' (=1531, clxxiiii).

[57] Ibid., vi(b) (=1531, vi), x(b) (=1531, x), xii (=1531, x(b)). Brecht, p. 71 n. 80, suggests that Rothmann's comments about chronicles discussing Nimrod's activities as the origins of secular authority are actually references to Franck's *Chronica*.

[58] Franck, *Chronica*, vi(b) (=1531, vi–vi(b)), xi (=1531, x): 'Es ist hie zu mercken/ das die herrschaft von der lincken/ gotlosen seitten vnd übel geraten kinder Noe herkumpt/ vnd nicht von der linien Christi/ noch von den glidern der gerechten/ derhalb sich Fürsten und Herren jrs herkummens bald gerümpt haben/ auch kein gottseliger Herr Keiser oder Fürst gewesen ist/ biß zü letst das volck Gottes mer auß fürwitz dann bedrengt/ umb ein künig vnd öberhand batten/ da wurden sie auß genaden/ nit auß verdienst/ etwa doch selten mit einem gottsäligen/ frummen künig versehen/ als David/ Ezechias. u. Darumb sprich ich ist der Herren herkommen nicht fast ehrlich/ vnd haben allzumal ein klein lob in der schrift/ vnnd haben fast all durch aus übel haußgehalten/ wie man noch sihet/ das ein frummer Fürst wiltpret im himmel ist/ ... '.

To reinforce his claims about the heathen nature of temporal authority, Franck, too, relates it to the origins of idolatry, which he traces to Nini. Elsewhere he notes that some have identified Nimrod with Saturn, although he does not appear to have noted the other identification of Bel with Jupiter.[59] While he does not state explicitly in the 1531 edition of the *Chronica* that the subsequent history of temporal authority should be understood according to the pattern established in the book of Daniel, Franck clearly adopts this pattern and on several occasions refers his readers to Daniel when discussing questions arising from attempts to calculate the length of historical ages. Within this context he treats the history of the Holy Roman Empire as a continuation of the fourth monarchy described in Daniel 2.[60] And his history of Imperial Rome goes into some detail in describing the vices of some of the more debauched Roman emperors. Included among these are unflattering portraits of Nero and Maximus Thrax.[61] One is tempted, then, to see Rothmann combing Franck's *Chronica* for material to fill out his emerging vision of the history of temporal authority. Certainly, the significant parallels in these two histories suggest more than a casual or coincidental relationship between them.

But to what extent does this amount to a significant influence of Franck on Rothmann? In other words, does it qualify as one of the channels by which the radicalism of the South German Reformation was conveyed to northerners? Cornelis Augustijn has cautioned students of Franck to be modest in their claims about the extent to which Franck influenced his contemporaries. In particular, Augustijn insists that we distinguish between those who merely plundered Franck's writings, especially his historical writings, for data to support their own agendas and those who breathed in the true spirit of Franck's message.[62] No amount of smoke and mirrors would suffice to make Rothmann into a legitimate heir of Franck's spiritual legacy.[63] Yet, Rothmann's

---

[59] Ibid., xiiii–xiiii(b) (=1531, xii), xx–xx(b) (=1531, xviii).

[60] See Franck's treatment of the Babylonian/Assyrian, Persian, Macedonian and Roman Empires, *Chronica* (1531), xxviii ff. Interestingly, in the 1536 edition he is quite explicit about his use of Daniel in charting the course of the world monarchies, xi(b)–xii(b).

[61] Ibid., cxliiii (=1531, cxxx–cxxx(b)), clv–clv(b) (=1531, cxliv–cxlv). In both cases the descriptions in the 1531 edition are lengthier, spell out in more detail the vices of the emperors and highlight their roles in the persecutions of the early church.

[62] Cornelis Augustijn and Theo Parmentier, 'Sebastian Franck in den nördlichen Niederlanden 1550 bis 1600' in Jan-Dirk Müller (ed.), *Sebastian Franck (1499–1542)* (Wiesbaden, 1993), p. 306.

[63] For example, see Franck's comments on the events in Münster in the 1536 edition of the *Chronica*, ccxci–ccxciiii.

reading of the *Chronica* appears to be more than just a cynical plundering of specific historical data to be plugged into a preexistent historical framework. Rather, Franck's detailed exposés on the origins and development of temporal authority provided a powerful remedy for Rothmann's conservative, 'quasi-Lutheran' theories of its origin. Although they put it to drastically different uses, Franck and Rothmann did share a common vision of the heathen nature and history of temporal authority. That vision, deriving originally from Franck, when grafted onto Hoffman's apocalyptic framework by Rothmann, produced explosive results.

CHAPTER SEVEN

Andreas von Karlstadt as a humanist theologian

Bill McNiel

Like many of his contemporaries, Andreas von Karlstadt was educated in the biblical humanist tradition, which emphasized the study of the ancients, the biblical languages, and the church fathers. Yet modern assessments of Karlstadt's thought rarely focus attention on his relationship to the humanist movement. Scholars who deal with his humanist background tend to minimize its long-term importance to Karlstadt's intellectual development.[1] One reason why the significance of his humanism has not been discussed more often is the acceptance of the once unquestioned notion that the Reformation and humanism were fundamentally opposed on the issue of human dignity and free will.[2] However,

---

[1] After citing several sources that reveal a humanist influence on Karlstadt, Hermann Barge concludes that the Reformer was swayed by the humanists' language and style, but not by their substantive thought. Hermann Barge, *Andreas Bodenstein von Karlstadt*, vol. 1, *Karlstadt und die Anfänge der Reformation* (Leipzig, 1905; reprint, Nieuwkoop, 1968), p. 170. Although he does not deal with the issue of Karlstadt's humanism comprehensively, Gordon Rupp makes the point that Karlstadt was a leader of the humanist campaign during the early Reformation to reform the Wittenberg curriculum. Gordon Rupp, *Patterns of Reformation* (Philadelphia, 1969), pp. 60–61. Like Barge, Ronald Sider argues that humanism had no more than a superficial influence on Karlstadt. Ronald J. Sider, *Andreas Bodenstein von Karlstadt: The Development of His Thought 1517–1525* (Leiden, 1974), pp. 10–11. Ulrich Bubenheimer argues in *Consonantia Theologiae et Iurisprudentiae* that humanism did not have a substantial impact on Karlstadt before his Swiss period. Ulrich Bubenheimer, *Consonantia Theologiae et Iurisprudentiae: Andreas Bodenstein von Karlstadt als Theologe und Jurist zwischen Scholastik und Reformation* (Tübingen, 1977), p. 286. In a 1987 article, however, Bubenheimer states that Karlstadt, Luther and Müntzer shared a similar humanist education. He identifies Karlstadt as a Reuchlinist at the beginning of the Reformation, and notes that he was influenced early in his career by Johannes Reuchlin and Pico della Mirandola, both of whom played a part in the development of his mystical piety. Ulrich Bubenheimer, 'Luther-Karlstadt-Müntzer: soziale Herkunft und humanistische Bildung. Ausgewählte Aspekte vergleichender Biographie,' *Amtsblatt Der Evangelisch-Lutherischen Kirche In Thüringen* 40 (April 1987), pp. 65–6, 68.

[2] Bernd Moeller, 'The German Humanists and the Beginnings of the Reformation', in H.C. Erik Midelford and Mark U. Edwards, Jr (eds and trans.), *Imperial Cities and the Reformation*, 2nd edn (Durham, NC, 1982), p. 29. Bernd Moeller argues that the most

both movements worked harmoniously in Karlstadt's mind throughout his career as a Reformer. The purpose of this chapter is to illuminate the neglected humanist side of Karlstadt's intellectual life, and therefore to reveal the close relationship between the Reformation and the humanist movement.

The compatibility of humanism and the Reformation becomes apparent when the beliefs of specific humanists are examined. For instance, the noted humanist Lorenzo Valla agreed with Luther that the *viator* had no free will *coram deo*.[3] Recent literature on Ulrich Zwingli and John Calvin establishes persuasively that both were simultaneously humanists and Reformers, despite their rejection of free will.[4] Moreover, humanists such as Philip Melanchthon, who joined Luther and Karlstadt against Rome, thought of themselves as fighting to restore the Scriptures to their ancient integrity, a notion which coincided completely with the aims of the Reformers.

It follows from our discussion that humanism was combined with a variety of theological and philosophical outlooks. Any definition of humanism should allow for this diversity of beliefs. Paul Oscar Kristeller argues that humanism was not a philosophical point of view, but a methodology.[5] Humanists devoted themselves to the recovery of the lost

---

influential followers of Martin Luther were the humanist government officials and scholars who broadcasted his ideas from town to town through their sodalities. Yet, according to Moeller, the core of humanism was its high regard for human dignity; a notion which ran counter to Luther's understanding of man as totally sinful. Moeller concludes that the humanists' support for Luther and the Reformation was 'a constructive misunderstanding'. Maria Grossmann, *Humanism in Wittenberg 1485–1517* (Nieuwkoop, 1975), p. 134. For Grossmann, humanism is an interesting interlude between the period of scholasticism's dominance and the Reformation: 'But the freedom of the Christian man as Luther preached it has little relation to the humanists' concept of man, and it is a dubious supposition to regard humanism as a natural ally of Protestantism. Nevertheless, by undermining scholasticism, humanism helped to bring about the transition to Protestantism.' Of course, contra Grossmann, Protestantism was not yet a confessional faith during the early years of the Reformation. The issue of free will was debated freely within church circles and sometimes even between humanists, such as Karlstadt and Johannes Eck.

[3] Ronald G. Witt, 'The Humanist Movement', in Thomas A. Brady Jr, Heiko A. Oberman and James D. Tracy (eds), *Handbook of European History, 1400–1600: Late Middle Ages, Renaissance, and Reformation*, vol. II, *Visions, Programs, and Outcomes* (Leiden, 1995), p. 108.

[4] James Stayer, 'Zwingli and the "viri multi et excellentes"', in E.J. Furcha and H.W. Pipkin (eds), *Prophet, Pastor, Protestant: the Work of Huldrych Zwingli after Five Hundred Years* (Allison, PA, 1984), pp. 137–54. W.J. Bouwsma, *Calvin: a Sixteenth Century Portrait* (New York, 1988), pp. 9–16.

[5] Paul Oscar Kristeller, *Renaissance Thought: the Classic, Scholastic and Humanist Strains* (New York, 1961), pp. 22, 74–5.

truths of antiquity. Their sources were the Greek and Roman authors, including the Greek and Latin church fathers, and the Bible, which they interpreted directly through its Hebrew and Greek texts. As defined by Kristeller, humanism was essentially empty of philosophical or theological content, thus explaining why Valla could disagree with Erasmus on the issue of free will, and why some humanists moved against Rome while others did not. Kristeller allows for the synthesis of humanism and Reformation.

Applying Kristeller's definition, this chapter will not be concerned directly with Karlstadt's theology, but with his methodology and rhetorical style. It is our understanding that Karlstadt was strongly influenced by humanism throughout his career. Even during his scholastic phase (c. 1505–17) and in his Orlamünde period (1523–25), signs of humanist influence were apparent. He made references to the ancients, used Greek and Hebrew, wrote flowery poems, epigrams and dedicatory letters. At his most spiritualistic, when he argued for the sufficiency of spiritual revelation, he remained devoted to humanist exegetical methods as a means toward spiritual truth.

Karlstadt was likely exposed to humanism while he studied at the University of Erfurt (1499–1503). During the period of his attendance, Maternus Pistoris and Nikolaus Marschalk were making Erfurt a centre for humanism. Although there is a lack of evidence, Hermann Barge speculates that Karlstadt owed to them his knowledge of Greek and his ability to write Latin poems in a typically ostentatious humanist style.[6]

At the University of Cologne (1503–04) Karlstadt studied the *via antiqua* and came to Wittenberg in 1505 as a Thomist with Scotist overtones. It was as a follower of the *via antiqua* that Karlstadt made his mark on the academic world. He lectured on Thomas and Aristotelian Metaphysics[7] and wrote two Thomist tracts. Yet Karlstadt's allegiance to the *via antiqua* did not subsume his humanist orientation. There were several signs of humanist influence in Karlstadt's earliest works. *De intentionibus* (1507) contains flowery epigrams with mythological references and a dedicatory letter.[8] In *Distinctiones Thomistarvm* (1507) Karlstadt began with a few words in Greek and ended with a

---

[6] Barge, vol. 1, pp. 4–5.

[7] Ibid., pp. 8–9. The *via antiqua* was a curriculum stream which, simply stated, emphasized the philosophical realism of Thomas Aquinas, as opposed to the *via moderna*'s stress on William of Occam and his followers. For a nuanced discussion of the fifteenth-century conflict between the two *viae* see James H. Overfield, *Humanism and Scholasticism in Late Medieval Germany* (Princeton, NJ, 1984), pp. 49–60.

[8] Ibid., pp. 9–10.

passage in Hebrew.[9] His use of Hebrew in *Distinctiones Thomistarvm* was dependent upon Johannes Reuchlin's *Capnion vel de verbo mirifico* (1494) and *Rudimenta hebraica* (1506), as well as a Jewish prayerbook.[10] It is clear that his study of Hebrew and Reuchlin's works began early in his career.

Moreover, as early as 1514, in a letter to Georg Spalatin, Karlstadt declared his support for Reuchlin, as Reuchlin fought against the proposed ban on Hebrew texts.[11] Again in 1516, he professed his allegiance to Reuchlin's cause in two letters to Spalatin, siding with the 'learned and pure Dr. Johannes Reuchlin'.[12] Clearly Karlstadt was both a scholastic and a humanist during his early Wittenberg period.

There was an emphasis on humanism in Wittenberg dating from the foundation of the university in 1502. The founder, Elector Frederick the Wise, was a patron of humanist studies, as evidenced by the numerous humanist books he and Spalatin collected for the Wittenberg library.[13] Martin Polich von Mellerstadt, the first rector of the university, had strong humanist credentials, along with the first dean of theology, Johann von Staupitz.[14] By 1513, the library contained many works by the church fathers, Greek and Latin classics, language and grammar manuals, and histories, as well as scholastic treatises.[15] From the time of Karlstadt's arrival in Wittenberg, he was working and studying in a humanist milieu.

---

[9] Gustav Bauch, 'Andreas Carlstadt als Scholastiker', *Zeitschrift für Kirchengeschichte* 18 (1898), p. 54. See also Barge, vol. 1, p. 28.

[10] Hans Peter Rüger, 'Karlstadt als Hebraist an der Universität zu Wittenberg', *ARG* 75 (1984), pp. 299–302. Rüger argues that Karlstadt's Hebrew citation was in part an adoption of Reuchlin's teaching on the three forms of the revelation of God: Schaddai (God in the form of nature), Jahwe (God in the form of law) and IHSVH (God in the form of grace and love, or Jesus).

[11] Andreas von Karlstadt, 'Letter to Spalatin (13 February 1514)', in Johann Friedrich Heckel (ed.), *Manipulus primus epistolarum singularium* (1695), pp. 17–20. See Sider, *Andreas Bodenstein von Karlstadt*, pp. 10–11 for the date and a quotation from the letter.

[12] Andreas von Karlstadt, 'Ad manus Celeberrimi ac Doctissimi Viri D. Spalatini, Charissimi Fautoris', Johann Gottfried Olearius (ed.), in *Scrinium antiquarium*, 2nd edn, (Jena and Arnstadt, 1698), pp. 2–3. Andreas von Karlstadt, 'Ad manus Celeberrimi Domini Georgii Spalatini Philosophiae Doctoris, Fautoris Colendissimi &c.', in *Scrinium antiquarium*, p. 3.

[13] Grossmann, pp. 100–12.

[14] If not a humanist, Staupitz was a friend of humanism. David Steinmetz argues that he did not have an adequate knowledge of Greek or Hebrew, only Latin. Thus, although he had good humanist friends, he can not himself be called a humanist. David Steinmetz, *Luther and Staupitz: An essay in the Intellectual Origins of the Protestant Reformation* (Durham, NC, 1980), pp. 38–9.

[15] Grossmann, p. 109.

Along with his philological and theological education, Karlstadt was versed in jurisprudence. His trip to Rome in 1515 was the culmination of a long interest in the study of law. It is known that he participated in a law disputation in 1511 and attended daily lectures on canon law by the provost of the Castle Church of All Saints, Henning Göde. Karlstadt was advanced enough in the study of jurisprudence by 1511 that a Wittenberg Professor of Law, Christoph Scheurl, was convinced that he would soon earn his doctorate in canon law.[16] After a stay in Rome at the *Sapienza*, he officially received his doctorate in both canon and civil jurisprudence.

In Wittenberg and in Rome, Karlstadt studied law under the influence of the *mos italicus*, which emphasized the citing of scholastic authorities, such as the medieval Italian jurists Bartolus de Saxoferrato (1314–57) and Accursius.[17] Yet, he was open to influence by the humanistically oriented *mos gallicus*. Karlstadt's commentary on Augustine's *De spiritu et litera* (1517–19)[18] contains references to Cicero, as well as to Bartolus and Accursius.[19] Here again Karlstadt synthesized humanist and scholastic influences.

This might seem like a major contradiction in Karlstadt's thought. Theoretically, humanism, with its emphasis on poetry, grammar, rhetoric, history and moral philosophy, was the antithesis of scholasticism, which had as its basis formal logic and Aristotelian philosophy. But the synthesis of humanism and scholasticism was not unusual among medieval and early modern thinkers,[20] and Karlstadt's contemporaries did not view it as an inconsistency. On 16 November 1508 Christoph Scheurl gave a eulogy in which he praised Karlstadt as 'a man very learned in Latin, Greek and Hebrew and noted as a philosopher, more noted as a theologian and most noted as a Thomist ... '.[21] Scheurl was not the only humanist to remark on Karlstadt's abilities. In 1514, an

---

[16] Bubenheimer, *Consonantia Theologiae et Iurisprudentiae*, pp. 14–15.

[17] Ibid., pp. 204–5.

[18] Karlstadt's *De spiritu et litera* was printed in stages from his dedicatory letter to Staupitz (18 November 1517) to the end of the commentary (end of January or beginning of February 1519). A complete publication history of the work can be found in Ernst Kähler (ed.), *Karlstadt und Augustin: Der Kommentar des Andreas Bodenstein von Karlstadt zu Augustins Schrift 'De spiritu et litera'*, (Halle (Saale), 1952), pp. 48–52.

[19] Andreas von Karlstadt, *De spiritu et litera*, in *Karlstadt und Augustin*, p. 18. See Andreas von Karlstadt, *Confutatio* (Wittenberg), BV for citations of Cicero. Bubenheimer, *Consonantia Theologiae et Iurisprudentiae*, pp. 206–13. According to Bubenheimer, during the period from 1517–19 Karlstadt rejected scholastic theology, but remained a scholastic in the field of jurisprudence.

[20] Barge, vol. 1, p. 9. See also Kristeller, p. 116 and Overfield, p. 330.

[21] *Oratio doctoris Scheurli attingens litterarum praesentiam, nec non laudem Ecclesie Collegiate Vittenburgensis* (Leipzig, 1509); quoted in Barge, vol. 1, p. 28.

anonymous visitor to Wittenberg described Karlstadt's diverse scholarly abilities:

> Andreas Bodenstein from Karlstadt ... doctor of arts and sacred theology, Archdeacon and Canon on the collegiate church of All Saints in Wittenberg, – a man experienced in the Holy Scripture and very learned in canon law as well as in Aristotelian philosophy: a highly renowned philosopher, speaker, poet and theologian. His mind is precise and quick to grasp; his style of speech impressive. In Hebrew, Greek and Latin, he is well skilled. Moreover, he is a highly sharp dialectic debater, and an exceedingly attentive follower of Thomas as well as Scotus. In addition, he is distinguished in verse and prose.[22]

This portrait of Karlstadt as an omnicompetent scholar is perhaps an exaggeration. But it reveals the intertwining of scholasticism and humanism, which exemplified German university culture during the late fifteenth and early sixteenth centuries. Karlstadt participated in this eclectic tradition.

That Karlstadt's interests were diverse is seen in an undated letter he wrote to Spalatin (after March 1517).[23] Here again we see his Reuchlinist allegiances:

> In addition, you would do me not a small favour ... if you would send my vulgar and boorish, though certainly affectionate, original letter together with your so refined and ingenious writing to our most learned and worthy Reuchlin. I can only express the highest praise for his *Cabbalistica*, with the exposition [of the Cabbala] of Giovanni Pico, Count of Mirandola, which I will explain next week to the admirable youths and men.[24]

This letter is important not only because it shows that Karlstadt had friendly contact with Reuchlin around 1517, but perhaps more importantly it reveals Karlstadt's interest in Hebrew mystical literature and theory, the Cabbala,[25] an interest which goes back at least as far as

---

[22] Joachim Johann Mader (ed.), *Scriptorum insignium qui in celeberrimis praesertim Lipsiensi, Wittenbergensi, Francofordiana ad Oderam academiis a fundatione ipsarum usque ad annum Christi 1515 floruerunt centuria* ... (Helmstedt, 1660), G 3 a f; quoted in Ernst Kähler, 'Karlstadts Protest gegen die theologische Wissenschaft', in *450 Jahre Martin-Luther-Universität Halle-Wittenberg*, vol. 1 (Halle-Wittenberg, 1952), pp. 299–300.

[23] Bubenheimer, 'Luther – Karlstadt – Müntzer: soziale Herkunft und humanistische Bildung.', p. 65.

[24] Andreas von Karlstadt, 'Doctissimo, amicissimoqve Spalatino, Fautori suo ex pectore colendo.', in *Scrinium antiquarium*, p. 82. See also Bubenheimer, 'Luther – Karlstadt – Müntzer: soziale Herkunft und humanistische Bildung.', p. 65.

[25] Cabbala is a Hebrew word meaning tradition. It was an esoteric Jewish system of exegesis, tending toward a gnostic view of the world. The *Cabbala* in the letter refers to Reuchlin's *De Arte Cabbalistica* (1517), in which he used Cabbalistic doctrines to interpret scriptures.

1507, and his apparent use of a Jewish prayerbook. As the letter suggests, he lectured on the Italian humanist Giovanni Pico della Mirandola's forays into the Cabbala. This certainly explains why he supported the Hebraists against Johann Pfefferkorn and the Dominicans of Cologne in 1514.[26]

Karlstadt's break with scholastic realist theology in 1517 was inspired mainly by a disagreement with Luther in 1516 over the authenticity of the pseudo-Augustinian work *De vera et falsa poenitentia*. At this point in his development, Karlstadt's knowledge of Augustine was probably limited to scholastic commentaries. His discussion with Luther led him to buy and read an edition of Augustine's works and Johannes von Staupitz's *Libellus de Executione eterne predestinationis*.[27] After reading Staupitz and Augustine, and under the influence of Luther, Karlstadt rejected the authority of the scholastic fathers in the realm of theology.

It was not humanism, but Luther's influence that led Karlstadt away from the *via antiqua* toward Augustinianism.[28] However, this transition was made within a humanist context. Both Karlstadt and Luther saw themselves as continuing the battle against the scholastics that Reuchlin and Erasmus had begun.[29] Like Reuchlin and Erasmus, they challenged

---

[26] Overfield explains that in the first several years of the Reuchlin affair (1509 to 1513) the focus of both Reuchlin and his detractors was on whether Jewish books should be confiscated from the synagogues and whether they were of any use to Christians. In 1513, Reuchlin launched a mild attack against what he perceived to be the Cologne theologians' puerile emphasis on logic, and for a short period suspected that their assault on him was really a conspiracy against humanistic studies. But the anti-Reuchlinists were anti-Jewish not anti-humanist. In fact, a leading supporter of Pfefferkorn's anti-Jewish campaign was Ortwin Grotius, a scholar with humanist credentials. Erasmus attempted to remain neutral in the affair at least partially because of his suspicion that the trend toward studying Hebrew literature might promote Jewish ceremonialism. The affair was simply not a conflict between humanist and scholastic forces. Overfield concludes that only one work associated with the affair, the *Letters of Obscure Men* (1515 and 1517) written by Ulrich von Hutten and Crotus Rubeanus, portrayed the controversy as if it were a cosmic struggle between humanism and scholasticism. Yet the work was criticized or ignored by many prominent humanists. Overfield, pp. 247–97.

[27] *Karlstadt und Augustin*, pp. 3–4.

[28] Bubenheimer, *Consonantia Theologiae et Iurisprudentiae*, p. 212.

[29] To understand that Luther viewed himself as treading in Reuchlin's footsteps one need only look at his letter to Reuchlin in 1518: 'I am now being attacked by the Behemoth, who are anxious to avenge upon me the disgrace they have suffered at your hands. Doubtless I am forced to encounter them with much feebler weapons of wit and learning, but with as much courage and delight as you. ... For God has achieved this through you – that the lord of the Sophists has found that the righteousness of God must be met with gentleness, so that Germany, through the teaching of the Holy Scriptures, which, alas, for so many hundred years has been smothered and suppressed, has again begun to breathe.' Martin Luther, *The Letters of Martin Luther* (London, 1908), p. 39.

the veracity of the scholastic commentators, and promoted the sufficiency of the biblical word.

In the *151 Theses* (26 April 1517), Karlstadt severed his ties with the scholastic commentators, opposing their mixing of Aristotelian philosophy with theology: 'the teaching of Aristotle in the schools of theology is a harmful mixture.'[30] Addressing himself to the students, he wrote in his preface to *De spiritu et litera* (1517) that they were privileged to have the Scriptures taught 'ex ipso fonte', as opposed to 'ex scholasticis'.[31] He bragged about Petrus Lupinus' lectures on St Ambrose, Johannes Rhagius Aesticampianus' on St Jerome,[32] and Luther's ability to use Greek and Hebrew to interpret Hebrews. At the same time that Karlstadt was raving about the possibility for humanist studies in Wittenberg, he and Luther were involved in a movement to purge the university of all scholastic studies, opening the door for more teaching on books of Scripture in the ancient languages and 'eminent' church fathers.[33]

On the issue of authority, he placed the Scriptures first and then the church fathers. When contradictions occurred within the patristic literature, the statements in question were to be judged in accordance with Scripture and reason.[34] Not even Augustine's opinions were reliable without biblical verification.[35]

This same theory of authority was expressed in his *370 Conclusiones* (May 1518). 'A text of the Bible quoted by an ecclesiastical doctor is stronger and proves more than the saying of the one quoting it.'[36] He continues in thesis 12 of the same work to argue that the Bible was not only above the church fathers, but the church as a whole.[37] Although Karlstadt put theoretical limits on the authority of the church, he did not reject its authority, nor its claim of infallibility. It was within the limits of canon law when he argued that the Pope could be declared in error if his

---

[30] Andreas von Karlstadt, *151 Theses*, in *Karlstadt und Augustin*, p. 34.

[31] Andreas von Karlstadt, *De spiritu et litera*, pp. 9–10.

[32] Petrus Wolff (Lupinus) from Radheim (d. 1521) was a professor of theology and curator and chancellor of All Saints in Wittenberg. For Lupinus see Bubenheimer, *Consonantia Theologiae et Iurisprudentiae*, p. 290 n. 3. Aesticampianus (d. 1520) had just joined the Wittenberg faculty in 1517, after already having had a controversial career as a poet and rhetorician. On Aesticampianus see Overfield, pp. 238–43.

[33] Martin Luther, 'To John Lang Wittenberg, 18 May 1517', in *LW*, 48, p. 42.

[34] Karlstadt, *151 Theses*, pp. 11–12. The same argument was made by Karlstadt in the first eleven theses of the *405 Concl.* (1518). See Bubenheimer, *Consonantia Theologiae et Iurisprudentiae*, p. 78.

[35] Ibid., p. 12. 'Sentencia Augustini in moralibus nulli cedit (contra canonistas).'

[36] Andreas von Karlstadt, 'CCCLXX et apologeticae conclusiones', in Valentin Ernst Löscher (ed.), *Vollständige Reformationes-Acta und Documenta*, vol. 2 (Leipzig, 1723), p. 79; quoted and translated in Sider, *Andreas Bodenstein von Karlstadt*, p. 48.

[37] Ibid., p. 80.

decrees contradicted the Scriptures.[38] Interestingly, he reiterated his belief in papal authority in an earlier thesis.[39] However, general councils were not infallible,[40] a notion which was shared by his fellow papal supporters. Like the councils, the church fathers were not without error, but their statements were not to be taken lightly. Karlstadt's works during this period were packed with positive references to the pre-scholastic fathers, along with Jean Gerson (1363–1429) and St Bernard (1090–1153). He cited Augustine to support his premise of biblical supremacy.[41]

1517 was a transition year for Karlstadt. He severed his ties with the scholastic fathers and began to focus strictly on the Bible and the church fathers as sources of truth. Still, his emphasis on biblical authority and the *fontes Augustini* did not overshadow his allegiance to the Pope. This change in Karlstadt's outlook should be placed within the context of the humanist movement. At this time, like many other humanists, he was shedding his scholastic dialectics in favour of a purely exegetically-based theology.

The debate between Johannes Eck and Karlstadt (1519) was a debate between a scholastic/ humanist and a humanist. Eck remained within the eclectic scholastic tradition that Karlstadt had jettisoned two years earlier. Karlstadt refused to accept Aristotle as a legitimate authority in the field of theology; and Eck justified his use of Aristotle, citing Cicero, Quintilian, and Plato in his defence.[42] In his writings against Eck, Karlstadt cited Cicero, Horace, Quintilian and Plinius, along with Erasmus, whom he ranked with Augustine and Ambrose as a great theologian.[43] He chided Eck for arguing that some parts of Scripture should not be opened to the unlearned by citing Erasmus' call for the laity to have access to the complete Scriptures in the vernacular.[44] In the same work, he recommended the reading of Jerome, Augustine and Chrysostom at the expense of his former teachers Thomas Aquinas and John Capreolus (*c.* 1380–1444).[45]

---

[38] Ibid., p. 99. Both Sider and Bubenheimer show that Karlstadt took this statement directly from canon law. Sider, *Andreas Bodenstein von Karlstadt*, p. 50. Bubenheimer, *Consonantia Theologiae et Iurisprudentiae*, p. 115.

[39] Ibid. Here, we agree with the arguments of Sider and Bubenheimer against Barge. Karlstadt did not reject papal authority in his *370 Conclusiones*, but in 1520.

[40] Ibid., p. 80; quoted and translated in Sider, *Andreas Bodenstein von Karlstadt*, p. 53.

[41] See note 35.

[42] Barge, vol. 1, p. 157.

[43] Andreas von Karlstadt, *Epistola Andree Carolostadii* (Wittenberg, 1519), CivV. See also Barge, vol. 1, p. 170.

[44] Andreas von Karlstadt, *Verba Dei* (Wittenberg, 1520), D. See also Barge, vol. 1, pp. 175–6.

[45] Karlstadt, *Verba Dei*, Gij. See also Barge, vol. 1, p. 177.

Karlstadt's humanism may have become more pronounced after his break with scholasticism, but this does not obscure the fact that he was a humanist before the transition. Moreover, we should not diminish the impact that humanism had on this development in his thought. His attacks on scholastic soteriology were Augustinian in content, but his turn toward the church fathers' writings (the *fontes Augustini*), and his attack on scholastic authorities, were within the context of the break between scholastic realism and humanism that occurred during the early Reformation.

The importance of humanism to Karlstadt's intellectual development is apparent again in his pivotal works of 1520. In *Weliche biecher Biblisch seint*, Karlstadt cited the Hebrew Bible and Jerome when deciding which books should be given the status of Holy Scripture.[46] He favoured Jerome over Augustine on this issue, because Augustine included books in his canon which were not in the Hebrew Bible. It was the Hebrew Bible that must be followed 'in doubtful or dark matters'.[47] In contrast to Luther, he argued for the canonicity of the epistle of James, citing Jerome, Augustine and the Greek text as support.

Karlstadt's reliance on the Hebrew text was evident again when he attempted to render a careful translation of Numbers 30 in his booklet on vows (1521). Translating from Latin to German, he tried to retain the original Hebrew language and meaning. He criticized the Latin Bible for its inadequacies:

> I do not want to hide the fact that the Latin Bible uses the term *statim* at this point which in Hebrew means *day*. Also, that it is written here, 'then he shall bear her iniquity,' which basically is the term which the translator puts into Latin as *afflixit*. I therefore stayed with the Hebrew truth. Likewise, the term for *ieiunium* is not found in the Hebrew [text]. I reckon that our text mixed a gloss in with the text – which happens often, though it is not praiseworthy.[48]

Here we see Karlstadt as a theologian and a philologist, searching diligently for the 'Hebrew truth'.

Karlstadt's desire to go back to the Greek and Hebrew texts of the Bible and his use of the church fathers were well within the biblical

---

[46] Andreas von Karlstadt, *Weliche biecher Biblisch seind* (Wittenberg, 1520), aiiV–aiiiV. Andreas von Karlstadt, *The Books That Are Holy and Biblical*, E.J. Furcha (ed. and trans.) [typed manuscript], pp. 6–9.

[47] Andreas von Karlstadt, *Weliche biecher Biblisch seind*, BV. Andreas von Karlstadt, *The Books That Are Holy and Biblical*, p. 15.

[48] Andreas von Karlstadt, *Regarding Vows*, in E.J. Furcha (ed. and trans.), *The Essential Carlstadt*, (Waterloo, Ont., 1995), p. 96. *The Essential Carlstadt* will hereafter be cited as *Carlstadt*. Andreas von Karlstadt, *Von gelubden vnterrichtung* (Wittenberg, 1521), HiiV.

humanist tradition. He drew a balance between the dominant authority
of the Bible and the supporting role of the church fathers. This balance
is revealed in his treatise on I Corinthians 1 (1521): 'When I want to use
Augustine, Jerome, Ambrose, and others while disputing over the evangelical mass, they must be in agreement with the text [the Bible] and say
nothing against it.'[49] The Scriptures were the basis upon which the
works of the fathers should be judged.

He ranked the church fathers slightly below the non-biblical, or
apocryphal, scriptures in his hierarchy of authorities. Like the apocryphal books, the church fathers served as unarmoured soldiers, unable to
stand on their own and vulnerable in serious battle, but adding to the
numbers and prestige of the army as it marched on parade or jousted
with the enemy.[50] Essentially, they were used to place one's arguments
into the context of church tradition and, thus, to protect one from the
accusation of heresy.

> In this way also I generally read my response and argument at
> Leipzig from the Bible and from the books of Augustine, Jerome,
> Ambrose, Bernhard, Gregory, Cyprian, Cyril and others – to stop,
> flee, and avert from me any suspicion of heresy.[51]

Like the Bible, patristic literature stemmed from a time before the church
had been corrupted by Aristotelian philosophy. To Karlstadt, this gave it
legitimacy. In the margin beside the statement quoted above, he asserted
that the 'Pope labels Augustine a heretic'.[52] It was important for Karlstadt,
as for all of the Reformers, to claim the patristic tradition as his own.

After the Papal Bull condemning Luther and Karlstadt arrived in
Wittenberg in 1520, Karlstadt openly rejected papal authority. He did
not, however, reject the authority of the ancient fathers. His argument

---

[49] Andreas von Karlstadt, *Sendbryff Andres Boden. von Carolstatt. Erklerung Pauli.*
(Wittenberg, 1521), Aiii. 'Wan ich mit Augusti. Hieroni. Ambro. vnn andern von
Ewangelischer Messe wolt disputirn/ musten sie mit den text tzefriden sein vnn dawider
nicht reden.'
[50] Karlstadt, *The Books That Are Holy and Biblical*, pp. 12–13. 'The biblical books
are the skilled and armed sentences; the others, which I mentioned earlier, are exposed,
naked and weak, but they add to the host and serve not badly in parades and skirmishes.
... I don't mean to say that these lowly and weak books contain lies (as someone may
assume). No, I say that no one who rejects these books should be regarded a heretic. I
hold to this in keeping with the teaching of St Jerome. While they do not put down, bind
or capture any enemies, they are better and stronger than the writings and teachings of St
Augustine, Jerome, Ambrose, Gregory, and the like.' Karlstadt, *Weliche biecher Biblisch
seind*, AivV–b.
[51] Andreas von Karlstadt, *Missiue vonn der aller hochste tugent gelassenheyt*
(Wittenberg, 1520), B. Andreas von Karlstadt, *Tract on the Supreme Virtue of Gelassenheit*
in *Carlstadt*, p. 33.
[52] Ibid.

against the Pope was based almost solely on the biblical word, but was bolstered, in some cases, by the patristic writings. To support his general argument that the Pope displayed too much pomp to be a Christian leader, Karlstadt cited the Greek father, St Cyril (*c.* AD 315–86). According to Karlstadt, St Cyril stated that the church should limit its birth or anniversary celebrations to the birthday of Christ. Thus, any church-sponsored celebration of the Pope's election and coronation was against ancient church tradition.[53] Here Karlstadt condemned what he perceived to be the overly elaborate celebrations of the papacy by referring to the contrary teachings of an ancient father of the church.

During the period from 1521–24, there is evidence that at least some contemporaries saw Karlstadt as a leader of the humanist evangelical movement, which emphasized biblical rather than papal authority. In *Ain Schöner dialogus* (1521), Martin Bucer placed Karlstadt alongside the learned leaders of the Reformation: Luther, Erasmus and Oecolampadius. These leaders, according to Bucer, were learned in Greek, Hebrew and Latin.[54] Like Bucer, the author of the dialogue *Cunz und der Fritz*[55] freely unites Karlstadt with Erasmus and Oecolampadius.[56] Moreover, the composer of the poem *Triumphus veritatis* (*c.* 1524) portrayed Karlstadt, Luther and Ulrich von Hutten as evangelical heroes.[57]

After being pushed aside by Luther in 1522, Karlstadt rejected the Wittenberg church and university hierarchies. He moved to Orlamünde

---

[53] Andreas von Karlstadt, *Von Bepstlicher Heylickeit*, FiiijV. 'Cyrillus saget/ das die kirchen keynes heyligen geburtstag sol feyhern/ auszgenonmenn Christum/ Nun ist der bapst yhe nit szo heylig als sanct Johannes der tauffer odder Jeremias/ aber Esaias/ dennest mussen vil Romer den iartag seiner erwelung vnd kronung feyhern/ vnd mit lichten vnd wachsz vnnd vassen/ puluer/ vnd puchszen gesang/ begehen.'

[54] Martin Bucer, *Ain Schöner dialogus* in Oskar Schader (ed.), *Satiren und Pasquille aus der Reformationszeit*, vol. 2 (Hannover, 1863), p. 140. Priest: 'Dann ich hör, es seyent sunst vil gelerter leüt auff seiner seytten, besonder Doctor Erasmus Rotterdam, der gschrift ain starcker egstain, des geleych Doctor Andreas Karolstat, ain kron der hailigen gschrifft, auch Eocolampadius vnd der noch vil mer. etc. Dann jch vernym, dise hochgelertten menner haben den rechten kern der gutten bücher in yebung, kriechisch, hebraisch, lateinisch vnd vylleycht kaldeysch; auss den allen, die dann bey kurtzen jaren her für kumen seind, Lygt (als ich hör) der recht schatz der hailigen gschrifft.'

[55] According to Oskar Schade, the author of *Cunz und der Fritz* was probably Urbanus Rhegius. It was probably published in either Ulm or Augsburg not before September of 1521. Oskar Schade (ed.), *Ain Schöner Dialogus. Cunz und der Fritz* in *Satiren und Pasquille*, vol. 2, p. 324.

[56] Ibid, pp. 119–24.

[57] Oskar Schade (ed.), *Triumphus Veritatis*, in *Satiren und Pasquille*, vol. 2, pp. 196–251. The author identifies himself as Hans Heinrich Freiermut. Calvin Pater argues that the poem was published in 1524; and that the author was probably Hans Sachs, the Nuremberg poet. Calvin Augustine Pater, *Karlstadt as the Father of the Baptist Movements: The Emergence of Lay Protestantism* (Toronto, 1984), pp. 295–300.

to become a 'new layman', and eventually gave up his Archdeaconate and university post. However, despite shunning the academic community, he did not rebuke learning as such, nor did he argue for its diminished usefulness. He merely objected to the pursuit of knowledge for selfish reasons rather than for the glory of God. Karlstadt found the pursuit of honours in university and church to be contrary to God's will:

> What does one seek in the higher schools than to be honoured by others? ... Yet, it cannot be that we believe and trust God while we receive such honours. Christ says, 'Not the one who seeks honour.' He narrows the scope and says, 'Whoever receives honour from another, cannot believe God.' ... What I said of universities also applies to bishops and priests.[58]

The objection here was not over the act of learning. The fact is that Karlstadt promoted the learning of God's word among the peasantry. It was the selfish pursuit of academic glory that needed to be purged.

The *Dialogue* (1524) has been seen as Karlstadt's most anti-intellectual/spiritualist tract. It is here that he argues for the sufficiency of spiritual revelation, through the words of the peasant Peter.[59] Yet Peter was not completely unlearned; he knew his Bible, and at one time had studied the biblical languages. All three of the characters in the *Dialogue* accepted that the Greek text was the true rendition of the word. There was no contradiction between the spiritual word and the scriptural word in Karlstadt's theology. The Spirit supported the Scriptures and the Scriptures the Spirit. All spiritual revelation had to be held against the clear word of Scripture. The Greek and Hebrew Bibles were the standard upon which any claim to scriptural authority should be based, and by which any claim to spiritual revelation should be assessed. In the *Dialogue*, Peter was pleased that his spiritual revelations were supported by the original Greek texts.[60] What he knew in his heart was known to anyone who understood the Greek New Testament.

Karlstadt displayed important humanist ideals throughout his career. This was not lost on contemporaries, who commented on his knowledge of the biblical languages and associated him with other humanists. His move toward Reformation evangelicalism should be seen as a product

---

[58] Andreas von Karlstadt, *The Meaning of the Term Gelassen and Where in Holy Scripture it is Found* in *Carlstadt*, pp. 161–2. Andreas von Karlstadt, *Was gesagt ist: Sich gelassen* (1523), eiiiV.

[59] Andreas von Karlstadt, *Dialogue or Discussion Booklet* in *Carlstadt*, p. 282. Andreas von Karlstadt, *Dialogus* in Erich Hertzsch (ed.), *Karlstadts Schriften aus den Jahren 1523–25*, vol. 2 (Halle (Saale), 1957), p. 18.

[60] Ibid.

of his humanist exegetical methods, and his study of the church fathers' original writings. Even during a period of moderate spiritualism, he remained devoted to a humanist approach. Humanism links Karlstadt's eclectic Thomist period with his period as a Radical Reformer in the same way that it links the Middle Ages with the Reformation.

CHAPTER EIGHT

Between the devil and the inquisitor: Anabaptists, diabolical conspiracies and magical beliefs in the sixteenth-century Netherlands

*Gary K. Waite**

This study explores the intersections between the heresy of Anabaptism and the supposedly even greater apostasy of demonic witchcraft. Anabaptism challenged the institutional church(es) because of its rejection of the official social structure and hierarchical understanding of the cosmos.[1] The early Anabaptists, moreover, depicted the ecclesiastical authorities in apocalyptical terms as the antichrist (the son of the devil), thereby turning the accusation of a diabolical conspiracy on its head.[2] However, once a relative truce had been declared with Lutherans, and

---

* The research for this paper was funded by the Social Sciences and Humanities Research Council of Canada and the University of New Brunswick. Most materials were examined during visits to the Doopsgezinde Bibliotheek, Universiteits-Bibliotheek Amsterdam, and the Acadia Centre for Baptist and Anabaptist Studies, Acadia University, Wolfville, NS.

[1] Willem Frijhof suggests that demonic possession cases were most prominent among new monastic orders practising new modes of spirituality, because their contemporaries, 'unable as yet to comprehend the new, recognise only the reversal to the old categories and postulate an intervention on the part of the devil. The fear of a structural attack on the institution explains the vigorousness of the persecution ... ', a vigorousness that was directed also against Anabaptists, because they challenged the survival of the old christianity and hence promoted their own cosmic structure and values. Willem M. Frijhof, 'Official and Popular Religion in Christianity. The Late Middle-Ages and Early Modern Times (13th–18th Centuries)', Pieter H. Vrijhof and Jacques Waardenburg (eds), *Official and Popular Religion: Analysis of a Theme for Religious Studies* (The Hague, 1979), pp. 71–116, esp. pp. 92–3. Note also the fascinating if controversial study by Lionel Rothkrug who posits a correspondence between witchcraft beliefs and peasant rebellion in the German lands; in 'Holy Shrines, Religious Dissonance and Satan in the Origins of the German Reformation', *Historical Reflections/ Réflexions Historiques*, 14 (1987), pp. 143–277.

[2] For an early example of this apocalyptical ideology from Holland Anabaptists, see Gary K. Waite and Samme Zijlstra, 'Antiochus Revisited: An Anonymous Anabaptist Letter to the Court at the Hague', *MQR*, 66 (1992), pp. 26–46.

Anabaptists had been persecuted into an underground and largely sectarian existence, it seems many authorities turned around 1560 to the suppression of magical deviance with increased fury and near unanimity. This chronological development leads to several related questions: first, did the perceived threat of Anabaptism have anything to do with this revival of diabolical conspiracies? Second, did the popular or official image of Anabaptists change in any way after the rise of witch-hunting? Third, was there any overlap in official perception of Anabaptists and witches during the critical decades of the 1540s to 1560s?

This much is agreed upon: the flare-up of the persecution of witches followed close upon the heals of the waning of large-scale heresy prosecution by 1565, although there were a number of individual cases of prosecution for witchcraft that took place coterminously with the trials against religious dissidents. However, it was not the isolated witch who brought periodic bouts of terror to the hearts of Europeans through the later sixteenth and seventeenth centuries, but the belief that witchcraft was a diabolical conspiracy between Satan and groups of women and men meeting secretly at night who performed perverse inversions of Christian rites, worshipped the devil, kidnapped and roasted unbaptized infants, and plotted the overthrow of Christian society. Certainly belief in magic and witchcraft was endemic to European society, but it was not until the fifteenth century that this stereotype of the diabolical and conspiratorial witch was fully developed. Even so, persecutions of these supposed diabolical agents seem to have died down by the end of the century, and soon the inquisitorial and secular courts were preoccupied with religious dissidents. Brian Levack's suggestion of a chronological intersection between heresy persecution and witchcraft trials has been recently pursued by William Monter, who has calculated that there were some 3 000 legally sanctioned executions for heresy from 1520 to c. 1565 and about two thirds of these victims were Anabaptists.[3] He argues that the apparent rise of Anabaptism from the ashes of the German Peasants' War of 1525 and the fear of further sedition provoked by these religious dissenters led to the secularization of heresy trials in the German Empire, the Low Countries and eventually elsewhere in Europe.[4] Monter asks why this momentous attack on heresy by secular states has not seriously

---

[3] Brian P. Levack, *The Witch-Hunt in Early Modern Europe* (2nd edn, London and New York, 1995), p. 120; William Monter, 'Heresy Executions in Reformation Europe, 1520–1565', in Ole Peter Grell and Bob Scribner (eds), *Tolerance and Intolerance in the European Reformation* (Cambridge, 1996), pp. 48–64, esp. p. 49.

[4] Monter, 'Heresy Executions', p. 50. For Anabaptism and the Peasants' War, see James M. Stayer, *The German Peasants' War and Anabaptist Community of Goods* (Montreal and Kingston, Ont., 1991).

been seen as contributing to the even more horrific assault on accused witches. The reason is perhaps quite simple: historians of the Reformation and historians of witchcraft, in Monter's words, 'rarely read each other's works',[5] a conclusion that is perhaps unfair in some cases[6] but is too often corroborated when reading the secondary literature in both fields.[7] It is this major gap in our understanding of the persecution of both heretics and witches that this chapter broaches, seeking to communicate to scholars of both the Reformation and the witch-hunts.

Given what we now know about early-modern popular culture, it seems likely that ordinary people who witnessed the fiery executions of both Anabaptists and accused witches would have confused the two sets of victims, especially since their contemporary polemicists condemned Anabaptists as a demonic sect threatening the Christian religion. Perhaps ordinary people also misconstrued some Anabaptist ideas or practices as somehow magical and demonic. Lutheran and Reformed polemicists showed little caution in demonizing their more radical opponents, and in some cases, associating them with sorcery. In his *Lectures on Galatians* Luther wrote the following in a passage about witchcraft:

> Thus in our day we, too, must labour with the Word of God against the fanatical opinions of the Anabaptists and the Sacramentarians ... For we have recalled many whom they had bewitched, and we have set them free from their bewitchment, from which they could never have been untangled by their own powers if they had not been admonished by us and recalled through the Word of God. ... So great is the efficacy of this satanic illusion in those who have been deluded this way that they would boast and swear that they have the most certain truth.[8]

Of course Luther distinguished between physical and 'spiritual' witchcraft. However, not all of his readers, or those who heard Luther's ideas

---

[5] Monter, 'Heresy Executions', p. 62.

[6] Heiko A. Oberman discusses the issue of tolerance in Early Modern Europe by presenting cases involving a pre-Reformation witch, a Jew and religious dissenters, but without making any conclusions about how each of these may have related to the other apart from acting as 'test cases' for the limits of tolerance. Oberman, 'The Travail of Tolerance: Containing Chaos in Early Modern Europe', in Grell and Scribner, *Tolerance and Intolerance*, pp. 13–31.

[7] For example, in two recent large surveys of the Reformation, there is barely a mention of witchcraft: Carter Lindberg refers to belief in witches only in the context of pre-Reformation superstitions (*The European Reformations* [Oxford, 1996], esp. pp. 61–2), and while Euan Cameron's tome includes a succinct discussion of the Reformation's suppression of popular culture, he does not once mention the horrific persecution of witches (*The European Reformation* [Oxford,1991], esp. pp. 408–10). I am working on a monograph on the subject tentatively entitled *Heresy, Magic and Witchcraft in Early Modern Europe* (Basingstoke, in preparation).

[8] LW, vol. 26, *Lectures on Galatians*, pp. 194–5.

second hand, made such careful distinctions.[9] That Menno Simons
(c. 1496–1561) found it necessary to respond to charges that he and his
fellow Mennonites were demon-possessed illustrates the potential ramifications of such polemical characterization.[10] Instead, Menno argued,
infant baptism was a 'ceremony of Antichrist, a public blasphemy, a
bewitching sin'. While this position may have led some opponents to
believe that Anabaptists were demon possessed, Menno responded that,

> We consider those possessed of the devil who speak the devil's
> words, who teach the devil's falsehood instead of truth, steal God's
> glory from Him, and sadly deceive souls ... we hate the word of the
> devil from our inmost souls ... . This is an evident sign that we are
> not possessed of the spirit of the devil but of that of the Lord. If we
> were of the devil as we are reviled, we would walk upon a broader
> road and be befriended by the world and not so resignedly offer
> our property and blood for the cause of the Word of the Lord.[11]

In other words, the true agents of the devil are the religious and civic
authorities that vigorously pursue the Anabaptists.

---

[9] Martin Luther certainly believed that his phrase 'Freedom of the Christian Man' had
been badly misused by the German peasants as a slogan of rebellion in 1525. Notwithstanding Luther's protest, the rebellious peasants 'thought of the enterprise as their
contribution to the Reformation'. Stayer, *The German Peasants' War*, p. 35.

[10] For Menno's defence, see his comments in 'Brief Defense to All Theologians' (1552),
John C. Wenger (ed.) and Leonard Verduin (trans.), *The Complete Writings* (Scottdale,
PA, 1956), p. 535, and in 'Reply to False Accusations' (1552), ibid., pp. 571–2. Later in
the sixteenth and seventeenth centuries several Dutch Mennonites joined the debate on
witchcraft prosecution, with at least three of them, Jan Jansz Deutel (d. 1657), Abraham
Palingh (1588/89–1682) and Antonius van Dale (1638–1708), rejecting the typical argu-
ments which had buttressed such vicious action for a century. See especially Marijke
Gijswijt-Hofstra, 'Doperse geluiden over magie en toverij: Twisck, Deutel, Palingh en
van Dale', A. Lambo (ed.), *Oecumennisme. Opstellen aangeboden aan Henk B. Kossen
ter gelegenheid van zijn afscheid als kerkelijk hoogleraar* (Amsterdam, 1989), pp. 69–83;
Hans de Waardt, 'Abraham Palingh en het demasqué van de duivel,' *Doopsgezinde
Bijdragen*, 17 (1991), pp. 75–100; Hans de Waardt, 'Abraham Palingh. Ein holländischer
Baptist und die Macht des Teufels', in Hartmut Lehmann and Otto Ulbricht (eds), *Vom
Unfug des Hexen-Processes: Gegner der Hexenverfolgungen von Johann Wyer bis Friedrich
Spee* (Wiesbaden, 1992), pp. 247–68; Gary K. Waite, 'From David Joris to Balthasar
Bekker?: The Radical Reformation and Scepticism towards the Devil in the Early Mod-
ern Netherlands (1540–1700)', *Fides et Historia*, 28 (1996), pp. 5–26; and Gary K.
Waite, 'David Joris en de opkomst van de sceptische traditie jegens de duivel in de vroeg-
moderne Nederlanden', in Gerard Rooijakkers, Lène Dresen-Coenders and Margreet
Geerdes (eds), *Duivelsbeelden in de Nederlanden* (Baarn, 1994), pp. 216–31 (chapter
translated by Pieter Visser).

[11] Menno, *The Complete Writings*, pp. 133, 140. For the original, see Menno Simons,
Opera Omnia Theologica of alle de Godtgeleerde Wercken van Menno Symons (1681
edn, Amsterdam, 1989); esp. *Een fundament en Klare Aenwysinge van de Salighmakende
Leere Jesu Christi*, p. 19; *Een Weemoedige ende Christelycke Ontschuldinge ende
Verantwoordinge*, p. 513.

Between the inquisitor and the devil: Anabaptists in the courts

A start to examining the implications of Anabaptist rejection of infant baptism can be found in the published court records relating to Dutch Anabaptists.[12] These are the records of the court officials, reflecting the interrogations as understood and recorded by the prosecutors. We can then turn to a source that presents the perspective of the arrested Anabaptists themselves as they underwent their interrogations and reflected on their final days. This is the martyr book *Het Offer des Heeren* (1570), and while the documents in this work too have undergone a complicated process of transmission and editing, they reflect the authentic voice of the persecuted. Both of these types of sources provide important information on the relationship between accused heretics on the one side and their official interrogators on the other.

Before tackling the persecution of Anabaptists, it might be useful to survey briefly how Lutherans and other early Evangelicals were treated and regarded in the courts prior to the arrival of Anabaptism in the Netherlands *c.* 1530. Examination of these published sources, which are admittedly incomplete, reveals that the authorities in the vast majority of cases regarded the early Lutheran movement as a form of academic heresy, as almost an 'in-house' conflict among clerical factions. This is especially the case between 1519 and 1521, for it was Luther's learned supporters within the Augustinian monasteries who won the greatest attention on the part of the authorities, leading them to become the first martyrs of the Reformation in the Netherlands.[13] Unlike the case with the later Anabaptists, the Lutherans' theological positions were taken seriously and rebutted in a learned manner by their orthodox opponents.[14] In only one of the published sources is there any serious attempt to link Luther's heresy with diabolical notions, and that was a response to Luther's own characterization of the Pope as antichrist. This reference occurred in Charles V's second placard against Lutheranism, issued 8 May 1521 (his first placard of 20 March 1521, made no such reference). In it Charles V's theologians note that Luther had scandalized the

---

[12] Albert F. Mellink (ed.), *Documenta Anabaptistica Neerlandica*, vol. I: *Friesland en Groningen 1530–1550* (Leiden, 1975); vol. II: *Amsterdam, 1536–1578* (Leiden, 1980); vol. V: *Amsterdam, 1531–1536* (Leiden, 1985); vol. VII: *Friesland (1551– 1601) and Groningen (1538–1601)*, completed by S. Zijlstra (Leiden, 1995); hereafter *DAN* and vol. number.

[13] Paul Fredericq (ed.), *Corpus Documentorum Haereticae Pravitatis Neerlandicae* (5 vols, Ghent and 's-Gravenhage, 1892–1906), esp. vols 4 and 5, which include sources up to 1528.

[14] For example, see the rebuttal of Luther's doctrines by the Universities of Cologne and Louvain, in Fredericq, *Corpus Documentorum* 4: docs 25 and 26 resp.

entire church, especially when he called the fifteenth-century Council of Constance, which had burned Jan Hus at the stake, the 'synagogue of Satan'. In response, and with intended irony, the writer concludes that 'the person of the aforesaid Martin is not a man, but a devil under the species of a man, bedecked in the habit of a religious, in order better and more easily to bring the human race into eternal death and damnation.'[15] Even this bit of scholastic gamesmanship, based as it was on Aristotelian logic and modelled after the very doctrine of transubstantiation rejected by Luther, was not taken up in later placards or apparently even by interrogators of early Lutherans to implicate the Lutheran Reformation seriously in a diabolical plot. Instead, Charles V's public commission to inquisitor Frans vander Hulst and accompanying placard of 23 April 1522 toned down the diabolical rhetoric, so that Luther and his ideas are listed as schismatic, heretical and leading to eternal damnation, but his person is no longer described as a demon.[16] As the evangelical movement became more popular and lost its learned leadership under the pressure of persecution, there may have been a tendency to characterize it as a greater diabolical threat, but the available published sources do not reveal this as a significant development. Despite the authorities' opposition to Luther's reform movement and heretical ideas, Lutherans could prove useful in opposing even more radical forms of heresy, such as that of the infamous slater Loy Pruystinck (de Schaliedecker), whose quite unorthodox opinions, including his rejection of hell, eternal punishment and the physical resurrection, as well as his affirmation that the Holy Spirit was none other than human reason resident in each individual, won many followers in Antwerp. In 1525 Pruystinck travelled to Wittenberg to convince Luther of his pantheistic notions but Luther's response was hardly positive, hastily dashing off a missive to his followers in Antwerp warning them of this mischievous spirit [polltergeyster] and his dangerous ideas.[17] Ironically, when in January of the following year Pruystinck and nine of his supporters were arrested for heresy, his crime was identified as 'Lutheranism' [heresie lutheriane], undoubtedly to Luther's chagrin.[18] In spite of his public recantation in February, Pruystinck continued to spread his ideas throughout the city, attracting not only an adoring crowd of poor sympathizers who bowed down when he passed

[15] Fredericq, *Corpus Documentorum* 4: doc. 47, p. 67.

[16] Fredericq, *Corpus Documentorum* 4: docs 72 and 79.

[17] 'Eyn brieff D. Martini Luther An die Christem zu Antorff', in Julius Friedrichs (ed.), *De Secte de Loïsten of Antwerpsche Libertijnen (1525–1545): Eligius Pruystinck (Loy de Schaliedecker) en zijn Aanhangers* (Ghent and The Hague, 1891), pp. 4–7.

[18] Frederichs, *De Secte der Loïsten*, pp. 8–9.

by adorned in his bejewelled rags, but also a number from the middle and upper social strata. In 1539, reform-minded dramatists in the city wrote a Lutheran play that opposed the more radical notions of Pruystinck, thus maintaining the support of the local authorities for their dramatic activities.[19] Finally in 1544 Pruystinck and several of his prominent supporters were arrested and executed.[20] This one example does help reveal why Luther's reform, however distasteful it may have seemed to orthodox theologians, did not elicit the same level of panic on the part of the authorities.

Anabaptists in the authorities' perspective

As with most secular court materials, the Anabaptist court records present very skimpy summaries of the proceedings; however, a few things can be gleaned from them. First, it appears that what most concerned court officials was the extraction of confessions about the principal beliefs of heretical Anabaptism, most notably its rejection of infant baptism and transubstantiation and the adoption of adult baptism. The records describe this latter act as a renunciation of one's original baptism, and hence of the church and Christian society. In most cases, the accused had come to regard infant baptism as ineffectual and the priestly consecrated Host as ordinary bread. Furthermore, some Anabaptist parents were discovered because they had not had their infants baptized, in itself a criminal act.[21] Given the physical obviousness of pregnancy, it must have been difficult to hide a pregnancy and

---

[19] G. Jo. Steenbergen, 'Het Spel der Violieren op het Gentse Landjuweel', *Jaarboek van de Koninklijke soevereine Hoofdkamer van Retorica 'De Fonteine' te Gent*, 4 (1946–47), pp. 15–26, affirms that the play is directed against the teachings of Pruystinck. See also Gary K. Waite, 'Reformers on Stage: Rhetorician Drama and Reformation Propaganda in the Netherlands of Charles V, 1519–1556', *ARG*, 83 (1992), pp. 209–39; also Gary K. Waite, 'Reformers on Stage: Popular Drama and Religious Propaganda in the Low Countries of Charles V, 1515–1556', book manuscript under consideration for publication.

[20] See also Norman Cohn, *The Pursuit of the Millennium* (London, 1970 [1957]), p. 170.

[21] For example, see the cases of Uulbe Claeszoon, of 8 May 1538 in the Court of Friesland, who was executed for refusing to baptize his infant, who unfortunately had died in an unbaptized state (and hence damned) 17 weeks after birth, *DAN* I, p. 55; and Pieter Pieterszoon (Beckgen), of 11 January 1569 in the Amsterdam court, who abducted his newborn daughter from her mother so that she could not be baptized, *DAN* II, pp. 272–87. See also *DAN* VII, p. 13, where on 10 January 1553 Joucke Sible was arrested for having allowed her seven or eight-year-old child to die unbaptized, claiming she had been forced to do so by her husband; also p. 26 where on 27 April 1553, Aucke Sieurdtsd. was arrested for not having her infant 'christianized'.

birth from the authorities. This may have been the reason why a ru-mour appeared during the height of Anabaptist activity in Amsterdam in 1534, suggesting midwives were smuggling newborn infants out of the city. Count Hoogstraten expressed considerable concern over this news, although Amsterdam's magistracy denied any knowledge of such occurrences, doubting that such was even possible.[22] The ability of many Anabaptists to hide their unbaptized infants from the authorities, however, may have led to increased suspicion regarding midwives, who, perhaps not surprisingly, figured largely in witchcraft beliefs.[23] As with the case of midwives suspected of witchcraft, the presumed collusion between midwives and Anabaptist parents finally led the Groningen authorities in 1569 to issue a decree ordering all midwives to be exam-ined by the States General to see 'if they are Catholic and of good reputation' before being allowed to perform their work in the region.[24]

Increasingly, especially after Anabaptists had successfully taken over Münster in 1534, authorities sought to uncover the conspiracy of Anabaptism, to extract from the accused the names of all others who had attended the secret meetings and who were also supposedly plotting insurrection.[25] Thus descriptions of the sect included the appellative 'seditious' as well as the more typical 'heretical'. The imperial placard

---

[22] *DAN* V, p. 52 (point 40), and the response, p. 61.

[23] See Anne Llewellyn Barstow, *Witchcraze: A New History of the European Witch Hunts* (San Francisco, 1994), p. 113; Levack, *The Witch-Hunt*, pp. 139–40. The *Malleus Maleficarum* had, in fact, already argued that midwives frequently offered up unbaptized infants to the devil. However, Robin Briggs (*Witches and Neighbors* [New York and Harmondsworth, 1996], pp. 77–8, 279–81), argues that there is no statistical evidence to support the argument that midwives were especially targeted as witches, and his research from the Lorraine trials shows that they were instead under-represented. Lyndal Roper (*Oedipus and the Devil: Witchcraft, Sexuality and Religion in Early Modern Europe* [Routledge, 1994], pp. 199–225), moreover, has shown that it was not midwives who were accused as witches when newborn infants died in Augsburg, but lying-in maids. For other recent discussions of the witch-hunts, see Bengt Ankarloo and Gustav Henningsen (eds), *Early Modern European Witchcraft: Centres and Peripheries* (Oxford, 1990); Jonathan Barry, Marianne Hester and Gareth Roberts (eds), *Witchcraft in Early Modern Europe: Studies in Culture and Belief* (Cambridge, 1996); Wolfgang Behringer, *Witchcraft Persecutions in Bavaria: Popular Magic, Religious Zealotry and the Reason of State in Early Modern Europe* (Cambridge, 1997); Geoffrey Scarre, *Witchcraft and Magic in 16th and 17th Century Europe* (Houndmills, England, 1987); Joseph Klaits, *Servants of Satan: The Age of the Witch Hunts* (Bloomington, IN, 1985); and Richard van Dülmen (ed.), *Hexenwelten: Magie und Imagination vom 16.–20. Jahrhundert* (Saarbrücken, 1991).

[24] *DAN* VII, p. 129.

[25] This is seen, for example, in the case of Andries Claeszoon of Doonrijp, tried on 16 March 1535 by the Court of Friesland, who freely confessed to rebaptism, to holding conventicles in his house, and who was convicted for being a member of the 'rebellious' sect of Anabaptists in Münster. *DAN* I, p. 27.

against Menno Simons of 7 December 1542, described him as deceiving
the simple people with his false teaching during secret, night-time meetings.[26] Like diabolical witchcraft, the crime of rebaptism, because of its
inherent social danger, was treated as an exceptional crime of '*lese
majestatis*', of treason against both divine and human authority.[27] The
concern over heresy had therefore been heightened to the level of a
secret and dangerous conspiracy. Mandate after mandate ordered local
officials and clergy to uncover people hiding in attics or cellars,[28] to
keep their eyes on any who did not attend yearly confession or mass
and to report on the kind of lives they led, those with whom they
associated, any 'secret meetings' at their homes, as well as to relate the
presence of any strangers in their midst.[29] Furthermore, on 6 January
1536, Karl van Egmond, Duke of Guelders, ordered all the clergy of his
domain to conduct a visitation in Drenthe and the region of Groningen
to discover any heretical beliefs.[30] To underscore the authorities' seri-
ousness regarding the presumed Anabaptist threat, in most areas of the
Low Countries those convicted of such heresy were, like convicted
witches, burned at the stake, although under certain conditions the
accused might be accorded the mercy of a drowning or beheading.

Fears of an Anabaptist conspiracy to overthrow Christendom did not
dissipate quickly. Two decades after the Münster debacle the court of
Friesland issued a placard denouncing the increase in dangerous heretics hiding in their midst who reject all the sacraments, steal from
people and churches, and secretly plot a godless revolt to expel and
exterminate Christians. To accentuate the danger of this threat, the
president of the court, Hippolitus Persijn, calls these Anabaptist heretics
'an evil race of men and monstrous creatures'.[31] Of course part of
Persijn's concern was to counteract the Batenburgers, a small group of
militant Anabaptists who commited acts of robbery and violence as a
means of visiting divine vengeance upon their persecutors.[32] Yet Persijn

[26] *DAN* I, p. 65.
[27] *DAN* II, p. 296.
[28] *DAN* V, p. 66, from 21 November 1534.
[29] On 2 February 1535, the Amsterdam authorities were forced to go so far as to
forbid any further 'mummery' or masking, activities usually enjoyed during Carnival or
similar frivolous events, in order to ensure Anabaptist conspirators did not take advantage of such opportunities to disguise their identities. *DAN* V, p. 108.
[30] *DAN* I, p. 140. For another example, see the missive from the Stadholder of
Friesland to the local officials of 24 May 1544, *DAN* I, p. 69.
[31] 'Boose geslachte van menschen ende monstreuse creatueren', *DAN* VII, pp. 14–21,
from 10 January 1553.
[32] For the Batenburgers, see Gary K. Waite, 'From Apocalyptic Crusaders to Anabaptist
Terrorists: Anabaptist Radicalism after Münster, 1535–1544', *ARG*, 80 (1989),
pp. 173–93.

makes no distinction between militant and peaceful Anabaptists, such as the Mennonites, presumably wishing to keep the size of the fearful conspiracy as large as possible. Three years later the stadholder of King Philip II attempted much the same thing in his attempts to force the city of Groningen to fall in with the king's policy of harsh suppression of Anabaptism, telling the city fathers that the Anabaptists and related sects were gaining the upper hand in the city and would soon overthrow it. The city council responded in a very interesting fashion: its members knew of some women who refused to baptize their children, but they did not consider these to be dangerous, nor were they aware of any portentous buildup in militant Anabaptist forces.[33] In other words, in this case the local civic authorities had become acquainted with their Mennonite residents and knew them to be no threat to law and order, whereas the more distant royal government continued to propagate a conspiratorial vision of these heretics. Interestingly enough, one of the worst outbreaks of executions in the Netherlands for witchcraft oc-curred in the Groningen Ommelanden, the rural area outside of the city, where twenty executions took place in 1547 and another five in 1562.[34] Unlike Friesland, where the Court of Friesland kept a firm hand over local courts and controlled heresy hunting, completely suppressing po-tential witch-hunts, the Ommelanden courts had a relatively free hand and were more easily manipulated by 'foreign' pressures to prosecute, such as the royal government or advocates of witch-hunting from East Frisia.[35] At the same time it seems both Groningen's and the Ommelanden's officials strongly resisted royal pressure to prosecute Mennonites, forcing the stadholder in 1567 to hire, without the

---

[33] *DAN* VII, pp. 153–64.

[34] Marijke Gijswijt-Hofstra, 'Six Centuries of Witchcraft in the Netherlands: Themes, Outlines, and Interpretations', Marijke Gijswijt-Hofstra and Willem Frijhoff (eds), *Witch-craft in the Netherlands from the Fourteenth to the Twentieth Century* (Rotterdam, 1991), pp. 1–36, esp. 26. See also Marijke Gijswijt-Hofstra, 'The European Witchcraft Debate and the Dutch Variant', *Social History*, 15 (1990), pp. 181–94. Excellent collec-tions of essays include Willem de Blécourt and Marijke Gijswijt-Hofstra (eds), *Kwade mensen. Toverij in Nederland* (Amsterdam, 1986); and Marijke Gijswijt-Hofstra and Willem Frijhoff (eds), *Nederland betoverd. Toverij en hekserij van de veertiende tot in de twintigste eeuw* (Amsterdam, 1987). For recent regional studies, see Willem de Blécourt, *Termen van toverij: de veranderende betekenis van toverij in Noordoost-Nederland tussen de zestiende en de twinigste eeuw* (Nijmegen, 1990); and Hans de Waardt, *Toverij en samenleving. Holland 1500–1800* (Den Haag, 1991).

[35] P. Gerbenzon, 'De vervolging van toverij in Groningen en Friesland, zestiende eeuw. "Buitenlandse" invloeden en de invloed van rechterlijke organisatie en procesrecht', in Gijswijt-Hofstra and Frijhoff, *Nederland betoverd*, pp. 124–32. See also Levack's discus-sion of the role of centralized courts in the witch-hunts, in Levack, *The Witch-hunt*, pp. 84–99.

approval of the local authorities, a band of mercenaries to 'rob, disturb and hunt down' Mennonites in the Ommelanden.[36] Evidently, in this region of the Netherlands, witchcraft was perceived as a much more serious threat to social order than was Anabaptism, royal propaganda notwithstanding. In neighbouring Friesland, however, it appears that judicial officials were content to limit their efforts in counteracting heresy to Anabaptism.

Such broad-ranging conspiracies usually had at their centre the leadership of the devil. Yet, the devil figures hardly at all in the published court records. Of course, this could simply mean that its presence and activity were assumed. It could also mean, as it did in many witchcraft cases, that the accused themselves did not mention the devil, even though the interrogators constantly attempted to put a demonological slant on the accused's confessions.[37] Before examining the applicability of this theory for Anabaptist trials, it will be illuminating first to examine the few cases where the devil is mentioned. Then we can turn to the *Het Offer*, where the devil figures more prominently.

In the four volumes examined, the name of the devil, or the adjective diabolical, appears only seven times, and in two volumes, not at all. Of all of these, only in one case was the name used by an accused Anabaptist. One of the reasons for the apparent neglect of the devil (at least in the official court records) has to do with the attitude of the accused themselves toward the magical and diabolical beliefs of their day. The Anabaptist rejection of all Catholic ritual led them to regard all sacraments as priestly magic. Anabaptists rejected the doctrine that Christ was corporeally present in the consecrated host, because they could not understand how Christ could be physically present both in heaven and in the bread. Most revealing is the confession of the Anabaptist leader Adraien 'the one eyed' Pieterszoon, who, on 12 May 1534, admitted to the Amsterdam magistrates that he had told some people walking to the 'Holy Place' [*Heilige Stede*, the shrine memorializing the city's miracle of the Host][38] that the bread and cheese in his hands were as good as the bread (Host) sitting in the shrine's monstrance. He also remarked to some others that if the body of Christ was indeed in the Host, then it should bleed when broken and he challenged these people to bring 'fifty gods' (Hosts) which he would stab with a knife and if they bled, he

---

[36] *DAN* VII, p. 206.

[37] See, for example, Willem de Blécourt, 'Typen van toverij', Peter te Boekhorst, Peter Burke and Willem Frijhoff (eds), *Cultuur en maatschappij in Nederland 1500–1850* (Boom, 1992), pp. 319–63, esp. p. 343.

[38] James D. Tracy, *Holland Under Habsburg Rule, 1506–1566: The Formation of a Body Politic* (Berkeley, CA, 1990), pp. 150–51.

would believe in the sacrament. Even more brazenly he had stated in the city hall that the Host is merely baked bread and priests cannot make gods, for God is in heaven. Apparently the city's bailiff [*schout*] had responded to Adriaen's disbelief by referring Adriaen to the miracles which took place on a daily basis at the Holy Place shrine. To this Adriaen replied, 'the devil can perform these miracles as well as God'.[39] This, the only reference to the devil recorded from the lips of an accused Anabaptist in these sources, reveals quite clearly the anti-miraculous (at least in the Catholic sense) perspective of many Anabaptists, perhaps even a commonsense scepticism which contrasts with both the miraculous and learned demonological theory. At the same time, Adraien's threat to desecrate the Host is not totally removed from the realm of magical beliefs; judging from accusations made against Jews in the later fifteenth and sixteenth centuries, it seems to have been widely believed that desecrated Hosts did bleed, confirming the reality of transubstantiation in the face of doubters.[40] Adriaen most assuredly knew of these beliefs, and his comments must therefore be seen as a direct challenge not to official theology, but to popular religion, to magical thinking.

That Anabaptists were not altogether successful in severing themselves completely from a magical universe is seen from the other references to the devil in these volumes. As noted, all of these came from the interrogators or hostile chroniclers. Several events, in both early Anabaptism and later Mennonitism reveal that visions and miraculous portents could be decisive in determining which direction Anabaptists would take.[41] We will look at only a couple of the more notorious

---

[39] *DAN* V, pp. 6–9, 40–41; as related to him by one of the city's now deceased aldermen, Pieter Aemszoon.

[40] R. Po-Chia Hsia, 'Jewish Magic in Early Modern Germany', in R. Po-Chia Hsia (ed.), *Religion and Culture in the Renaissance and Reformation* (London and Ronceverte, 1987), pp. 81–97; see also his *The Myth of Ritual Murder: Jews and Magic in Reformation Germany* (New Haven, CT, and London, 1988). At the same time, Adriaen and his cohorts were able to tap into a rising tide of scepticism regarding the catholic miraculous tradition; in the same year as Adriaen's boast, city fathers heard several complaints about Amsterdamers who closed their doors and windows when the processional priests carrying the blessed Host in a monstrance to the 'Holy Place' passed by. *DAN* V, pp. 7–8. Another example was provided by an anticlerical actor who had commissioned an artist to paint a backdrop to a play, both of which depicted demons dressed as monks fishing for money. Here the devil was used to mock the clergy, creating, according to the city officials, much murmuring among people of all sorts in the city and a ridiculing of Amsterdam's clergy. *DAN* V, p. 43.

[41] Two of the most widely reported portents were those seen over Münster, especially the times the inhabitants saw 'three suns' and, more dramatically, a portent in the sky of a man with bloody hands; reported on 17 May 1535, by Jacob van Campen to the Amsterdam authorities, *DAN* V, p. 156. In Amsterdam, some Anabaptists expected the sign of a three-day cloud of darkness that was to divide Amsterdam in half (between the

incidents of early Dutch Anabaptism: the 'naked runners' of Amsterdam and the 't Zandt affair.

On the evening of 11 February 1535, a small group of eleven Anabaptists (seven men and four women) was led by their prophet, the tailor and actor Heynrick Heynricxz, to remove and burn their clothes in the upstairs of a house and then run out onto the streets of the city, crying 'woe, woe over the world and the godless', proclaiming the 'naked truth'.[42] Prior to this act, the prophet had claimed not only to have seen and spoken to God, but to having visited heaven and hell. Another of his disciples had put a burning coal in his mouth, believing it would not burn him and that by doing so he would no longer require food. During their interrogation, the defendants refused to put on any clothing and said strange things that so puzzled Gerrit van Assendelft, president of the Court of Holland in The Hague, that he wondered if the accused were possessed:

> It is a strange thing to see these naked people, springing like wild folk. It leads one to think that they are in part possessed by the devil, although they speak pertinently, with good understanding, and say strange, unheard of things which would take too long to write.[43]

Evidently this high official of the central court had considered a diagnosis of diabolical possession, but ultimately rejected it because the accused did not exhibit all of the known characteristics of possession, appearing

---

old and new sides) and herald the bloodless victory over the godless, *DAN* V, p. 88. The validity of such 'signs and wonders', however, was determined by an established criteria of authenticity relating to the movement's apocalyptical framework; that is, a vision was a bona fide one if it confirmed the teachings of the prophet, whether Melchior Hoffman or Jan Matthijs, and confirmed the nearness of the end and the righteousness of the Anabaptist cause. Within this structure, however, there could be considerable room for interesting developments. See Gary K. Waite, 'Talking Animals, Preserved Corpses and Venusberg: The Sixteenth-Century Worldview and Popular Conceptions of the Spiritualist David Joris (1501–1556)', *Social History*, 20 (1995), pp. 137–56; for later incidents, see Gary K. Waite, 'Demonic Affliction or Divine Chastisement? Conceptions of Illness and Healing amongst Spiritualists and Mennonites in Holland, c.1530–c.1630', in Marijke Gijswijt-Hofstra, Hilary Marland and Hans de Waardt (eds), *Illness and Healing Alternatives in Western Europe*, Routledge Studies in the Social History of Medicine Series (London and New York, 1997), pp. 59–79.

[42] *DAN* V, pp. 109–16; see also A.F. Mellink, *Amsterdam en de Wederdopers* (Nijmegen, 1978); Gary K. Waite, 'Popular Drama and Radical Religion: The Chambers of Rhetoric and Anabaptism in the Netherlands', *MQR*, 65 (1991), pp. 227–55.

[43] 'Tis een vreempt dinck dese naeckte luyden te zien ende springen gelijcken wilt volck, ende is te beduchten dat zij van den duvel eensdeels beseten zijn, hoewel zijluyden pertinentelicken spreken met goeden verstande, ende seggen vreempde ongehoorde dingen die te lanck zoude vallen te scrijven.' *DAN* V, p. 112.

instead to maintain their faculty of reason.[44] It must also be noted here that if the Anabaptists had been declared possessed, they would have been regarded as victims and treated with exorcisms. Such was obviously not the case.

Judging from these published accounts, suspicion of diabolical possession came up only once more, this time in the reports about the supposed 'Son of God' of 't Zandt, Cornelis int Kershof, and the 'Father', Herman Schoenmaker. These two managed to take over leadership of the Anabaptists who had gathered in early 1535 at a farmhouse in 't Zandt, Groningen, waiting for a messenger to lead them into Münster. According to the later account of the Reformed preacher of East Frisia, Gerardus Nicolai, Schoenmaker had told Cornelis to take the mug of beer from his hand and to drink in the Holy Spirit. Upon doing so, Cornelis sprang from his bed and ran among the believers, shouting 'kill your flesh, kill your flesh, your flesh is your devil, your flesh is your devil'.[45] Eventually an old woman came into Cornelis's room and witnessing his leaping about and ranting, went out to the people crying, 'oppose the possessed man'.[46] However, she was consequently convinced and became another spokesperson of the Son, telling the people to get rid of all fancy clothes, money and weapons, for God would defeat the godless without the assistance of material supports. When some doubters kept back possessions, she told the audience to 'cast out the oppressing devil', that is, reliance on gold and silver. However, the doubters could not be silenced and apparently one of them grabbed the Son and shoved him 'up to his ears in dung' in the barnyard, saying 'now you lay in the pit of hell'.[47] When the Münster messenger Antonis Kistemaker arrived, he was dismayed at the turn of events, and with the doubters literally kicked Cornelis out of the house. According to the

---

[44] The classic signs of possession included convulsive movements or seizures, speaking in a voice different from one's own, expressing horrible blasphemies, and exhibiting eyes that bug out, a grossly extended tongue, and a head wrenched nearly backward facing. See H.C. Erik Midelfort, 'The Devil and the German People: Reflections on the Popularity of Demon Possession in Sixteenth-Century Germany', in Steven Ozment (ed.), *Religion and Culture in the Renaissance and Reformation*, Sixteenth Century Essays and Studies 11 (Kirksville, MO, 1989), pp. 99–119, esp. 112.

[45] *DAN* I, pp. 115–22.

[46] 'Daerbeneven quam daer oock noch een oude bedaechde vrouw in, dewelcke van dat loopen ende crijten des Soons verwondert ende verschrickt zijnde, seyde: Stuert den beseten mensche, stuert den beseten mensche, etc.' *DAN* I, p. 116.

[47] 'Als nu de sommige hierover begonsten te twijfelen, ende een van hen zijne twijfelinge wat opentlyck bekende, ende daertegen sprack, so grijpt hem de Sone aen, ende stoot hem in de koegruppe tot over zijn ooren in den koedreck, seggende: daer lighstu in den afgront der hellen.' When the people witnessed this drama, some began to say 'ghewisselyck wij zijn hiermede alle te samen alsoo vuylyck bescheten'. *DAN* I, p. 117.

reports, Nicolai records that Cornelis flew so quickly over the frozen watering hole that some said 'the devil must have carried him over'.[48] In any event, the Anabaptists dispersed once they heard that the stadholder of Groningen, Karl van Guelders (the bastard son of Duke Karl van Egmond) was coming with an armed force.

Can these reports of strange activities be believed? Certainly Nicolai was no friend of Anabaptists, and he sought to portray them in the darkest possible colours. Learned writers may also have been at a loss to explain such unusual religious behaviour without recourse to theories of possession; Phillip Melanchthon, Luther's lieutenant, could explain the behaviour of the Münster Anabaptists, with their strange kingdom, polygamy and community of goods, only by diagnosing them as possessed by the devil.[49] At the same time, there is little doubt about the veracity of the accounts of the naked runners and there seems no reason to dispute Nicolai's report out of hand. However, what is most important for our purposes is not to determine if the accounts are completely accurate, but to learn from them what the authorities believed about Anabaptists and their supposed connection with the devil. It does not appear that the Erasmian-minded authorities of Amsterdam (at least before the notorious Anabaptist assault on the city hall on 10 May 1535) took very seriously a diabolical conspiracy. The trial accounts recorded by the Anabaptists themselves suggests a somewhat different picture elsewhere.

The Anabaptists' perspective

The accounts of Mennonite trials composed by the victims and collected by an anonymous editor as *Het Offer des Heeren* [*The Offering of the Lord*], fill in the picture of the official accounts of interrogations.[50] Unfortunately, only a handful of *Het Offer's* martyrs appear in the published sources surveyed above and merely one of these, the trial of Lysbet Dircxdochter in Leeuwaarden, Friesland, in 1549, adds considerable new detail.[51] In this account of the interrogation of Lysbet, a

---

[48] 'Over dewelcke hij so snellyck vlooch, alsof hem de duyvel (seyden sij) daerover gevoert hadde', for it was over twenty feet wide. *DAN* I, p. 118.

[49] D. Jonathan Grieser, 'Seducers of the Simple Folk: The Polemical War against Anabaptism (1525–1540)' (ThD diss., Harvard University, 1993), pp. 321–22.

[50] 'Dit Boeck wort genaemt: Het offer des Heeren ... ', 1570 (first published in 1563), S. Cramer (ed.), *Bibliotheca Reformatoria Neerlandica* ('s-Gravenhage, 1904), vol. II. Hereafter *BRN* II.

[51] *BRN* II, pp. 91–4; *DAN* I, p. 85. When citing solely from *BRN*, I will list the page numbers in the body of this chapter.

former nun executed for her rejection of the sacraments of the church, the authorities ask her what she believed about the 'most worthy, holy sacrament'. In her own account, she responds that she had read nothing of a holy sacrament in the Scriptures, only of a Lord's Supper. To this the gentlemen of the court respond, 'Silence, for the devil speaks from your mouth.' Preparing her for torture, they strip her against her pleas to force her to confess the names of her associates.[52] She holds firm and is drowned as a heretic. Lysbet's experience in the interrogation room was not far removed from that of accused witches; she was questioned according to a set script, stripped and tortured to uncover her cohorts, and accused of diabolical inspiration. We must not forget, in spite of our proclivity to make sharp distinctions between different fields of study such as heresy and witchcraft – reflected in the practice of pulling Anabaptist records out of their juridical contexts and publishing them separately – that it was often the same court officials who tried both sets of victims, sometimes conducting such seemingly distinct trials during the same week. One would therefore expect the interrogators to carry over techniques and ideas from one interrogation to another, although in most cases the Dutch authorities were able to distinguish clearly between those accused of Anabaptist heresy and those charged with diabolical witchcraft. As seen in the case of Lysbet, and a few of the other cases from *Het Offer* which we will examine now, accusations of diabolical guidance provided one common thread between the two sets of judicial victims.

Another case is that of Claesken Gaeledochter, executed by the Court of Friesland on 14 March 1559. Claesken records that she was asked the standard questions, what she believed about baptism, who had baptized her, why she had not baptized her children. Then she adds, 'these are the questions which he [the inquisitor] asked me. But he had many more words, and when I did not answer him well, then he said that I had the mute devil in me, for the devil places himself as an angel of light in us, which was true of all heretics' (p. 324). (This would have been a reference to a specific demon whose job it was to cause its servants to remain mute when questioned by the authorities.)[53] When two monks were brought in to convince her of her errors, Claesken notes that because of her stubbornness, they too insisted she was controlled by the devil: 'The beginning and end was that I had the devil in

---

[52] Mayken Boosers, burned at Doornick on 18 September 1564, was at least allowed to strip herself before her torture. *BRN* II, p. 412.

[53] There were dozens of such demons noted in the various 'devil's books' of the sixteenth century. See Ria Stambaugh (ed.), *Teufelbücher in Auswahl* (5 vols, Berlin, 1970–80).

me, and that I was deceived' (p. 328). After the inquisitor compared her rebaptism with the baptism of a Jew – which by this time was believed to be of little effect[54] – Claesken writes that 'all that he kept saying was that we had it all from the devil, and that we had the proud devil in us'. Faced with Claesken's intransigence, the inquisitor concluded that the devil had called her. She refuted this conclusion by asking, 'is the devil now of such a nature that he rejects the evil and does the good?', for that is what she and her colleagues have done in their baptism (p. 336).

That by the middle of the century the authorities took very seriously the rumour that Mennonites were possessed by the devil is seen also in the case of Jan Geertsz, tried in The Hague in 1564 (burned there on 15 December). Hanging by his wrists tied behind his back, Jan refuses to give the names of his co-religionists. The interrogator orders him lowered to the floor, so that the 'dumb devil might speak more easily'. When that fails to loosen Jan's tongue, the president of the court apparently exclaimed, 'Have you no stout guards who can drive out this dumb demon?' (p. 407). Evidently in this case the authorities believed that the heretic must have been possessed by a devil of muteness in order to withstand the torture. Apparently even further torture could not cast out this stubborn devil (p. 408). For his part, Jan credited his silence to the assistance of God.

If the accounts presumably composed by the victims themselves can be trusted (and there seems little reason to doubt their veracity on this point), it appears that the devil was a more prominent figure in interrogations than the brief trial summaries provided by the authorities would lead us to believe. Anabaptists were apparently accused of being under the lordship of the devil, even to the degree of possession. Their response, as noted not only in Claesken's stance but also in Menno Simons's published comments mentioned earlier, was that their godly lives gave the lie to this allegation. Those in league with or possessed by the devil hardly committed acts of charity toward their fellow humans.[55]

---

[54] Jerome Friedman, 'Jewish Conversion, the Spanish Pure Blood Laws and Reformation: A Revisionist View of Racial and Religious Antisemitism', *The Sixteenth Century Journal*, 18 (1987), pp. 3–30.

[55] For a discussion of notions of sainthood among the Anabaptists and how these may have further contributed to accusations against them of demonic inspiration, see Gary K. Waite, 'Anabaptist Anticlericalism and the Laicization of Sainthood: Anabaptist Saints and Sanctity in the Netherlands', presented at the conference 'Confessional Sanctity', Dordrecht, 5–7 November 1998, and forthcoming in a volume on 'Confessional Sanctity' in the series *Veröffentlichungen des Institus für Europäische Geschichte Mainz, Beiheft* (Mainz, Philipp von Zabern) and in Dutch translation in the *Doopsgezinde Bijdragen*.

In several instances, Anabaptists charged their interrogators with being those truly in league with the devil. Hans van Ouerdamme, tried in Ghent in 1550, apparently answered the monks who demanded he swear on his baptism and faith to tell the truth: 'What, will you swear much? I regard not your swearing, for it is a craft of the sorcerers [*toouenaers*], who swear against the truth.' He notes that three of his co-religionists had been returned to the Catholic fold in the course of their trials, something that Hans blamed on the monks' 'bewitched swearing, that they did not keep themselves from the devil's deception', for they did not have the gift of disputation (p. 110). He compares his opponents to the Egyptian sorcerers who opposed Moses, and concludes his remarks to the gentlemen of the court, 'now understand, you noble sirs, the misuse and abuses of your state or ministry, for we confess it not to be of God, but of the devil, and that the antichrist has so bewitched and blinded your eyes, through the deceit of the devil, that you do not perceive yourselves to be what you are' (p. 114). Similarly, after his interrogation in the prison of Antwerp in August 1551, Jeronimus Segersz wrote to his wife that 'we must oppose the princes and mighty of this world, yes the spirits that work in the air, which is the old serpent and Satan' (p. 134). He warns her of the devil which seeks to damn their souls and of the false prophets which have only the teaching of the demons (pp. 145–6). Peter van Weruick, imprisoned in Ghent in 1552, writes to his sisters and brothers that they must distinguish between what is the worship of God and that which is really the worship of the devil and idolatry. Those who perform righteousness are the children of God, he continues, while those who sin are from the devil (p. 188). Peter was not reticent to make his opinion known to his interrogators; he reports that he told them 'perhaps your teaching is the teaching of the devil, for it is against the truth' (p. 190). Another Anabaptist, Claes de Praet, who was eventually executed in Ghent in 1556, was told by Pieter Titelmans, the infamous inquisitor of Flanders, that he had been deceived by the devil and misled by artisans and that he should now be instructed by the learned. Claes responded, 'why then do they [the learned] lead the life of a devil?' (p. 244).

One of the fullest interrogation accounts is provided by Jacques, a Mennonite interrogated in Leeuwarden several times in January and February 1558. Here the issue of the presence of the body of Christ in the consecrated wafer evoked a heated discussion, with Jacques calling the host an idol and the inquisitor Lindannus affirming the power inherent in the sacrament.[56] From the beginning the commissioner of

---

[56] In an interesting aside, Jacques remarks to his reader that his opponents 'hebben in haer doopsel tegen de schriftuere, ende van dat doopsel der wijser vroeyvrouwen, hoe dat

the court told Jacques that Mennonite leaders such as Menno and Leonard Bouwens had deceived him and his co-religionists, 'leading them to all the demons and damnation' (p. 274). When the inquisitor argued that the sacrament worked by virtue of the power inherent in the words spoken originally by Christ, regardless of the moral state of the priest, Jacques argued that 'the power does not lay in the words, for that would be sorcery' (p. 292). Exasperated, the inquisitor blurted out that Jacques's words were from Satan, not God, a charge that the accused regarded as blasphemy. The real work of Satan, the Anabaptist later mentioned, was to get people caught up in 'vain disputations' in order to lead them into foolishness (p. 311). In other words, the true agents of the devil were the learned theologians who opposed the clear understanding of Scripture on the part of the Anabaptists.

The Anabaptist belief that Catholic practices were witchcraft (or sorcery) seems to have been widespread. The lengths that Anabaptists would go to avoid baptizing their infants suggests that they viewed the Catholic rite as one that would, at the very least, taint their children with the diabolical. (On the other hand, spiritualists like David Joris depreciated the importance of externals such as water baptism while at the same time denying the physical existence of the devil.)[57] In 1553 in Kortrijk Joos Kint was interrogated by inquisitor Titelmans. She confronted him bravely, responding to his demand she renounce her rebaptism by stating 'my faith and baptism I know, but I have nothing to do with your swearing [besweeringe], I would then confess to you sorcerers [Ic soude daer aen v toouenaers bekennen].' She then warns him not to tell others that she had recanted or that she had a devil in her, not to mention that she was damned among the simple folk. Several times, in fact, she told her accusers to 'get behind me Satan' (pp. 224–26). For these courageous souls facing their own destruction, it was quite clear who were truly in league with the devil.

Were there any incidents wherein the authorities conflated beliefs about witches and those about Anabaptists? Joke Spaans has recently discovered some intriguing evidence from Amsterdam witchcraft trials of the 1550s and 1560s where under torture two accused witches appear to have changed their accounts of a meeting with a Mennonite

---

zijt voor goet houden, ende herdoopen noch eens, daerom seyde ic, dat sy Wederdoopers waren' (p. 284). In his defence of the mass, Lindanus apparently went to the extreme of saying 'Al waert de erchste mensche vander werelt, iae al waert een Turck, oft een Heyden, waert dat hy quame tot dat Sacrament, hy soude ontfangen dat lichaem ende dat bloet Christi, soo wel als een ander, ia dat meer is, al waert oock een Beeste.' BRN II, p. 290.

[57] Gary K. Waite, '"Man is a Devil to Himself": David Joris and the Rise of a Sceptical Tradition towards the Devil in the Early Modern Netherlands, 1540–1600', Nederlands Archief voor Kerkgeschiedenis / Dutch Review of Church History, 75 (1995), pp. 1–30.

or other sectarian leader in order to conform to their interrogators' views of the devil. One of the accused, Volckgen Harmansdr. of Blokzijl, was executed in 1564 because 'before the enemy she had denied her baptism and christendom [*doopsel ende chrisdom*]'. In her first testimony, Volckgen describes this 'enemy' as a weaver from the Waterland. Spaans plausibly suggests that this could have been a Mennonite, for a relatively high proportion of both Waterlanders and weavers were attracted to this branch of radical reform. In the Amsterdam court records there were also numerous reports during this period of Waterland Mennonites proselytizing in the port city.[58] In any event, in her later confession Volckgen changes the character of the 'enemy' to fit the accepted appearance of the devil. Spaans also rightly points out that those who underwent sectarian 'rebaptism' were like witches charged with having denied their original baptism and Christian faith.[59] In other words, both Anabaptists and supposed witches were accused of renouncing their original baptism and hence opening themselves to demonic control. The difference is that Anabaptists were not, as far as I have been able to determine, charged explicitly with making a pact with the devil, the key charge against witches.

Conclusions

It is much easier to describe what this investigation into one form of sixteenth-century religious heresy and witchcraft belief has not shown rather than what it has proven. Certainly I do not wish to revive the old 'witchcraft as heresy school' – that witchcraft was a Christian heresy which developed out of French Catharism – so well demolished by Norman Cohn and Richard Kieckhefer, who discovered that the fourteenth-century documents providing the link between heretical Cathars and the earliest witchcraft trials were forgeries.[60] As far as I have been

---

[58] See, for example, the case of Willem Jansz from Waterland, in *DAN* II, pp. 287– 90.

[59] Joke Spaans, 'Toverijprocessen in Amsterdam en Haarlem, ca. 1540–1620', in Gijswijt-Hofstra and Frijhof, *Nederland betoverd*, pp. 69–79, esp. 76–8. I am in the process of analysing these records as well. They involve the cases of Meyns Cornelisdr. of Purmerend (1555), in Gemeente Archief Amsterdam, Rechterlijk Archief, 5061: 567 – 'Justitieboek' (1523–66), fol. 228v; and 271 – 'Confessieboek' (1553–64), fols 38r-51r; and of Volckgen Harmansdr. of Blokzijl (1564), in 272 – 'Confessieboek' (1564–67), fols 32v-32r.

[60] Norman Cohn, *Europe's Inner Demons* (London, 1975), and Richard Kieckhefer, *European Witch Trials. Their Foundations in Popular and Learned Culture, 1300–1500* (London, 1976). See also H.C. Erik Midelfort, 'Witchcraft, Magic and the Occult,' Steven Ozment (ed.), *Reformation Europe: A Guide to Research* (St Louis, MO, 1982), pp. 189–90.

able to determine, of all the major religious traditions of the sixteenth century, Anabaptists were the least caught up in magical beliefs or practices (apart from those, I suppose, who emphasized immediate revelation).[61] On the other hand, I think it fair to suggest that scholars have been too reluctant to return to the question of the relationship between heresy and supposed demonic sects, especially in the sixteenth century. At least at the level of officialdom, and perhaps too of popular perception, the prosecution of sixteenth-century Anabaptism and of magical deviance had much in common. For one thing, rejection of infant baptism carried with it, in the minds of sixteenth-century people, several diabolical ramifications, not the least of which was the increase in the number of unbaptized and 'unexorcised' individuals who were presumed to be much more susceptible to diabolical influence. Perhaps too the supposed collusion of midwives in assisting Anabaptist parents avoid baptizing their newborn infants helped rekindle suspicions that midwives were in league with the devil to supply it with unbaptized infants. These and many other parallels between persecution of Anabaptists and witches appeared during the decades of the 1540s to 1560s, precisely the moment when authorities across Europe were becoming less concerned with Anabaptism but even more worried about the menace of witchcraft.

---

[61] Stuart Clark, *Thinking with Demons: The Idea of Witchcraft in Early Modern Europe* (Oxford, 1997), p. 543.

PART THREE

The theory and practice of writing histories of radical or non-conformist religious groups

Stepchildren of the Reformation or heralds of modernity: Ernst Troeltsch on sixteenth-century Anabaptists, sectarians and Spiritualists

Sonia Riddoch

Historical judgements regarding the Anabaptist movement have ranged over a broad spectrum of opinion, and have reflected the period in which they were written along with the interests of their authors. In the sixteenth century, Anabaptism was associated in the public mind with the horrors of Münster. To Martin Luther, Anabaptists were *Schwärmer*, fanatics, enthusiasts, zealots and the target of some of his most vitriolic condemnations. As the events of the Reformation receded, however, a more temperate attitude towards Anabaptism emerged, marked by an interest in sectarianism as a legitimate dimension of the Reformation era and a readiness to acknowledge the Anabaptists' contribution to Western culture. A somewhat effusive example of the latter trait was the claim made by the nineteenth-century English Catholic writer, Lord Acton, who claimed that Anabaptism and the sects were 'one of the great generative factors in modern history and a turning point in the epic of modern history'.[1] In the mid-nineteenth century, the most significant publication was the *History of Pietism* (1880–86), by Lutheran theologian and church historian, Albrecht Ritschl, who placed Anabaptism in a broad context of Catholic religious history. Ritschl noted parallels between Anabaptism and medieval religion and hypothesized that a direct connection existed between Anabaptism and Franciscan tertiaries.[2] He found little of value in their theology; nevertheless, Ritschl's relatively dispassionate analysis of Anabaptist origins signified that the polemics of the sixteenth century had been left behind in Lutheran historiography – although an essay by

---

[1] A.G. Dickens and John Tonkin with the assistance of Kenneth Powell, *The Reformation in Historical Thought* (London, 1985), p. 216.

[2] Ibid.

Karl Holl, 'Luther und die Schwärmer' (1922), echoing Martin Luther's dismissive judgement, indicated that a negative attitude towards sectarians in Lutheranism had not entirely disappeared. In North America a growing interest within the Mennonite community in its history stimulated further research into sixteenth-century Mennonite origins and the movement's historical significance.[3] Mennonite historian Harold Bender argued that 'the great principles of freedom of conscience, separation of church and state ... so essential to democracy, ultimately are derived from the Anabaptists of the Reformation period'[4] and Roland Bainton ranked sixteenth-century Anabaptism and Columbus's discovery of America as events of equal world-historical significance.[5]

The writings of theologian Ernst Troeltsch on the Anabaptist and sectarian movement have generally been regarded as part of the positive re-valuation of Anabaptism. And indeed, in his first public statement on Anabaptism, Troeltsch sounded as if he were an early exponent of Bender's Anabaptist vision. The occasion was a congress of German historians in 1906 at Stuttgart. Originally Max Weber had been scheduled to address the gathering but at the last minute was unable to fulfil his commitment and asked Troeltsch, his friend and colleague at the University of Heidelberg, to take his place. Despite Troeltsch's different professional background the choice of Troeltsch as a replacement for Weber was a natural one. Both belonged to the *Eranos Kreis*, a group of scholars at Heidelberg united by a common interest in investigating the role of religion in European history.[6] They had travelled together to the United States in 1904 while Weber was gathering material for his articles on *The Protestant Ethic and the Spirit of Capitalism*, and, more importantly, Weber had drawn on Troeltsch's expertise for the theological literature he used in his *Protestant Ethic*.[7] Troeltsch's speech, which appeared later that year in the *Historische Zeitschrift* with the title 'Die Bedeutung des Protestantismus für der Entstehung der modernen Welt', explored the connections between Protestantism and modern culture. Adopting a position in direct opposition to the accepted historiographical wisdom that regarded Martin Luther and the Reformation as the departure point for modernity,[8] Troeltsch argued that early Protestantism was

---

[3] Ibid., p. 221.

[4] Harold S. Bender, 'The Anabaptist Vision', *Church History*, 8 (1944), pp. 23–4.

[5] Roland H. Bainton, *Studies on the Reformation* (Boston, 1963), p. 119.

[6] Friedrich Wilhelm Graf, 'Friendship Between Experts: Notes on Weber and Troeltsch', in Wolfgang J. Mommsen and Jürgen Osterhammel (eds), *Max Weber and His Contemporaries* (London, 1987), p. 220.

[7] Ibid., p. 221.

[8] For a comprehensive survey of these interpretations, see Heinrich Bornkamm, *Luther im Spiegel der deutschen Geistesgeschichte* (Göttingen, 1970), pp. 199–455.

a continuation of the medieval ideal of a church-dominated civilization
or at very most it was a transitional period, 'the confessional age' of
European history. The closest any groups came to being harbingers of
modernity were the seventeenth-century English sectarians, and to a
limited extent, their spiritual ancestors in the Reformation, the
Anabaptists [*Taüfer*] and Spiritualists, for it was with these groups that
the conceptions of freedom of conscience and separation of church and
state originated.[9] As Troeltsch put it,

> the father of human rights is not really Protestantism but Baptism
> [*Täufertum*], which Protestantism hated and drove out to the New
> World. North American Baptism and Quakerism grew out of Inde-
> pendency, the great religious movement of the English Revolution.
> This independency was strongly influenced by continental
> Anabaptists who had fled from Holland ... Out of this episode
> have come the great ideas of the separation of church and state,
> religious tolerance, the principle of voluntarism in church member-
> ship, and freedom of conscience.[10]

Troeltsch's comments on this occasion provoked a more spirited negative reaction than any other of his works did, or would do.[11] To elevate
sectarians, and English sectarians at that, to world-historical importance while at the same time questioning the primacy of Luther, however
moderately, was unpatriotic and minimized the German contribution to
the evolution of European civilization. The impetus for this particular
appraisal of Anabaptism was the by-product of a debate on the nature
of Wilhelmine political culture. Twentieth-century scholars have debated the extent to which Germany was illiberal and questioned the
existence of a non-liberal German *Sonderweg* but to Troeltsch and his
circle there was no doubt that this was the case. Germany lacked a
strong liberal tradition and its political institutions were backward
compared to those in Britain and the United States. One possible reason
for the difference lay in the religious history of the respective countries.
Germany had had its reformation in the sixteenth century but, unlike
England and other societies where the influence of Calvinism was more
marked, Germany did not experience the same degree of sectarianism
typical of the Calvinist culture areas. And it was these sectarian structures which, from the perspective of Troeltsch and his circle, played a
crucial role in the modernization characteristic of English-speaking

---

[9] Ernst Troeltsch, 'Die Bedeutung des Protestantismus für die Entstehung der modernen
Welt', *Historische Zeitschrift*, 97 (1906), p. 29.

[10] Ibid., pp. 40–41.

[11] Manfred Wichelhaus, *Kirchengeschichtsschreibung und Soziologie im neunzehnten
Jahrhundert und bei Ernst Troeltsch* (Heidelberg, 1965), p. 178.

nations.[12] In his subsequent work particularly his monumental survey of Christian history, *The Social Teachings of the Christian Churches and Groups*, Troeltsch investigated these connections in greater depth. As will be seen, the outcome of his research resulted in a modification of the position expressed in his 1906 speech and article. The importance of Anabaptism receded in Troeltsch's thinking; he placed more emphasis on the contribution of neo-Calvinism and the role of spiritual and mystical religion in the development of Western political culture.

Before examining his work on the sectarian movement, its relation to Calvinism and spiritual religion in greater detail, it would be useful to review Troeltsch's understanding of church and sect as he developed them in *The Social Teachings*. Usually the difference is expressed thus: 'one is born into a church but joins a sect'. This particular statement, though true enough, does not address the religious distinctions between church and sect. The church-type has its roots in the universalism of Jesus' Gospel; it regards Christ as Redeemer whose Atonement provided the basis for the justification of all sinners.[13] The grace which flows from the act of Atonement is dispensed through the sacraments, meaning that there is no salvation outside the church and, secondly, that the church is the sole custodian of religious truth.[14] On the question of ethics, the church is prepared to compromise in order to accommodate the masses since in this way it is able to make an imprint on social values and create a unified Christian society, or what Troeltsch termed the *Corpus Christianum*. 'The Church is an institution which has been endowed with grace and salvation as a result of the work of Redemption; it is able to receive the masses, and to adjust itself to the world.'[15] The primary example, 'the pure, logical form of the church-type'[16] in Christian history, was the Roman Catholic church and Lutheranism was essentially similar. Calvinism, on the other hand, evolved along a different path. Primitive Calvinism was the 'daughter of Lutheranism';[17] however, the emphasis Calvin gave to certain religious ideas common to them both changed the nature of the Calvinist variant of the church-type. Calvin stressed the idea of election and the need to prove one's membership among the elect, resulting in a new conception of the calling.[18] Whereas in Catholicism and Lutheran-

---

[12] Benjamin Nelson, 'Max Weber, Ernst Troeltsch, Georg Jellinek as Comparative Historical Sociologists', *Sociological Analysis*, 36 (1975), p. 234.

[13] Ernst Troeltsch, *The Social Teachings of the Christian Churches and Groups*, Olive Wyon (trans.), (Chicago, 1981), p. 994.

[14] Ibid., p. 95.

[15] Ibid., p. 993.

[16] Ibid., p. 1007.

[17] Ibid., p. 579.

[18] Ibid., p. 611.

ism the calling was interpreted as 'one's appointed destiny',[19] in life, thus reinforcing a tendency to social conservatism, Calvinist Christians were expected to work zealously at transforming the world. This conception of the calling had an activist edge. Secondly, the Calvinist conception of biblical law differed. In Lutheranism, law served as a stimulus to repentance, whereas in Calvinism law was regarded as a positive moral law to be followed; it was a 'rule required for sanctification which flows from the grace of election'.[20] Thus, in sociological terms, the church was not just an organ of salvation but a means of sanctification, 'a holy community',[21] the aim of which was to mould life according to biblical ideals. Both these elements gave Calvinism a more reformist character than was typical of Catholic and Lutheran churches and served as bridges to sectarian movements. In seventeenth-century neo-Calvinism, the concept of a holy community was expressed in what Troeltsch called 'free church': religious bodies that held to an absolute conception of the truth but accepted the voluntary principle of church membership and the separation of church and state.[22]

As for the sect, its origins, too, lie in primitive Christianity. Theologically the sect emphasizes law above grace and regards Christ as law maker and exemplar.[23] In regard to ethics, the sectarian tendency arises from what Troeltsch termed the 'individualism' of the Gospel. It is based on a believer's personal relationship with God which in turn finds practical expression in following a strict gospel ethic expressed primarily in the Sermon on the Mount. Such an ethic is potentially revolutionary; in fact sectarianism with its innate bias towards a radical ethic might be compared to a coiled spring, which, if not properly tied down, is capable of ripping through the fabric of any church community. In social terms sectarianism appeals primarily to small groups of people who choose to detach themselves from a sinful world even if doing so entails suffering and persecution. Unlike the church-type, the sect resolutely rejects compromise of any kind and insists on a high level of personal perfection. Throughout Christian history the sectarian tendency has asserted itself in numerous forms. In early Christianity the ascetic movement was the primary expression of the sectarian tendency, one that the church with great difficulty succeeded in subduing into monasticism;[24] the Donatist and Montanist movements were other

---

[19] Ibid., p. 610.
[20] Ibid., p. 594.
[21] Ibid., p. 591.
[22] Ibid., pp. 656–7.
[23] Ibid., p. 994.
[24] Ibid., p. 240.

examples. Sectarianism is more pronounced during times of social up-
heaval and crisis as was the case in the period before the Reformation
when a profusion of sects and sect-type groups emerged. These included
Waldensians, Cathari, Franciscans among others in Southern Europe,
and Lollardy and John Wycliff's reform movement in the northern
portion of the continent. These were examples of the non-aggressive
sect prepared to suffer persecution patiently in expectation of the imminent end of the world. Such was not the case with the Hussite and
Taborite movements. They sought to change the world radically and
were prepared to use violence to do so; the recourse to violence, noted
Troeltsch, was 'something new'.[25]

The sixteenth-century Anabaptist movement represented yet another
phase in the development of the sectarian tendency. Popular religion
'under the stimulus of the Reformation' was marked by 'an enormous
number of small groups of earnest Christians, living apart from "the
world", claiming complete civil and religious freedom ... Their outward
symbol was Adult Baptism, which implied the voluntary principle.'[26]
Reformation sectarianism's first manifestation was in Zurich, 1521,
among those to whom 'Zwingli's application of the Scriptures seemed
inadequate'.[27] First-generation leaders were former Lutherans,
Zwinglians, humanists and biblically-informed laity who had been attracted by the Protestant Reformers' emphasis on the authority of the
Bible and the ethics embodied in the Sermon on the Mount; later, they
would draw into their ranks people dissatisfied with the compromises
made by Calvinism. For these reasons the sixteenth-century sectarian
movement, insisted Troeltsch, 'belonged to the Reformation, was caused
by the Reformation, and appealed to its ideals'.[28] Anabaptist communities practised a scriptural form of worship: strict church discipline
including the excommunication of deviant members, the literal application of the Sermon on the Mount, the refusal to swear oaths, rejection
of the sacramental church and adult baptism, which was 'the motto of
the movement'. The embryonic nature of the Protestant movement as
well as its inherent affinity with sectarianism allowed Anabaptism to
mushroom and before long the 'whole of Central Europe [was] covered
with a network of Anabaptist communities',[29] the chief centres being
Augsburg, Moravia, Strasbourg, and later Frisia and the Netherlands.
By 1526, individual Anabaptist groups 'began to organize their own

---

[25] Ibid., p. 364.
[26] Ibid., p. 695.
[27] Ibid., p. 703.
[28] Ibid., p. 699.
[29] Ibid., p. 704.

religious system ... with all the unlimited possibilities of ecclesiastical organization which seemed to be opening up in many directions, it looked as though there were a sphere and a future for the Anabaptist movement.'[30] In terms of social origins, Anabaptism consisted of people from the lower ranks of society such as miners and manual labourers but their early leaders were educated people [*Theologe*] who quickly learned to appeal to the 'democratic instincts of the masses'. Troeltsch also hinted that a link existed between Anabaptists and the participants in the Peasants' War although he did not make the connections clear. In the end, this phase of Anabaptism represented a 'premature triumph of the sectarian principles of the free churches'.[31]

Both Catholics and Protestants undertook energetic measures to eradicate Anabaptism, targeting the leaders first, then the masses. Persecution drove them into 'emotional chiliasm' and the horrors of Münster. Out of this confusion Menno Simons succeeded in gathering the surviving Anabaptists into a peaceful community. In it, the model established by the Zurichers predominated although some aspects of Menno's theological programme had affinities with medieval evangelical sects. He insisted on fidelity to the spirit of the Sermon on the Mount, equality, strict discipline, excommunication of erring members and separation from non-Anabaptist spouses even if doing so led to the breakup of families.[32] For some time they were the object of persecution but by the seventeenth century the divisions between the 'stepchildren of the Reformation' and the Calvinist majority had softened with the result that Anabaptists were allowed back into the Protestant family. For their part, Anabaptists accepted the Calvinist idea of the 'calling' and became willing to participate in the society around them. Troeltsch cited a statement by William of Orange praising Mennonites' 'submissive and peaceful spirit, their perfect obedience to their superiors, and willingness to contribute to the upkeep of society.'[33] Calvinists moderated their

---

[30] Ibid., p. 704. The basis of Troeltsch's account in this instance is a passage from Sebastian Franck who wrote that 'in the year 1526, both during and after the Peasants' Revolt, there arose a new sect and a separate church founded upon the letter of Scripture which some call Anabaptist and others Baptists, who began to separate themselves from others with a particular baptism and to despise all others as unchristian ... Their overseer and bishop was first Balthasar Hübner, then Melchior Rinck, followed by Joh. Hut, Joh. Denck, Ludwig Hetzer.' Ibid., p. 951 fn.

[31] Ibid., p. 704.

[32] Ibid., p. 705. The English version of *The Social Teachings* contains a mistranslation in describing Menno Simons's theological programme. It reads 'Menno Simons gave the leading position in the movement to the Zurich section'; Troeltsch's German text describes Menno's movement as being similar to the Zurich model.

[33] Ibid., p. 953 fn.

opposition to Anabaptists and agreed to extend them the civil rights that applied to citizens. What persecution was unable to accomplish came about through mutual willingness to compromise, with the result that continental Anabaptism – as a discrete movement – faded from history.

The continental experience was not the end of Reformation sectarianism, however. An analogous development appeared in England a century later, and in retrospect it would have a more momentous impact on European history. Both the peaceful and the aggressive branches in England had tenuous connections with continental sectarians. The founder of the peaceful variant was John Smyth, who established a Congregational church in 1602. Shortly afterwards Smyth relocated his church to Amsterdam where he became increasingly drawn into the Dutch Baptist and Mennonite communities.[34] One portion of his congregation, however, returned to England and founded a church from which arose the church of the General Baptists. It combined the principle of voluntary church membership and baptism by immersion with a willingness to swear in courts of law and to accept military service in time of war.[35] Eventually, the General Baptists moved closer to Calvinism and the free churches by accepting the Calvinist conception of the calling and recognizing the state, thus making their peace with the secular world. In this form, noted Troeltsch in a generalizing leap that spanned centuries of history, they 'affected the whole of the political and social life of America as well as that of the English middle classes'.[36]

As for the 'radical Baptist' movement in England, its origins went back to 1530. Dutch immigrants fleeing persecution at home arrived in England and, joining with Lollards, established communities of the 'chiliastic-Hoffmann type', though they later became Mennonite. They suffered persecution but received their chance to play a role on the historical stage during the English Civil War. In the Barebones Parliament, [Major-General Thomas] Harrison represented 'the radical Baptist spirit'. He and his followers wanted to abolish all legal institutions and the organized church, end tithing and abolish private property in order to prepare the people for the advent of Christ which he believed to be imminent.[37] Had his demands been carried out, the whole of English society would have been transformed. But the moderates, led by General Monk, refused to collaborate with him and Harrison's hopes were shattered. His insurrection represented 'the last great period of Baptist

---

34 Ibid., p. 706.
35 Ibid., p. 707.
36 Ibid., p. 708.
37 Ibid., p. 709.

revolt' in England and in broader terms it embodied the 'last important wave of chiliasm, the last return of the spirit of the Hussites and of the Peasants' War'.[38]

Towards the end of the decade of war, 'politico-social' parties appeared. The most notable included the Levellers, Diggers and Millenarians, all of whom developed a more explicitly political programme based on religious values. The Levellers, led by John Lilburn, drew their support from the radical middle classes and workers. They insisted on a complete Christianization of the political and social order. At the same time their spiritualized conception of Christianity prompted a call for the separation of church and state; the connection between spiritual religion and political freedom was hinted at in these passages but would be explained more fully in the sections dealing with mystical religion. Taking as their model Jesus, whom they described as the first Leveller, they proposed a system of worship based on free and self-supporting congregations and a radical democracy based on equality before the law. When their proposals met with little approval, the Levellers responded by encouraging assassinations and conspiracies against the government, and, not surprisingly, were forcibly suppressed. The Diggers, the socialists and communists of their day, drew their support from the rural proletariat. Their leader, Gerard Winstanley, was inspired by a vision of a prelapsarian social order marked by equality, freedom and brotherhood. Any accommodation to existing conditions he rejected as an error or a legitimation of class interests. Carrying out his ideal would have entailed a distribution of common lands, a quasi-communistic land ownership system and the establishment of an absolute democracy. In contrast to the Levellers, the Diggers did not approve the use of force. The Millenarians were inspired by an apocalyptic vision of history which drew on the Book of Daniel with its succession of world-monarchies. After the final judgment 'an anarchy of love' would prevail. The more radical of the Millenarians constituted what Troeltsch referred to as the 'genuine religious fanatics' in the Barebones Parliament. When the English Interregnum ended, so did the 'last great period of Baptist revolt'. John Lilburn joined the Quakers, as did Gerard Winstanley; his ideas influenced John Bellars,[39] whose proposals for cooperative societies in turn had an impact on Richard Owen and modern socialism. Thus the aggressive sub-type of the sect ended up, as had the peaceful variant, by indirectly influencing the modern world through its synergistic association with neo-Calvinism. 'It helped

---

[38] Ibid.
[39] Ibid., p. 783.

loosen the connection between church and state' and in doing so, the radical sectarian movement made 'the formation of the free churches possible and helped to Christianize the ethical and social interests of the English people' without resorting to 'dogmatic compulsion'.[40] As was the case with the ascetic movement in medieval Christian history, radical sects with their revolutionary ethics had little direct impact on society if they chose to remain separate from or hostile to the world.

While preparing *The Social Teachings* for publication, Troeltsch turned his attention increasingly to the study of mystical and spiritual religion. This shift may have been connected with the evolution of his own 'mystical-spiritual viewpoint' or it may have reflected a broader concern. At the turn of the century there was an upsurge of interest in mystical religion, understood not as contemplation or renunciation of the world but as a means of establishing spiritual values appropriate for a capitalist society,[41] and Troeltsch, with his keen eye for cultural trends, was not unaware of such developments. In any event, the lengthy section dealing with mysticism in *The Social Teachings* testifies to its importance in Troeltsch's evaluation of Christian social teachings. Mysticism too had its origins in early Christianity although in a very broad sense it is part of every religious tradition. At the core of mysticism is the idea of a divine seed or spark in human nature that seeks a union with God; it focuses on inward religious experience and minimizes the importance of dogma and traditional theology. Mysticism believes in a universal religious consciousness in which the gulf between Christian and non-Christian evaporates. During the Reformation a Protestant mysticism arose which was 'a conscious, active, and independent principle of religious knowledge, inward experience, and morality'.[42] The impact of mysticism was greatest in the Netherlands and in England during the seventeenth and eighteenth centuries.

It had been a commonplace in German religious history that mystical religion and Anabaptism were one and the same phenomena. Troeltsch challenged this view, seeing the two religious formations as essentially different entities. Baptists focused on the law of Christ interpreted literally; spiritual reformers were almost antinomian, believing instead in obeying the light of conscience as revealed by the indwelling Christ. Baptists viewed the Word as a literal rule of life; Spiritualists believed in

---

[40] Ibid., p. 714.

[41] Gangolf Hübinger, 'Kulturkritik und Kulturpolitik des Eugen-Diedrichs-Verlags in Wilhelmismus, Auswege aus der Krise der Modern?', in Horst Renz and Friedrich Wilhelm Graf (eds), *Umstrittene Modern. Die Zukunft der Neuzeit im Urteil der Epoche Ernst Troeltschs: Troeltsch-Studien*, vol. 4 (Gütersloh, 1987), p. 102.

[42] Troeltsch, *The Social Teachings*, p. 740.

an inner Word, a divine spark in the individual. Baptists objectified religion: they insisted on baptism, relied on external organizations and ceremonies, among them, the Lord's Supper and washing of feet. Spiritualists did not care about external baptism, preferring instead the baptism of the Spirit, and did not feel the need for ceremonial forms of worship. Anabaptists organized communities and congregations, whereas the Spiritualists had no formal structures of any kind. Baptists believed in the imminent arrival of the apocalypse; the Spiritualists adopted a spiritualized interpretation of that event.[43] Nevertheless, there were some connections. Troeltsch conceded that mysticism or spiritual religion intersected with Anabaptism in those cases where, as he put it, Anabaptists felt the need for a theology but the most significant exception were the Quakers, 'a curious blend of sectarianism and spiritual religion'. They were

> descendants of the spirituality of the Reformation period, heralds of the inner light, of an individual rebirth through the eternal Christ in whose message the Spirit in the regenerate soul and in the Bible is one, heralds of the presence of the Divine Light which lightens every man coming into the world and which is only released from the prison house of the flesh when it comes into contact with the Bible.[44]

Quakerism represented the union of this mystical doctrine with the Baptist ideal of a holy community based on genuine conversion and separation from the state. The Quakers adopted the Mennonite constitution and evolved a structured organization consisting of an inner and outer circle of believers, elders and overseers of poor relief. They did not insist on adult baptism as a token of membership although the prospective member needed to show evidence of being born again or having experienced spiritual renewal. In their ethical teachings the Quakers avoided antinomianism by adopting the ideals of the Sermon on the Mount. They also rejected war, participation in worldly affairs, and administration of justice. In fact, for a while, the Quakers epitomized 'the purest form of the Anabaptist movement' before they too became bourgeois and became integrated into the larger society.

Troeltsch's researches into mysticism resulted in a re-evaluation of the sectarian impact on political thought in particular on the issues of freedom of conscience and toleration. The Anabaptist justification for living apart from the world rested on the religious principle embedded in sectarian Christianity; that is, the freedom they sought was freedom from compulsion and had nothing to do with the espousal of human

---

[43] Ibid., pp. 742–3.
[44] Ibid., p. 780.

rights as a general principle. Anabaptists were not early exponents of an abstract principle of separation of church and state. Anabaptists and sectarians, as did the churches, held to an absolute conception of religious truth; only among 'spiritual reformers' was there liberty of conscience within the religious community. Spiritualists sought toleration not because they wanted freedom of worship for themselves but because they believed that each individual had the right to his own convictions. For this reason, the Spiritualists, not Anabaptists or Baptists, were the logical point of origin of the modern conception of freedom of conscience and toleration.

In the notes accompanying his analysis of spiritual religion, Troeltsch drew attention to the change in his thinking. Referring to his article on 'The Separation of Church and State' (1906), he stated

> at that time (1906) I did not recognize sufficiently the difference between the Baptist movement and *Spiritualismus* ... As the Church is connected with a definite conception of the truth so also the sect and *Spiritualismus* are connected with a definite conception of truth. The sect renounces compulsion and conformity, but not the absolute character of the conception of truth; *Spiritualismus* makes it relative in various forms of expression of a truth which is only to be attained spiritually and inwardly.[45]

The shift which occurred in *The Social Teachings* is also apparent in the 1912 version of 'Die Bedeutung'. Whereas in 1906 Troeltsch identified the Baptists as the originators of political rights, in his 1912 revision he credited Baptists and *Spiritualists* (emphasis mine) with political modernity. Roger Williams, the governor of the Massachusetts colony and early proponent of freedom of religion, 'went over to the Baptists, and thence to an undogmatic Spiritualism'. Pennsylvania, the second home of 'liberty of conscience', had both Baptist and Spiritualist roots. The 'parent of human rights' was no longer simply Baptism, but 'Sectarianism and Spiritualism'.[46]

The decline of sectarianism and mysticism did not mean that these movements had no lasting impact on Western culture. Both contributed to a religious formation Troeltsch described as Ascetic Protestantism. It harmonized the divergent traits of Calvinism both old and new, English Baptists, continental Anabaptism, the free church tendency, Pietism, Puritanism and spiritual religion to create an entity that incorporated some features from all these religious formations. Unlike medieval Catholicism, Ascetic Protestantism was more accurately described as a

---

[45] Ibid., pp. 965–6.

[46] Ernst Troeltsch, *Protestantism and Progress: The Significance of Protestantism fro the Rise of the Modern World*, W. Montgomery (trans.), (Philadelphia, 1986), p. 67.

common ethos than a new ecclesiastical order; nevertheless, the Christian social philosophy of Ascetic Protestantism, as Troeltsch called it, was 'a great unity, which, for historical significance can only be compared with the social philosophy of the Middle Ages.' In other words the stepchildren of the Reformation did receive a chance to play their part on the stage of world history but only in a supporting role in a drama dominated by more powerful characters.

How are we to evaluate Troeltsch as an historian? In the first place, Troeltsch was not a diligent empirical investigator who focused on specific historical issues or personalities and scrutinized primary documents. He was interested in individuals but the individuals who played key roles in his analysis were collectivities: the medieval Catholic Church, Lutheranism, Calvinism, Anabaptists and Spiritualists; individual personalities – Calvin, Luther, sectarian leaders – played only a supporting role. This helps explain the cursory and sketchy overviews he provided of individuals such as Thomas Müntzer, Andreas Karlstadt, Sebastian Franck and other Reformation figures. Troeltsch did not deny this aspect of his work; however, he did not see it as a failing. Empirical history, he once wrote, 'can only provide knowledge of the external side of things; it is the veil behind which a deeper life moves'.[47] The task of the historian was to discern the broad patterns of development with the aim of understanding the present. In these respects, Troeltsch exemplified the German historicist tradition.

Troeltsch's particular interest in the past concerned the role of religion in shaping modern culture. He insisted that religious ideas have their own inner dialectic and cannot be reduced to epiphenomena of economic forces as some historians would do. At the same time, however, the context in which ideas arise determines how they will play themselves out. Adapting an insight from Marx, he noted that 'spiritual values are conditioned by the setting in which they arise'.[48] The democratic impulses in Calvinism originated at a time when western European political systems were undergoing significant change. Anabaptist insistence on separation from the secular world had no bearing on the question of separation of church and state until the eighteenth century, by which time European society was no longer as marked by the kind of intense religious controversy typical of the Reformation period, and the central insights of spiritual religion as well as the political implications of these ideas could not be realized until a more secular atmosphere had emerged in Western culture. In other words, Troeltsch was not so naïve

---

[47] Ernst Troeltsch, *The Christian Faith*, Gertrud von le Fort (ed.), Garrett E. Paul (trans.), (Minneapolis, 1991), 258.
[48] Troeltsch, *The Social Teachings*, p. 88.

as to claim that there was a direct link between religious ideas and modern conceptions of human rights, but by examining the context in which they arose, he drew attention to the fact that religious beliefs and practices contributed in some measure to the formulation of those conceptions.

CHAPTER TEN

Crossing Max Weber's 'Great Divide': comparing early modern Jewish and Anabaptist histories

Michael Driedger

David Sorkin began a recent essay on early modern Judaism entitled 'The Case for Comparison' with reflections about the state of current scholarship on the subject. He wrote that, because of dissatisfaction with 'the parochial vision' of Jewish studies,

> in the past two decades scholars have attempted to restore Jewish history to the 'context' of the larger society, examining in minute details the series of relationships – economic, social, political and cultural – through which Jews at once created their own history as a minority group and participated in that of the broader society.[1]

With perhaps a few minor modifications to account for the obvious differences separating a religious community with an ancient tradition from a newly emerging set of Protestant groups, this observation applies equally well to the historiography of early sixteenth-century Anabaptists. For example, since the 1970s scholars including Hans-Jürgen Goertz, Werner Packull and James Stayer have located early Anabaptist histories in the broader narrative of the 'Radical Reformation'. The consequences will be well known to most readers: on the one hand, a departure from the denominational, early-twentieth-century Mennonite historiography of 'normative' Anabaptism; and, on the other, an expanded understanding of the early Reformation as a whole, focusing on the diversity and dynamism of early Reformation movements and cultures, as opposed to a picture of the early Reformation centred around a single great leader.

To a more limited extent, Sorkin's observation also applies to the historiography of early modern European Mennonitism. This subject of research is beginning to attract more attention in scholarly circles today, following a general trend in Reformation studies toward the examination

---

[1] David Sorkin, 'The Case for Comparison: Moses Mendelssohn and the Religious Enlightenment', *Modern Judaism*, 14: 2 (1994), pp. 121–38; the quotation is from p. 122.

of the long-term consequences of the Protestant challenge to the Roman church. Scholars interested in Mennonitism should, of course, strive to place Mennonite groups in as rich and broad an historical context as possible.

Nonetheless, to avoid falling back in a parochial mind-set of Mennonite history, a further cautionary note from Sorkin's essay is worth attention:

> Such study of the 'context' of Jewish history breaches only the outer perimeter that ghettoized the discipline. The inner perimeter that remains intact is the assumption, usually tacit, that Jewish history is somehow singular – that its peculiar nature either resists the categories historians use for other peoples or requires that those categories be so significantly modified as to be qualitatively different.[2]

Mennonite history too has its inner perimeter, which can sometimes make a strongly contextualized, socio-historical study of the Mennonite past difficult. Expressed in a clear form, this inner perimeter consists of the idea that Anabaptist-Mennonite history, despite containing seemingly endless schisms and a variety of separate institutional and cultural traditions, is one history from the sixteenth century up until the present; that the early sixteenth century was the time when Anabaptism was practised in its most pure and true form; that later forms of Anabaptism in the early modern period generally were a departure from the original, pure spirit of the founding fathers; and that historical study can teach Mennonites today who they are or should be as a people. It is an old and limiting habit of Mennonite historiographical thinking dating back to early modern martyrologies to place past adult baptizers in the 'vertical', internal, denominational contexts of forebears and successors rather than a 'horizontal', socio-historical context of neighbours and contemporaries.

What contextualizations, especially ones organized vertically, make it difficult for us to study is the extent to which Anabaptist patterns of historical development were actually unique – or not so unique. Sorkin offers a solution for a similar problem in Jewish studies: 'To try to breach this inner perimeter it might be salutary to complement the study of "context" with "comparison", supplementing questions of influence and relationship with ones about homologous trends, parallel changes and common developments.'[3] An approach similar to Sorkin's has already been applied to a limited extent to Mennonite studies. In an essay published in the same year as Sorkin's comments about context and comparison, Daphne Winland argued that there are parallel

---

[2] Ibid., p. 122.
[3] Ibid.

structures in modern Mennonite and Jewish historiographies and sociologies.[4] This observation begs a further question: can we find parallel structures in Anabaptist and Jewish history and society? To consider comparative questions like this one seriously is the best antidote to the perpetuation of a parochial vision in Mennonite studies.

Excursus: Max Weber and the 'Great Divide'

Before beginning the project of comparing Jewish and Anabaptist histories, I want to address a potential problem with historical and sociological comparisons. While Sorkin emphasizes that comparison can help move scholars beyond the narrow perspectives of parochial histories, the opposite can also be true. The best example of (apparently) comparative thinking[5] which helps reinforce rather than breach the inner perimeter of ghettoized scholarship is Max Weber's sociology of religion. This claim requires a thorough explanation.

In texts like *The Protestant Ethic and the Spirit of Capitalism*, *The Protestant Sects and the Spirit of Capitalism* and *Ancient Judaism*, Weber presented a comparative analysis of the everyday sociopsychological pressures that the major European religious communities placed on their rank-and-file members. In the introductory remarks to his studies in the sociology of world religions, written near the end of his life, he claimed that this comparative approach can *help* account for the following observations.[6] Capitalism has existed everywhere and for as long as people have lived in organized societies. Modern, bourgeois, industrial capitalism on the other hand is a recent social form, characterized by rational, methodical organization of a formally free labour force. This social form has been made possible in large part by the conviction that work is its own reward. The conviction first gained acceptance among a mass audience in western Europe and North America and spread from there. By the beginning of the twentieth century, when Weber wrote about it, it had already become widespread.

Weber's writings on the sociology of world religions are in large part an attempt to trace the long-forgotten and tangled roots of this modern

---

[4] Daphne Winland, 'Native Scholarship: The Enigma of Self-Definition among Jewish and Mennonite Scholars', *Journal of Historical Sociology*, 5: 4 (1992), pp. 431–61.

[5] See, for example, Stephen Kalberg, *Max Weber's Comparative-Historical Sociology* (Cambridge, 1994).

[6] Max Weber, *The Protestant Ethic and the Spirit of Capitalism*, Talcott Parsons (trans.), (London, 1967 [1930]), pp. 13–31. To save space, I have avoided citing the German originals of Weber's texts.

conviction, 'the spirit of capitalism'. By the end of his career, Weber saw his essays on world religions in an even broader context – the history of a social world organized rationally in all its facets: lifestyle, law, business, government, science and fine arts. There were several important stages in the development of rational social forms in the European west, including the antimagical tendencies in ancient Jewish religion. But most important was the appearance of early modern Puritan and sectarian Protestantism. These groups cultivated a way of life, 'the Protestant ethic', which helped nurture 'the spirit of capitalism' at an early stage of its development.

Weber's work had an important methodological component. In the first decade of the twentieth century, around the same time he was completing his initial essays outlining the famous Protestant ethic thesis, Weber was also writing on the methods appropriate for studying cultural phenomena. Of special interest here is his essay on '"Objectivity" in Social Science and Social Policy'. In this essay his central focus was what he called ideal types or evaluative ideas. An ideal type, which we might also call a model, is neither a systematic summary of a form of social life nor a purely historical concept. Weber wrote that 'The goal of ideal-typical concept-construction is always to make clearly explicit not the class or average character but rather the unique individual character of cultural phenomena.'[7] Weber intended that ideal types should be treated, to quote Fritz Ringer, as 'simplifications or "one-sidedly" exaggerated characterizations of complex phenomena that can be hypothetically posited and then "compared" with the realities they are meant to elucidate'.[8] Armed with this kind of 'heuristic device',[9] researchers can make connections and see hitherto unnoticed patterns of cultural significance in the 'inexhaustible diversity to be found in all historical material'.[10]

Weber wanted to avoid the pitfalls of historical positivism, the idea that, given enough correctly gathered information, we can discover the way things really were in the past. The advantage of his method is that it forces us to confront a truth which positivism tries to deny: in the process of trying to understand a subject of social research, the scholar plays an unavoidably active role in shaping that subject. Ideal types

---

[7] Weber, '"Objectivity" in Social Science and Social Policy', in Edward A. Shils and Henry A. Finch (trans and eds), *The Methodology of the Social Sciences* (New York, 1964 [1949]), pp. 49–112; the quotation is from p. 101.

[8] Fritz Ringer, *Max Weber's Methodology: The Unification of the Cultural and Social Sciences* (Cambridge, MA, and London, 1997), p. 5.

[9] Weber, '"Objectivity" in Social Science and Social Policy', p. 102.

[10] Weber, *The Protestant Ethic*, p. 45. Also see '"Objectivity" in Social Science and Social Policy', p. 84.

used in a responsible and sophisticated way should lead to both interpretive insights about the subject of study *and* critical reflection about
the conceptual tools which make these insights possible.

Weber was, however, aware of potential problems with his ideal-
typical methodology. He stressed in 'Objectivity' that researchers need
to distinguish carefully between ideal-typical constructs and historical
reality. He warned against methodological sloppiness in this regard, for
failure to keep the distinction clear would negate the method's benefits:

> The eminent, indeed unique, *heuristic* significance of these ideal
> types when they are used for the *assessment* of reality is known to
> everyone who has ever employed Marxian concepts and hypoth-
> eses. Similarly, their perniciousness, as soon as they are thought of
> as empirically valid or as real (*i.e.*, truly metaphysical) 'effective
> forces,' 'tendencies,' etc. is likewise known to those who have used
> them.[11]

The point has already been made but deserves emphasis: models should
remain nothing more than provisional tools for helping us make sense
of the rich and complex diversity which makes up social reality.

Using something approaching this method to analyse western European religious culture, Weber argued that Catholic, Lutheran, ascetic
Protestant and Jewish traditions each had a unique social character
which can be expressed ideal-typically. His view was based on the
assumption that religious motives or ethics unique to a specific group
shaped the practical, everyday actions of members of that group.

For example, Weber interpreted Judaism as the religion of a 'pariah
people'. A pariah community in Weber's sense was a group whose
position of social subordination was a result only partially of exclusion
enforced by hostile external circumstances. More important was voluntary separation from an ungodly world. This was the result of ethical
motivations, in particular the high premium placed on present suffering
which a believer endured faithfully and obediently in the hope of future
compensation from God. There was an important element of historical
development in this Jewish pariah ethic. Under Babylonian rule the
ancient Hebrews were filled with hatred and resentment directed toward their godless oppressors. These feelings were expressed in their
most honest and primitive form in ancient religious texts like the Psalms.
Collective resentment and the accompanying impractical desire for active vengeance was eventually replaced with an abiding hope in future,
other-worldly rewards. Revenge was left to God. To secure their future
rewards, the Jews collectively through the centuries had to obey God's
law, even if this meant suffering injustices and living apart from the

---

[11] '"Objectivity" in Social Science and Social Policy', p. 103.

ungodly masses who did not recognize divine commandments. In short, separateness and collective suffering became the highest expressions of faith for the obedient Jew. Disprivilege and hardship in the present were to be translated into salvation in the future. Ancient Judaism had helped contribute to the rise of modern rationalism, since as a religion of rules and regulations it could be understandable to all believers. Thus it was an important initial step towards freeing Western religion and society from a reliance on magical explanations. Nonetheless, the world-historical significance of the long-surviving ethic of ancient Judaism was limited. Jewish capitalism, for example, remained through the generations a kind of self-segregating pariah capitalism which did not encourage key developments like the rational organization of labour in the mainstream of society.[12]

By contrast, within the category of ascetic Protestantism Weber distinguished 'sectarians' (which he used in a sociologically 'neutral' sense) from predestinarian Calvinists. Predestinarian Calvinists and sectarian Protestants had played a special role in the rise of modern capitalism, each for different reasons. Together with Baptists and Quakers, Weber saw Mennonites and their Anabaptist forebears as prime examples of sectarian Protestantism. In Anabaptist groups the Protestant ethic of hard work in a worldly calling was driven by at least two main, ideal-typical traits: 1) voluntary membership in a community of believers, which was confirmed by adult baptism administered upon a person's public profession of faith; and 2) strict moral discipline. Once they had achieved membership in these small, voluntary Christian groups, believers had to prove their upright ethical status again and again by continued success or at least blameless conduct in day-to-day affairs. They otherwise risked losing favour with their peers *and* God, which, in concrete terms, meant exclusion from the sacrament of communion or even expulsion from the community of faith. In this way, modern economic virtues were instilled in the early modern sectarian Protestant rank-and-file by religious demands built into the very constitution of the community.[13]

---

[12] For these arguments, see primarily Weber's *Ancient Judaism*, Hans H. Gerth and Don Martindale (eds and trans), (Glencoe, 1952). Among secondary interpretations, one essay is worth particular attention: Arnaldo Momigliano, 'A Note on Max Weber's Definition of Judaism as a Pariah-Religion', *History and Theory*, 19: 3 (1980), pp. 313–18.

[13] For these arguments, see primarily Weber's *The Protestant Sects and the Spirit of Capitalism* as well as The Protestant Sects and the Spirit of Capitalism in Hans H. Gerth and C. Wright Mills (eds and trans), *From Max Weber* (New York, 1958 [1946]). Among secondary interpretations, one essay is of particular note: Stephen Berger, 'The Sects and the Breakthrough into the Modern World: On the Centrality of the Sects in Weber's Protestant Ethic Thesis', *Sociological Quarterly*, 12 (1971), pp. 486–99.

A fundamental question arises from the material reviewed so far: is Weber's sociology of religion an example of the strong and successful implementation of his ideal-typical methodology? Fritz Ringer, in his 1997 study of *Max Weber's Methodology*, draws a positive balance. According to Ringer, Weber's approach allowed him 1) to maintain that individual persons and their actions are the basic elements of sociological analysis, while at the same time 2) striving first and foremost for an understanding of 'the actions and beliefs of social *groups* and even of whole *cultures*'.[14] This balancing act between individual and collective levels of analysis was successful because 'Weber does not need to argue that the type [for example, the heuristic model of Calvinist ethical behaviour or dogma] is fully applicable to any single individual' nor even 'that any individual actually believed in it – or acted accordingly'.[15] 'All he must show is that it correctly identifies significant aspects of Protestant orientations.'[16] While individual Protestants acted in many and often contrary ways, models isolate what is typical and noteworthy about Protestant actions as a whole.

Ringer's defence of Weber seems strong only if we, like Ringer, examine Weber's sociology of Protestantism in isolation from the rest of his sociology of religion. Weber himself always insisted that his interpretation of Protestantism was closely linked with his interpretation of other western European religious groups. Especially in the revised version of *The Protestant Ethic and the Spirit of Capitalism* from 1920 he made it absolutely clear that Protestantism and Judaism had absolutely distinct socio-ethical orientations.[17] And in another essay on *The Social Psychology of the World Religions* he summarized his approach to the sociology of religion in the following manner: 'The author has always underscored those features in the total picture of a religion which have been decisive for the fashioning of the *practical* way of life, as well as those which distinguish one religion from another.'[18] The reason for this approach was that a crystal-clear distinction between Jewish and Protestant (as well as Catholic) ethical orientations was essential to the logic of his arguments about the rise of the spirit of modern capitalism.

---

[14] Ringer, p. 158.

[15] Ibid., p. 166.

[16] Ibid., pp. 166–7.

[17] See Gary Abraham, *Max Weber and the Jewish Question: A Study in the Social Outlook of His Sociology* (Urbana, IL, and Chicago, 1992). Especially in his chapter on the debates between Weber and his colleague Werner Sombart, Abraham describes the processes by which Weber came to clarify and intensify his arguments about the distinct ethical character of Judaism.

[18] Weber, 'The Social Psychology of the World Religions', *From Max Weber*, p. 294.

Methodological problems become apparent when we examine Weber's claims about Protestantism in the broader context of his comparative sociology. It is no longer sufficient, as Ringer claims, to show that an ideal type of Protestantism 'correctly identifies significant aspects of Protestant orientations'. Because Weber insisted that there were fundamental ethical differences between major religious traditions, a thorough-going Weberian analysis must also show that an ideal type of Protestantism (or Judaism) does *not* correctly identify *any* significant aspect of real Jewish (or Protestant) orientations, and so on.

Although Weber insisted that ideal types of world religions were themselves not real, he also insisted that each one can or should only be applied to a limited field of real historical events and people.[19] In so doing he blurred the line between mere heuristic concepts and historical reality. In his essay on '"Objectivity" in Social Science and Social Policy' Weber had warned against this very kind of methodological imprecision:

> In the interest of the concrete demonstration of an ideal type or of an ideal-typical developmental sequence, one seeks to *make it clear* by the use of concrete illustrative material drawn from empirical-historical reality. The danger of this procedure which in itself is entirely legitimate lies in the fact that historical knowledge here appears as a *servant* of theory instead of the opposite role. It is a great temptation for the theorist to regard this relationship either as the normal one or, far worse, to mix theory with history and indeed to confuse them with each other. ... The logical classification of analytical concepts on the one hand and the empirical arrangement of the events thus conceptualized in space, time and causal relationship, on the other, appear to be so bound together that there is an almost irresistible temptation to do violence to reality in order to prove the real validity of the construct.[20]

Weber was guilty of the very mistakes he warned against. He used evidence from the complex histories of Protestants and Jews to try to show that arbitrary and artificially clear ideal-typical constructs of Protestantism and Judaism were distinct.

---

[19] This is a conclusion based on the comparison of Weber's arguments in '"Objectivity"' with his later practice of this method in works like *Ancient Judaism*, *Economy and Society* and the revised edition of *The Protestant Ethic*. Supporting my observation is an essay by Tore Lindbekk, 'The Weberian Ideal-type: Development and Continuities', *Acta Sociologica*, 35 (1992), pp. 285–97. Lindbekk writes (p. 295) that in Weber's later methodological writings 'The "ideal", therefore, was very close to the "real"'. The reason for this apparent shift was Weber's growing interest in the institutionalization of systems of rationality.

[20] Weber, '"Objectivity" in Social Science and Social Policy', pp. 102–3. In the same essay, also see p. 94.

To make a more convincing case that Weber used historical knowledge arbitrarily as a servant of theory, it is necessary to show that we could usefully conceive of the relationship between Weber's ideal types and historical evidence differently. Leaving aside the controversial question about whether the pariah typology applies to historical Jews,[21] we could pose a different set of questions occasioned by Weber's ideal types. Does the typology of (Protestant) sectarianism identify at least some significant aspects of practical Jewish *ways* of life? To keep the discussion brief, I will focus on one aspect of that ideal type, the role of peer discipline in promoting hard work in a worldly calling.

Community-organized discipline of a sort not too different from that practised by groups like the Mennonites was important in Jewish life in early modern Europe. Three types of disciplinary sanctions are worth attention: *nezifah*, a temporary reprimand; *niddui*, community shunning, usually lasting for month-long periods, during which time an individual was excluded from religious privileges; and *herem*, permanent excommunication. *Niddui* especially could have been used to enforce what we might interpret as an inner-worldly work ethic, because, in addition to being imposed in cases where religious law generally was broken, it also was imposed in cases of fraud, debt, theft and bankruptcy.[22] In Jewish communities like the one in seventeenth-century Frankfurt, for example, expulsion from participation in synagogue ceremonies was one of the punishments used against bankrupt believers. Bankruptcy victims were even declared 'violators of God's name'.[23] This brief review has an important implication, especially if we also continue to take Weber's ideas about peer discipline as applied to Anabaptists seriously. For it now seems plausible and even productive to begin a research project comparing Protestant and Jewish community discipline in the early modern period. But such a project from an orthodox Weberian point of view would be unimportant, because it has already decided in advance for us that we need not pay attention to these (purportedly) insignificant details of Jewish culture.

The corresponding inversion or extension of Weber's analyses would be to investigate Protestants like the Anabaptists through the interpretive

---

[21] For a particularly critical view, see Abraham, p. 20: 'Weber's sociology of the Jews is not merely out of date; it is, rather, fundamentally flawed because it is guided by the need to select and interpret evidence so as to confirm a thesis that cannot be sustained. In other words, the Weber thesis ought to be considered to be conclusively discredited, rather than to be marred by mere shortcomings that have to do with the limited evidence that might have been available to Weber.'

[22] See 'Herem', *Encyclopaedia Judaica*, vol. 8 (Jerusalem, 1972), columns 350–55.

[23] I. Kracauer, *Geschichte der Juden in Frankfurt a.M. (1150–1824)*, vol. 2 (Frankfurt, 1927), p. 44.

lens of voluntary pariahdom. In the middle of the sixteenth century adult baptizers in continental Europe faced the real possibility of government-sponsored persecution. Menno Simons, for example, lived the life of a hunted man. He did manage to console himself and his followers by reminding them of their favoured place before God. As an example, we can take the following two verses of a hymn probably written by Menno around 1540:[24]

> I'd rather choose the sorrow sore,
>   And suffer as of God the child,
> Than have from Pharaoh all his store,
>   To revel in for one brief while;
>   The realm of Pharaoh cannot last,
>   Christ keeps His kingdom sure and fast;
>   Around His child His arm He casts.
> In this world, ye saints, you'll be defamed,
>   Let this be cause for pious glee;
> Christ Jesus too was much disdained;
>   Whereby he wrought to set us free;
>   He took away of sin the bill
>   Held by the foe. Now if you will
>   You too may enter heaven still!

We can think of patient suffering as having been a central theme in Anabaptist and Mennonite self-awareness. Evidence is easy to find. Martyrologies invoking the steadfastness and selflessness of early adult baptizers have been very popular through the generations in Amish and Mennonite households in Europe and North America. Even when intolerance and mild legal disadvantages replaced the threat of real persecution in the seventeenth and eighteenth centuries, leaders could encourage conformity to the ethic of patient suffering in order to try to maintain ritual boundaries separating the ungodly world from 'the true church' – as some Anabaptist groups have seen themselves. Anabaptists have in some ways acted as Weber claimed Jews did.

What should be clear from the material discussed so far is that Max Weber's sociology of religion establishes the illusion of comparison. For by directing scholars to look for quality X when studying Jews and quality Y when studying Protestants, he was in effect counselling against the use of comparative methods for comparing historical groups. Perhaps surprisingly, although he insisted that historical reality was rich and complex, he never took seriously the real possibility that the ideal-typical qualities X and Y each identified significant cultural characteristics of *numerous* historical groups. In order to strengthen his theories about

---

[24] *The Complete Writings of Menno Simons*, Leonard Verduin (trans.), J.C. Wenger (ed.), (Scottdale, PA, and Kitchener, Ont., 1986), pp. 1063–5, verses 5 and 6.

the rise of modern rationalism, Weber theorized a Great Divide,[25] a fundamental and qualitative cultural boundary, separating Jews from Protestants. His methods were well-tailored to arrive at preconceived conclusions which serve to constrict inquiry and foster clichés. Instead of promoting conventional Weberian conclusions, we should work to free ourselves to think new thoughts. In short, we should abandon altogether the segregationist project of Weber's sociology of religion.[26]

Comparing early modern European Jews and Anabaptists

Despite the fundamental problems to be found in Weber's sociology of religion, I think nonetheless that some main elements of his ideal-typical methodology are worth rescuing. Such a rescue action requires slight adjustments or modifications to Weber's initial recommendations. One of the reasons Weber's implementation of the ideal-typical methodology was so problem-ridden is that he insisted on drafting ideal types of discrete cultural phenomena, a procedure somewhat at odds with his original intention of using typologies as mere heuristic devices, never to be confused with reality. A more consistent application of the heuristic principle is necessary. Instead of drafting separate ideal types of Judaism or Protestantism or other historical groups, however large or small, we should be prepared to use ideal types which are not group-specific. Each ideal type should in theory be able to focus our attention on an important facet found in several groups, and, conversely, by applying several different ideal types to a single historical group we should be able to see that group in more complex terms.[27]

   The suggestion in this vein on which I would like to elaborate might seem at first glance preposterous: one of the best books written in recent years which helps us understand early modern European Anabaptist history is Jonathan Israel's *European Jewry in an Age of*

[25] I am using the term in a way similar to that used by Jack Goody, *The Domestication of the Savage Mind* (Cambridge, 1977); and Bruno Latour, *Science in Action: How to Follow Scientists and Engineers through Society* (Cambridge, MA, 1987).

[26] Abandoning Weber's preferred method of sociology of religion also implies abandoning his aim of explaining the rise of the spirit of modern capitalism. For a critique of Weber's distinction between the historical phenomenon of capitalism and 'the spirit of capitalism', see Alasdair MacIntyre, 'A Mistake about Causality in Social Science', in Peter Laslett and W.G. Runciman (eds), *Philosophy, Politics and Society* (Second Series) (Oxford, 1969), pp. 48–70.

[27] For a similar conclusion, see Johan Galtung, 'Theory Formation in Social Research: A Plea for Pluralism', in Else Oyen (ed.), *Comparative Methodology: Theory and Practice in International Social Research* (London, 1990), pp. 96–112.

Mercantilism.[28] This statement should not be misunderstood. Israel rarely mentions Anabaptists in his study. Furthermore, we should not forget some basic truths. Most obviously, Judaism is an ancient tradition, while continental European adult Baptist traditions developed first in the early sixteenth century. And, in the several hundred years that members of both backgrounds have lived in fairly close geographic proximity, there seem to have been few significant contacts. For the most part, Anabaptists and Jews – as long as both have existed side by side – have had different theologies, different religious offices, different ceremonies, different places of worship, different family connections, and an awareness of belonging to different historical traditions. In short, Jews are not Anabaptists.

Empirical observations like these should not, however, stop us from using common interpretive concepts to evaluate different concrete and individual historical groups. Such an application of a common concept to groups as historically and socially distinct as Hutterites and Waterlanders is the ideal type of 'the Anabaptist-Mennonite tradition'. Although there are affinities between this kind of ideal type and Weber's category of sectarian Protestantism,[29] the category of 'the Anabaptist-Mennonite tradition' is meant first and foremost to help us see traits shared by all those of Anabaptist descent. Because it is meant first and foremost to include rather than to divide, it is to be distinguished from Weber's aim of contrasting different religious traditions. But, although there is nothing intrinsically wrong with the ideal type of 'the Anabaptist-Mennonite tradition', we let ourselves get caught in an intellectual rut if we place too much value in it. There are other heuristically valuable ways of interpreting the Anabaptist past. These include an extension of Jonathan Israel's categories of forced migration, crisis and turning point, and partial reintegration.

Forced migration

Israel begins his outline of Jewish history in Christian Europe by describing a period of widespread persecution and expulsion lasting from

---

[28] Jonathan Israel, *European Jewry in an Age of Mercantilism* (Oxford, 1989). I have used the second edition, which the author modified in some regards significantly in response to criticism of the first version. Readers interested in this book are advised to look at both editions.

[29] It was no accident that Mennonite historians in the middle of the twentieth-century saw Max Weber's work as one of 'the foundations of an objective Anabaptist historiography ... ' (Guy F. Hershberger, 'Introduction', in Guy F. Hershberger (ed.), *The Recovery of the Anabaptist Vision* [Scottdale, PA, 1957], p. 5).

about 1470 until 1570. This century of forced migration, during which regimes tried to impose religious uniformity as seldom before, caused a violent transformation of medieval Jewish society. Jewish populations, once more or less settled, were forced to the peripheries of western Europe.

The Reformation of the early sixteenth century was also a period of the often violent transformation of European Christian society. The history of Anabaptist groups, which began as part of this Reformation context, is also dominated by themes of persecution and exile. Early Anabaptists were among the radical Christian reformers set on reorganizing society using the Bible, not accepted practice, as a model. They were quickly associated in the popular and official imagination with the Peasants' War of 1525 and the Münsterite kingdom of 1535, and therefore with fanaticism, excess, heresy, and social and political chaos. Governments allied with the old church as well as the new were horrified by the idea of lay Christianity spreading beyond the control of the proper authorities. At the Imperial Diet of Speyer in 1529 Anabaptism was even declared a capital crime. To escape violent persecution, committed Anabaptists moved from the southern German-speaking highlands and the southern Low Countries, the early strong points of Anabaptist movements, to places like Moravia, the northern Netherlands, northern Germany and the Vistula River delta. The second and subsequent generations of Anabaptists did their best to distance themselves from their revolutionary roots and come to terms with their inheritance of social and political disprivilege.

In short, the sixteenth century was a period of sudden and traumatic reorientation of Jewish and Christian cultures. Jewish and Anabaptist contemporaries suffered and reacted in similar ways to similar pressures. Many began searching for safer territories in which to practice their nonconformist beliefs, while others adopted Nicodemian strategies of survival.

Crisis and turning-point

Especially in the sixteenth century, many ecclesiastical and secular governments treated religious minorities as fundamental threats to order. Anabaptists and Jews, being in the minority almost everywhere they lived, tended to be easy targets of state control or clergy-incited popular hatred.

In the violent rhetoric of mainstream clergymen, religious nonconformists were sometimes even lumped together into one category. Here are two examples, the first from Joannes Schröter, a Jesuit priest of the late seventeenth century: 'O dear people, you hate the Jews as enemies of Christ and so should you hate their offspring, the Mennonites.'[30] Schröter hoped to stir up popular indignation against non-Catholic minorities. Similarly, orthodox Lutheran clergymen in central Europe campaigned from the pulpit and in formal political circles to have all non-Lutherans expelled from their regions. Their official position, summarized in the following prayer found at the beginning of a polemical pamphlet from 1702, 'The Frightening Brotherhood', was that non-Lutherans presented a looming and immediate danger to the spiritual and social order: 'Keep us by your Word, o Lord, and deflect the murderous intentions of the Quakers, Jews and Turks, who desire to dethrone your Son, Jesus Christ. Also defend us against all gangs, sects and scandals. Hear our prayers, dear Lord God!'[31] Statements like these had immense rhetorical power in an earlier age when Judaism and adult baptism were illegal in many European jurisdictions.[32]

Both of these examples are from around the turn of the eighteenth century. By this time, dreams of Christian institutional reunification were not shared so universally, for they were impractical, especially in the highly fragmented German-speaking territories. The erosion of these dreams had begun even earlier. Israel argues that the responses of secular governments toward Jews in Europe, once more uniformly negative, seem to have changed quite suddenly around 1570, after which point the full support of state violence began to accompany the violent rhetoric of orthodox preachers much less frequently. Scepticism had gained a stronger hold across Europe. Europe's Christians were having to cope with a growing spiritual crisis resulting from the Babel of voices claiming to represent the same truth. One increasingly common way for governments to deal with confessional division was to value political stability and conformity above religious conformity. Pragmatic reasons of state began to trump the values of orthodox clergymen. Given these

---

[30] *Stammbuch Der Mennistischen Ketzerey Sambt dero Gespanschafften Lehr und Sitten* (Neyß, 1691), p. 24.

[31] See the title page of *Erschröckliche Brüderschafft der Alten und Neuen Wiedertäuffer/ Quäcker/ Schwärmer und Frey-Geister/ mit Denen Heil- und Gottlosen Juden*, found in *Anabaptisticum et Ethusiasticum Pantheon* (1702). Lutheran pastors included Mennonites in their definition of 'sects'. In the section of *Anabaptisticum et Ethusiasticum Pantheon* which was compiled by Hamburg's Lutheran church representatives, there is a copy of a Prussian Mennonite confession of faith from 1660 as well as a Mennonite catechism from 1690.

[32] For further examples, see Heinold Fast, 'Die Mennoniten und die Gründung von Neustadtgödens', *MGBl*, 52 (1995), p. 97, note 16. The idea that Christian nonconformists and Jews conspired in their attacks on Christ and his church is an old one; see R.I. Moore, *The Formation of a Persecuting Society: Power and Deviance in Western Europe, 950–1250* (Oxford and Cambridge, MA, 1987).

changing attitudes it was now relatively easier for Jewish communities to find territories in which to settle and establish roots.

I find Israel's turning-point argument all the more convincing because of parallel conclusions arrived at independently by James Stayer. According to Stayer, the 'Radical Reformation', the active attempts begun in the early sixteenth century by Anabaptists and other activist Christians to change the world according to the biblical model, can be considered to have ended by the 1560s and 1570s. Stayer writes: 'After the religious peace of Augsburg (1555) and even more after the accession of Emperor Maximillian II (1564), Hutterites enjoyed *de facto* toleration by common consent of the Moravian aristocracy and the [Imperial] court at Vienna.'[33] And in the northern Netherlands of William of Orange the Mennonites had achieved a status of 'legitimate nonconformity' by the 1570s.[34]

A major problem facing rulers and church leaders across Europe after the middle of the sixteenth century was not so much how to achieve confessional purity but how to cope with confessional plurality. Because of similar reactions by secular authorities, the degree of persecution with which early modern Anabaptists and Jews had to cope diminished at around the same time.

Partial reintegration

According to Israel, the period from the end of the sixteenth century until the beginning of the eighteenth was the high point of early modern Jewish life in western Europe. More precisely, it was a time of Jewish reintegration into a society from which Jews had earlier been almost completely expelled as well as a time when European Jewry strengthened its own sense of a unique social and cultural identity.

The vibrancy of economic life was crucial for this period of relative prosperity. Jewish financiers in eastern and western Europe kept contacts with coreligionists in the Levant and Persia. These financiers were the rich élite in well-developed trade networks involving many more Jewish businessmen and tinkers, who together could transfer capital at relatively great speeds over long distances. It could be attractive to an early modern ruler to provide Jews with concessions in return for access to these economic networks. Limited toleration was motivated by interests of state, which in turn allowed the Jews to become partially

---

[33] James M. Stayer, 'The Radical Reformation', in Thomas A. Brady, Heiko A. Oberman and James D. Tracy (eds), *Handbook of European History, 1400–1600*, vol. 2 (Leiden, 1995), p. 266.

[34] Ibid., pp. 273–4.

reintegrated into European society while still remaining uniquely Jewish.

While he does not discuss the history of Jewish refugees, the German historian Heinz Schilling – in essays on 'confessional migration'[35] – makes similar points. Schilling's subjects are Lutherans and Calvinists and to a lesser extent Anabaptists from the Low Countries. According to Schilling what was typical about social arrangements after the Reformation was that the once strong connection between ruling classes and commercial classes was greatly diminished. Exile communities played a central role in this development. Expelled from their homelands because they refused to conform to the state-sanctioned church, refugees often found themselves treated only slightly better in the towns and cities in which they resettled. But, writes Schilling, '[t]he confessional anchoring of the exiles made them prepared not only to bear the disadvantages of a refugee's life. It unleashed further forces of religious, economic and social self-assertion, as well as the unconditional will to persevere in the face of all earthly obstacles.'[36] Schilling's statement does point to an important pattern. Confessional exiles often settled in towns and cities in which their religious beliefs and practices did not conform to the norms of the majority. For any number of reasons, mostly political or economic, they were nonetheless afforded varying degrees of toleration. They were not, however, allowed access to political offices. A whole community's resources and energies, limited though they might have been, were therefore concentrated in closely-knit family, church and market spheres.

Exclusion from mainstream political life played a role in shaping more than just the economic behaviour of religious nonconformists. Because they were rarely tolerated for principled religious or philosophical reasons, minority groups had to try to keep a low profile and live particularly faultless lives. In effect, the only way for religious nonconformists to preserve the stability of community life was to be social and political conformists. To do this successfully, community leaders had to maintain order in their own communities. To quote Israel:

---

[35] See the following two articles by Schilling: 'Die niederländischen Exulanten des 16. Jahrhunderts. Ein Beitrag zum Typus der frühneuzeitlichen Konfessionsmigration,' *Geschichte in Wissenschaft und Unterricht*, 43: 2 (1992), pp. 67–78; and 'Innovation through Migration: The Settlements of Calvinist Netherlanders in Sixteenth- and Seventeenth-Century Central and Western Europe,' *Histoire sociale – Social History*, (Ottawa) 16 (1983), pp. 7–33. For a similar typology, see Leo Driedger's use in *Mennonite Identity in Conflict* (Lewiston and Queenston, 1988) of Pierre van den Berghe's category 'middleman minority'.

[36] Schilling, 'Die niederländische Exulanten', p. 77. The translation is mine.

The universal precariousness of Jewish life militated strongly in favour of subjection to discipline and authority. It was not simply a question of upholding the Torah and pursuing the moral ideals of Judaism. Anything likely to exacerbate the ever-present reality of popular hatred was deemed a threat to the community. Unseemly conduct, licentiousness, extravagance, the presence of too many beggars, any sort of provocative behaviour was liable to be promptly suppressed. The boards of the elders kept a vigilant eye on costume, morals, and every aspect of life-style and this congregants had no choice but to accept.[37]

In short, nonconformists had to be acutely aware of what the seventeenth-century philosopher Thomas Hobbes called 'the mutual relation between protection and obedience'.[38]

Considerations like these could provide a good guide for scholars of northern European Mennonites looking to examine old material from a broader perspective. As was the case with other nonconforming Christians and Jews, the main reason rulers tolerated Anabaptists and Mennonites was economic self-interest. The scattered Mennonite communities in northern continental Europe were not as extensive as their counterparts from other religious traditions, but they were nonetheless important economically. Despite factional disputes, Mennonite communities remained joined across northern continental Europe by familial and ecclesiastical bonds, which helped foster close business connections between congregations in the economically prosperous Netherlands and the resource-rich Baltic. In addition to growing in economic strength, Mennonite communities after the middle or end of the sixteenth century also refined and elaborated on their own collective confessional identity through shared histories, interregional meetings, theological discussion and argument, the exchange of preachers, the movement of members between congregations, and community emergency aid programmes. This developing sense of community was made possible only because of government toleration, limited though it was. Mennonite leaders sought to remain on good terms with these leaders, and they justified their obedience as a moral duty flowing from the Anabaptist norm of Christian nonresistance.[39] The irony that Israel and Schilling highlight – that

---

[37] Israel, p. 198.

[38] *Leviathan*, concluding chapter.

[39] See Michael Driedger, 'Mennonites? Heretics? Obedient Citizens?' (PhD Diss., Queen's University at Kingston, 1996), chap. 4. Also see Hans-Jürgen Goertz, 'Zucht und Ordnung in nonkonformistischer Manier. Kleruskritik, Kirchenzucht und Sozialdisziplinierung in den Bewegungen der Täufer', *Antiklerikalismus und Reformation. Sozialgeschichtliche Untersuchungen* (Göttingen, 1995), pp. 103–14; an earlier version of this essay is found in Heinz Schilling (ed.), *Kirchenzucht und Sozialdisziplinierung im frühneuzeitlichen Europa* (Berlin, 1994), pp. 183–98.

is, that early modern exiles often thrived under the still adverse conditions of limited toleration – also applies to early modern Mennonites.

Conclusion

Although Israel's interpretation of Jewish history ends in the early part of the eighteenth century, the historiography about Judaism in the following generations is particularly rich. It too could serve as a guide for scholars studying European Mennonites in the eighteenth, nineteenth and twentieth centuries.[40] The point of such comparisons of Jewish and Anabaptist histories is not to suggest that they alone display close parallels. It is merely one particularly productive example of comparative studies of the kind advocated by David Sorkin.[41] This kind of search for commonalities promises to be a valuable tool for scholars of European Anabaptists because it can lead us to recognize that important trends in Anabaptist and Mennonite histories were often just one expression of more general trends in European and even world history. Although careful reflection about the heuristic value of ideal types can be useful in such investigations, it is not essential. What is essential, however, is a readiness to look for innovative new questions or interpretations in neighbouring historiographies, as well as a stubborn desire not to be trapped in restrictive modes of thought of the kind advocated by Max Weber. Rather than reinforcing Weber's Great Divide, we should be prepared to cross it and explore new intellectual territory.

---

[40] I will suggest very briefly only two of several possibilities: 'the religious Enlightenment' of the eighteenth century (see the following note); and nineteenth- and early twentieth-century Jewish nationalism and patriotism in Germany.

[41] In his own contributions to comparative studies, Sorkin has examined parallels between eighteenth-century European Jewish and Catholic communities, as well as developing the historiographical concept of 'the religious Enlightenment'. Three of his essays are worth particular note: 'From Context to Comparison. The German Haskalah and Reform Catholicism', *Tel Aviver Jahrbuch für deutsche Geschichte*, 20 (1991), pp. 23–58; 'The Case for Comparison' (already cited above); and 'Juden und Katholiken: Deutsch-jüdische Kultur im Vergleich 1750–1850', in Shulamit Volkov (ed.), *Deutsche Juden und die Moderne* (Munich, 1994), pp. 9–30.

CHAPTER ELEVEN

Are Mormons Anabaptists? The case of the Mormons and heirs of the Anabaptist tradition on the American frontier, *c.* 1840

Clyde R. Forsberg Jr

Introduction

In 1830, a young charismatic of New England ancestry, Joseph Smith Jr, announced his intentions to reform antebellum America along anti-evangelical lines. He organized a church, at first simply calling it 'The Church of Christ' and then later 'The Church of Jesus Christ of Latter-day Saints'. This coincided with his publication of an addendum to the Bible, naming it after its mesoamerican 'redactor', Mormon, and assigning himself a lesser role – that of 'translator'. The Book of Mormon's criticisms of evangelical religion would become the basis for a new religion, composed largely of anticlericals and outsiders of various types. Within a few short years, moreover, what had begun as an alternative to evangelical piety escalated into a revolutionary movement which seemed to pose a serious threat to Christianity in America.[1] Mormons begged to differ and were promptly invited to love their native, Protestant America or leave her. The mob would help pack, in any event. (The murder of Joseph Smith by vigilantes in 1844 drove home that point.) To antebellum America's great surprise, indeed relief, Mormons simply buried their prophet and left the country, journeying to the shores of the Great Salt Lake where they would build the kingdom of God anew and practise polygamy – a major tenet of the faith – with impunity.[2] In truth, Christendom in America had no intentions of sharing a border with Mormondom, standing idly by as the 'State of Deseret' (on behalf of the Mormon political kingdom of God) gobbled up precious land

---

[1] Klaus J. Hansen, *Quest for Empire: The Political Kingdom of God and the Council of Fifty in Mormon History* (Lincoln, NB, 1967).

[2] B. Carmon Hardy, *Solemn Covenant: The Mormon Polygamous Passage* (Urbana, IL, and Chicago, 1992).

which Americans proper believed had been set aside by the Deity for *their* exclusive socio-economic aggrandizement. However problematic the Mormon flight from American pluralism might have been,[3] it allowed two generations of Mormons to live in relative peace, institutionalize polygamy and other uniquely Mormon beliefs and practices in hopes of, at very least, providing a viable alternative to Evangelicalism. Mormonism's evangelical-minded foes in the United States Congress drafted anti-bigamy legislation beginning in the 1880s intended to drive Mormons into the sea and dash their political dreams of empire on the rocks of middle-class sensibility once and for all. Remarkably, by giving up polygamy and the political kingdom of God, Mormonism would live to fight another day, winning a victory of sorts.[4]

More remarkable still is the modern metamorphosis of Mormonism from quintessential radical, anti-evangelical, social, political and economic outsider to a very respectable and essentially Christian denomination in which to worship and raise one's children. Mormonism's premier intellectual phalanx, the Mormon History Association, has waged a brilliant defensive war by downplaying and, in some cases, ignoring the revolutionary beginnings of early Mormonism altogether, focusing instead on orthodox beliefs and practices. Several influential and decidedly pro-evangelical interpretations of early Mormonism are cases in point.[5] In this sense, Mormon and Mennonite historical writing has much in common; in particular, both groups ascribe normative, evangelical beliefs and practices to their respective charter members.[6] Indeed, Mormons and Mennonites (despite their differences) have much in common, too – a fact neither community has been eager to explore let alone consider seriously. The Mormon experience, its theology and even such thorny social practices and political institutions as polygamy and the political kingdom of God respectively, have an Anabaptist ring to them. Indeed, if, as Rufus M. Jones says, Anabaptism 'is the spiritual soil out of which all nonconformist sects have sprung' (quoted with approbation by none other than Harold S. Bender as 'one of the best characterizations of

---

[3] See in this connection, Marvin S. Hill, *Quest for Refuge: The Mormon Flight from American Pluralism* (Salt Lake City, UT, 1989).

[4] Klaus J. Hansen, 'The Metamorphosis of the Kingdom of God', in D. Michael Quinn (ed.), *The New Mormon History* (Salt Lake City, UT, 1992).

[5] See in particular Philip L. Barlow, *Mormons and the Bible: The Place of the Latter-day Saints in American Religion* (New York, 1991), Grant Underwood, *The Millenarian World of Early Mormonism* (Urbana, IL, and Chicago, 1993) and Jan Shipps and John Welch, *The Journals of William E. McLellin* (Urbana, IL, Chicago and Provo, UT, 1995).

[6] See in this connection, Harold S. Bender, 'The Anabaptist Vision', in James M. Stayer and Werner O. Packull (eds), *The Anabaptists and Thomas Müntzer* (Toronto, 1980), pp. 13–22.

Anabaptism'), then it would seem Mormonism is at very least a prime candidate for inclusion in the Anabaptist garden.[7]

The matter is far more complicated than that, of course. While Mormon–Anabaptist parallels are striking, especially in the case of early Mormonism and revolutionary Anabaptism, this does not constitute proof of a genetic relationship. To say that Anabaptism caused Mormonism would surely be another instance of the infamous *post hoc ergo propter hoc* fallacy. At most, we may speak of a correlation of belief and practice between two ostensibly disparate anticlerical movements. However, the value of a comparative study of these two movements is already clear in Michael Driedger's call to supplement research based on 'questions of influence with one's investigating homologous trends, parallel changes and common development'.[8] Because Mormons and Anabaptists were separated by centuries and oceans, and therefore Mormonism has no real claim on the Anabaptist tradition, the parallels between them have much to tell us about such 'homologous trends' in sectarian religion.

In addition, such a study allows us to understand better a hitherto infrequently acknowledged phenomenon: the large-scale conversion of radical Dunkers, heirs of the Anabaptist tradition on the American frontier, to Mormonism in the 1840s. Mormon missionaries encountered Dunkers in the course of their journeys, converting many, but not all, to the cause. The most significant meeting of Mormons and Dunkers took place in Illinois in the 1840s. The Mormon capital Nauvoo was not far from a large Dunker settlement in Adams County, Illinois. Vigorous theological debate ensued as missionaries from both communities butted heads and cracked Bibles. Brethren leaders D.B. Sturgis and George Wolfe II repelled the Mormon advance, but not before losing such influential Adams County Dunkers as the Abraham Hunsaker family.[9] Frederick S. Buchanan's essay, 'Mormons Meet the Mennonites: A View From 1884', argues that the failure of the Mormon mission to the Mennonites in the 1880s suggests that Mormons were not likely to convert significant numbers of Anabaptists in America at any time or under any circumstances. The Mormon mission to the Mennonites was doomed to fail for the simple reason that Mormonism, at that time,

---

[7] Bender, 'The Anabaptist Vision', p. 13.

[8] Michael Driedger, 'Crossing Max Weber's Great Divide: Comparing Early Modern Jewish and Anabaptist Histories', above, pp. 157–74.

[9] D. Durnbaugh, *Fruit of the Vine: A History of the Brethren, 1708–1995* (Elgin, IL, 1997), pp. 177–80. Also see David B. Eller, 'Church of Jesus Christ of Latter-Day [*sic*] Saints', in Donald F. Durnbaugh (ed.), *The Brethren Encyclopedia*, (Philadelphia/Oak Brook, IL, 1983/84), p. 298.

clearly represented everything spiritualist and/or Münsterite which
Menno Simons's disciples in Europe *and* America had come to reject –
extra canonical revelations, theocracy, polygamy, millenarian and apocalyptic prognosticating and the like.[10] However, Mormonism did not
pose the same difficulties for heirs of the Anabaptist tradition living on
the frontier four decades earlier – an alienated and disgruntled younger
generation of Dunkers for whom Mormon Nauvoo in the 1840s (a
veritable theocracy) and eventually Salt Lake City seemed a more ame-
nable religious home than Germantown. Mormonism offered *these*
Anabaptists one last chance to reclaim their sectarian/spiritualist identity but not their heritage *per se* by joining a new religious tradition
which rightly claimed to be neither Catholic nor Protestant.[11]

The historiographical conundrum

The reliance on 'normative visions' of the founding fathers of both
Anabaptist and Mormon traditions has seriously influenced historical
understandings of those traditions. Largely as a response to unfriendly
charges of critics of their religious affiliations, Mormon and Mennonite
historians have been reticent about recognizing the parallels between the
two movements. The first to see in Mormons a certain Anabaptist flair
was Alexander Campbell. In a work, entitled *Delusions: An Analysis of
the Book of Mormon; With an Examination of the Internal and External
Evidences*, he attacked the *Book of Mormon* as a combination of Yankee
artifice and Anabaptist 'tomfoolery'.[12] Writing in 1832, long before the
Mormon settlement of Nauvoo and what became a full-blown Mormon
theocracy complete with polygamy, Campbell characterized Mormonism
as a religious descendant of Anabaptist Münster. Anti-Mormon LaRoy
Sunderland arrived at the same conclusion a few years later, the same
year of the infamous Mormon War in Missouri in 1838.[13] And the
Protestant clergyman Joseph P. Thompson certainly had the luxury of
hindsight when he wrote in 1873 that '[t]he Anabaptists of Germany in
the sixteenth century had most of the characteristic features of Mormonism.

[10] Frederick S. Buchanan, 'Mormons Meet the Mennonites: A View from 1884',
MQR, 62 (1988), pp. 159–166.
[11] See in this connection, Walter Klassen, *Neither Catholic nor Protestant* (Waterloo,
Ont., 1973).
[12] Alexander Campbell, *Delusions: An Analysis of the Book of Mormon; With an
Examination of the Internal and External Evidences* (Boston, 1832).
[13] LaRoy Sunderland, *Mormonism Exposed and Refuted* (New York, 1838), p. 11. See
Stephen C. LeSueur, *The 1838 Mormon War In Missouri* (Columbia, MO, 1987).

They claimed to be inspired; they refused to acknowledge the civil government; they established a theocracy, calling Münster "Mount Zion"; they collected tithes and practised polygamy.'[14] In 1953, American historian David Brion Davis, then a graduate student, published what can rightly be called the first academic discussion of the possible relationship between Mormonism and Anabaptism, 'The New England Origins of Mormonism', favouring a more positive relationship between the two movements.[15] For their own reasons, and in light of the harsh tone of much of the above scholarship, Mormons have been reluctant to sue for patrimony, and Mennonite scholars have been no quicker to recognize Mormons as their spiritual heirs.

Mennonite scholarship on this subject, which is scant, favours an interpretation which admits the possibility of theological overlap, even striking parallels, without reducing Mormonism to a scion of sixteenth-century Anabaptism. William Juhnke's 1985 article in *Mennonite Life*, entitled 'Anabaptism and Mormonism: A Study in Comparative History', is a case in point. Extremely critical of the Mormon belief in additional revelations, Juhnke also attacks the alleged early Mormon conflation of church and state and, of course, polygamy. And while Juhnke admits that Mormons suffered terribly at the hands of magisterial religion, he suggests that all such depredations were justified given Mormonism's heretical beliefs and practices.[16]

Mormon scholarship is no less guilty of emphasizing the differences between these two traditions. Again, the corpus is not voluminous. Robert J. McCue's 1959 Brigham Young University MA thesis, 'Similarities and Differences in the Anabaptist and the Mormon Restoration', stood alone for some time, arriving at the only conclusion possible given the state of the question at this early juncture in the historiography.[17] 'The Restitution of the Sixteen century, and the Mormon Restoration of the Nineteenth century,' he writes, 'although they do have much in common, remain unique in their own right.'[18] The most striking difference between Anabaptists and Mormons, according to McCue, is the Mormon belief in private revelations. 'Whereas the former attempted a revival based on an appeal to the scriptures, the latter

---

[14] Cited in Joseph P. Thompson, *Church and State in the United States* (Boston, 1873), pp. 138–9.

[15] David Brion Davis, 'The New England Origins of Mormonism', *New England Quarterly*, 26 (1953), pp. 148–9, 156–7, 165.

[16] William Juhnke, 'Anabaptism and Mormonism: A Study in Comparative History', *Mennonite Life*, 40 (1985), pp. 22–5.

[17] Robert J. McCue, 'Similarities and Differences in the Anabaptist and the Mormon Restoration' (MA thesis, Brigham Young University, 1959).

[18] Ibid., p. 92.

claimed a restoration which made its own scriptures.'[19] Ironically, McCue's argument is not that different from Juhnke's discussed earlier.

In 1971, Robert Bruce Flanders of the Reorganized Church of Jesus Christ of Latter Day Saints (that 'Mormon' faction which did not follow Brigham Young to Utah or accept polygamy and other radical Mormon beliefs and practices) briefly noted that, '[w]ithout knowing it, Mormons thus stood somewhat in the same radical Christian tradition as the Donatists, the Montanists, the followers of Joachim of Fiore, the Anabaptists of Münster, and a heritage with which they were more familiar, the Massachusetts Bay Colony'.[20] In this vein, D. Michael Quinn published an article in 1987 entitled 'Socioreligious Radicalism of the Mormon Church: A Parallel to the Anabaptists'. Mormons and Anabaptists, Quinn argues, advocate believers' baptism (and thus deny infant baptism). Early in their respective histories, both were prone to exclusiveness and separation, Mormons even more so, Quinn claims, than Anabaptists. To maintain separation, both require believers to keep the commandments (discipleship) and both excommunicate wayward members (the ban). Mormonism is a theology of works not unlike Anabaptism, consistent with the visible church ideal which the two traditions also have in common. Mormonism's chiliastic eschatology recalls the apocalypticism of Dutch and South German-Austrian Anabaptists.[21]

In order to make a consistent argument for the Anabaptist character of Mormonism, Quinn's discussion of Mormons and the sword quite naturally gravitates to what he regarded as the Anabaptist periphery, the Waterlanders and Pilgramites – who believed Christians could participate in government, pay taxes and the like in good conscience – and, of course, Anabaptist Münster. Joseph Smith's candidacy for presidency of the United States in 1844 and his secret anointing as 'King Priest and Ruler over Israel on the earth, over Zion & the Kingdom of Christ our King of Kings' recalls King Jan of Leyden's coronation and theocratic tendencies, to be sure. Nonresistance is a more difficult issue – the Mormon War in Missouri in 1838 (the Haun's Mill Massacre in particular) and Mormon participation in the Spanish-American War of 1898 stand at odds with the alleged pacifism central to the Anabaptist

---

[19] Ibid., p. 11.

[20] Cited in D. Michael Quinn, 'Socioreligious Radicalism of the Mormon Church: A Parallel to the Anabaptists', in Davis Bitton and Maureen Ursenbach Beecher (eds), *New Views of Mormon History: Essays in Honor of Leonard J. Arrington*, (Salt Lake City, UT, 1987), p. 363.

[21] See in this connection, Werner O. Packull, *Mysticism and the Early South German-Austrian Anabaptist Movement, 1525–1531* (Scottdale, PA, 1977).

tradition. He perhaps should have included the Mountain Meadows Massacre as well.[22] However, Quinn notes that Mormons

> pacifistically withdrew in masse from the capital, Nauvoo, in 1846, to flee from their enemies in the wilderness ... used all military means short of bloodshed to ward off a federal regiment invading Utah in 1857–58, only to prepare another pacifistic withdrawal into the wilderness when a scorched earth policy failed; remained essentially neutral during the American Civil War ... .[23]

Quinn concludes that 'Mormonism and Anabaptism are qualitatively, rather than causally, related as counter cultural religious groups that sought to radicalize religion and society by reaffirming rejected practices of the past and by rejecting sacrosanct groups of the present.'[24] The founder of Mormonism clearly had a textbook knowledge of Anabaptism, donating a personal copy of Mosheim's *Ecclesiastical History* to the Nauvoo public library in 1844.[25] Yet, despite these similarities, Quinn doubts whether Anabaptism had a strong influence on Smith's religious orientation during the formative part of his career. For such a decidedly New Englander, Restorationism not Anabaptism seems a more likely source for his radicalism.

The theme of the relationship between 'restorationist' or 'restitutionist' themes in Mormonism and Anabaptism is taken up by Richard T. Hughes in 'A Comparison of the Restitution Motifs of the Campbells (1809–1830) and the Anabaptists (1524–1560)'. In this work, the author distinguishes between Campbellite ecumenism and Anabaptist sectarianism. The Campbellites derive their name from the American Restorationist and former Baptist, Alexander Campbell. Campbell's movement is important to Mormon history because of the conversion of the former Campbellite preacher, Sidney Rigdon, and his entire congregation to Mormonism at a crucial point in the history of the church. Mormonism is thought to represent the radical wing of the American Restorationist movement which Campbell allegedly authored. Whether Mormonism came out of Campbellite Restorationism is an important question which comes and goes and is related to the question of Mormonism's relationship to Anabaptism.[26] The relationship

---

[22] See in this connection, Juanita Brooks, *The Mountain Meadows Massacre* (Norman, OK, 1962).

[23] Ibid., pp. 372–3.

[24] Quinn, 'Socioreligious Radicalism of the Mormon Church', p. 379.

[25] See Kenneth W. Godfrey, 'Note on the Nauvoo Library and Literary Institute', *BYU Studies* (1974), p. 388.

[26] See in this connection, Marvin S. Hill, 'The Role of Christian Primitivism in the Origin and Development of the Mormon Kingdom, 1830–1844' (PhD diss., University of Chicago, 1968.) Cf. Jan Shipps, *Mormonism: The Story of A New Religious Tradition*

between Restorationism and Anabaptism is important. The two movements, Hughes argues, 'emerged in actual practice on opposite ends of the restitution spectrum ... . The explanation for this difference is clear: restitution was for the Campbells a means to Christian unity while the Anabaptists were seeking a revival of the pure *corpus Christi*.'[27] Quinn, citing Hughes, seems to assume that Mormonism and the Campbells constitute a more likely genetic lineage, especially in light of the conversion of Campbellite minister Sidney Rigdon and his entire Ohio congregation to Mormonism, the new religion's first evangelistic windfall.[28] Logically, Mormonism and Anabaptism, then, are opposites.

Underlying such conclusions remain normative visions of Anabaptism and Mormonism which, by their very definitions, preclude the possibility of any significant parallels between the two traditions. In particular, assumptions about the rigid biblicism of normative 'Evangelical Anabaptism' continue to encourage scholars to draw sharp lines of demarcation between the Anabaptists and the Mormons with their more mystical, extra-scriptural commitments. Dan Vogel's *Religious Seekers and the Advent of Mormonism* is a case in point.[29] Vogel argues that Mormon beliefs and practices have most in common with those of Seekers, the self-professed intellectual descendants, in his view at least, of such sixteenth-century, continental Anabaptists as Hans Denck, Sebastian Franck [sic], Kasper Schwenckfeld [sic] and Dirk Coornhertz [sic] via the English Seekers Walter, Thomas and Bartholomew Legate, John Wilkinson and Edward Wightman, John Everard (who translated portions of Denck's, Franck's and Castellio's works into English), Roger Brierly, John Webster and John Saltmarsh. In England, many Anabaptists joined ranks with the Seekers before siding with George Fox's Society of Friends (Quakers) in the 1650s. Joseph Smith Jr had an uncle who laboured as an itinerant Seeker minister his entire life, foregoing marriage and family in order to fulfil his onerous religious mandate. The Mormon prophet's mother, Lucy Mack, was herself a Seeker.[30] In fact, the entire Smith family were partial, it seems, to a wide array of European, British and American Anabaptist/Seeker/Quaker anti-evangelical ideas, in particular those of radical Baptist Roger Williams. Williams

(Urbana, IL, and Chicago, 1985) and Dan Vogel, *Religious Seekers and the Advent of Mormonism* (Salt Lake City, UT, 1988).

[27] Richard T. Hughes, 'Comparison of the Restitution Motifs of the Campbells (1809–1830) and the Anabaptists (1524–1560)', *MQR*, 45 (1971), p. 317.

[28] See in this connection, Hill, 'Christian Primitivism in the Origin and Development of the Mormon Kingdom'.

[29] Vogel, *Religious Seekers and the Advent of Mormonism*, pp. 1–47.

[30] See Lucy Mack Smith, *Biographical Sketches of Joseph Smith the Prophet and His Progenitors for Many Generations* (Lamoni, IA, 1912), pp. 9–11.

favoured a literalist as opposed to a spiritualist understanding – a visible church ideal, the performance of ordinances such as believers' baptism by duly authorized individuals, and the premillennial and thus bodily advent of Jesus Christ. For this reason perhaps, Williams's amounted to little more than a stalled believers' church. Lacking the necessary charisma, too, he could only wait for Jesus to make his premillennial appearance and restore His primitive *ecclesia* by means of a divinely reconstituted quorum of twelve apostles and prophets. Joseph Smith Jr, in the popular Mormon literature, had both the charisma, sense of mission and, most important of all, permission from on high to make good Williams's dreams of eschatological empire in particular.

However, relying on the normative 'Evangelical Anabaptist' type, Vogel distinguishes between biblicists and spiritualists, Anabaptists and Seekers. Yet revisionist literature on Anabaptist origins has long ago rejected the notion of such a normative definition.[31] As a result, the characteristics used to distinguish Mormonism from Anabaptism no longer qualify as norms applicable to all Anabaptists. For example, Vogel's sharp distinction between spiritualists and biblicists is hardly tenable in light of Werner Packull's research into south German/Austrian Anabaptistm or Klaus Deppermann's into Melchior Hoffman.[32] Similarly, the distinction between Mormon belief in self-defence and Anabaptist pacifism has long since collapsed with James Stayer's destruction of accepted opinions about Anabaptist teaching on the sword. Even the most distinctive feature of Mormonism, in popular opinion at least, is not without its parallels in Anabaptist history when one escapes the normative vision of 'Evangelical Anabaptism'. As Cornelius Krahn noted, there are parallels between Mormon and Münsterite thinking on polygamous marriage: 'Developing this thought [that is, polygamous union] the Münsterites, and later the Latter Day Saints [*sic*], came to the conclusion that every woman must be attached to a man in order to be saved, just as a man is subject to Christ'.[33] Indeed, the post-Münster, Melchiorite debate on marriage between David Joris and Johannes Eisenburg has a decidedly Mormon ring to it. As Gary B. Waite explains, Joris's brand of polygamy can be seen as a kind of puritanical

---

[31] James M. Stayer, Werner O. Packull and Klaus Deppermann, 'From Monogenesis to Polygenesis: The Historical Discussion of Anabaptist Origins', *MQR*, 49 (1975), pp. 83–121.

[32] Packull, *Mysticism*; Klaus Deppermann, *Melchior Hoffman: Social Unrest and Apocalyptic Visions in the Age of Reformation*, Malcolm Wren (trans.) and Benjamin Drewery (ed.), (Edinburgh, 1987).

[33] Cornelius Krahn, *Dutch Anabaptism: Origin, Spread, Life and Thought (1450–1600)* (The Hague, 1968), p. 144.

polygamy 'motivated by the love of God rather than by the lusts of the flesh'.[34] Joris thought marriages to unbelievers were not binding and that polygamy solved the otherwise thorny issue of believers yoking themselves only to believers. Above all, Joris, in concert with Bernhard Rothmann, believed that polygamous union was not only a superior form of connubial relations but produced superior offspring, a spiritual as well as biological core of holy children 'who would add to the number of saints in the kingdom, the 144 000 of Revelation 7'.[35] Children born of spiritual, that is of polygamous marriage, were already regenerate. And finally, polygamy for Joris was the basis of a patriarchal system of family government. B. Carmon Hardy's discussion of Mormon polygamous beliefs and practices, *Solemn Covenant: The Mormon Polygamous Passage*, contains precisely these arguments.[36]

Early Mormon economic belief and practice really span the broad reach of the communitarian spectrum. Anabaptist community of goods, as Stayer has shown, meant different things to different Anabaptist communities. Community of goods was not the exclusive domain of Hutterites, for example. Swiss Brethren, the Marpeck brotherhood and Mennonite mutual aid constitute a type of community of goods.[37] Importantly, early Mormon economic theory and practice, despite appearances, was of the Christian mutual aid type. And although the members of select Utah Mormon communities to the south, such as Orderville, literally had 'all things in common', the bulk of the church's cooperative stores and industries operated according to a modified joint-stock plan.[38]

The relationship between Mormonism and heirs of Anabaptists in America is a more difficult problem. The American scene involves a litany of theological controversies all its own. Richard Hughes's contention that Restorationists (Campbell's movement) and Anabaptists are fundamentally different, the latter a sectarian movement, the former an ecumenical one, is the old normative vision in new garb. It also might be said to support *and* contradict a Mormon-Anabaptist nexus. Mormons are Restorationists and, therefore, not Anabaptists. However, Mormonism is sectarian not ecumenical, locating it alongside

---

[34] Gary B. Waite, 'The Post-Münster Melchiorite Debate on Marriage: David Joris's Response to Johannes Eisenburg, 1537', *MQR*, 63 (1989), pp. 370–71.

[35] Ibid., p. 372.

[36] Hardy, *Solemn Covenant*, pp. 84–126.

[37] James M. Stayer, *The German Peasants' War and Anabaptist Community of Goods* (Kingston, Ont., and Montreal, 1991), p. 9.

[38] See in this connection, Leonard J. Arrington et al., *Building the City of God: Community and Cooperation among the Mormons* (Urbana, IL, 1992).

'sectarian' Anabaptism. In fact, the matter is further complicated by the fact that American Restorationism owes its existence not to Alexander Campbell and radical, breakaway Baptists exclusively, but to radical, breakaway Anabaptists as well – more so the latter, in fact. It seems that the Restorationist movement in nineteenth-century America, a more suitable rubric for Mormonism was started by Anabaptists. And if so, then Mormonism's undeniable connection to American Restorationism via renegade Disciple of Christ Sidney Rigdon suggests a contemporaneous Anabaptist antecedent.

David B. Eller's PhD dissertation, 'The Brethren in the Western Ohio Valley, 1790–1850: German Baptist Settlement and Frontier Accommodation', argues that Campbell purloined much of his Restorationist theology from decidedly German and Pennsylvanian sources. Indeed, American Restorationism traces its origins to none other than the radical Universalist Brethren, and Joseph Hostetler in particular.[39] Moreover, the movement began in 1828 following a historic unity conference of Brethren, Primitivist and New Light Baptists who, Eller explains, 'agreed to participate in a unified Restoration movement' which the Campbells did not join until four years later, in 1832.[40] The Disciples of Christ, Alexander Campbell's denomination, was, in fact, a subsequent merger. At this point, Eller opines, Brethren left the Anabaptist fold to become ecumenical Christians under Campbell.

However, another option or merger took place on the frontier about the same time which allowed many of Anabaptist lineage to become Americans but remain outside the pale of evangelical America. On the frontier, with the prospect of rejoining the eastern annual conference a remote impossibility, many prominent Brethren, in fact, converted to Mormonism instead. Moreover, by the time they found Mormonism and Mormonism found them, there was precious little to argue about.

Mormons meet the Dunkers, c. 1840

The First and Second Great Awakenings caused many Pennsylvania Mennonites in particular to break with tradition. Revivalism preached a warm pietism and ecumenical gospel at odds with Anabaptism, luring many Pennsylvania German and Dutch sectarians into the ranks of the American denominational mainstream. Some who left went from the

---

[39] David B. Eller, 'The Brethren in the Western Ohio Valley, 1790–1850: German Baptist Settlement and Frontier Accommodation' (PhD diss., Miami Ohio University, 1976), pp. 191 ff.

[40] Ibid., p. 199.

pan into the fire, espousing radical mystical and communitarian ideas out of step with Evangelicalism *and* Mennonitica, reminiscent of the apocalyptic heresies of Melchior Hoffmann, Jan of Leyden, Bernhard Rothmann and Jan van Batenburg.

Beulah Stauffer Hostetler discusses the wide array of competing Anabaptist visions in America during the eighteenth and nineteenth centuries in her book, *American Mennonites and Protestant Movements*.[41] Pennsylvania, in the wake of revivalist ferment, she points out, housed religious separatists of many national origins – Mennonites, Quakers, German Lutherans, German Reformed, German Schwenkfelders, Amish and so on; Radical Pietist Separatists of all kinds – Moravians, Brethren in Christ or River Brethren and German Baptists or Dunkers; and far more radical, mystical splinter groups such as the Contented of the God-loving Soul, the Inspirationalists and, of course, the Seven-Day Baptists of Ephrata.

Mormons and River Brethren both began as a consequence of mutual baptism in the Susquehanna River. The perhaps apocryphal story of Jacob Engel and a companion (with the same last name as one of Joseph Smith's early companions, Witmer/Whitmer) who consult a Dunker minister, Elder George Miller, and are told, 'if you want to start something of your own you better baptize yourselves' which Dunkers had done in Germany, seemed somehow more than mere coincidence.[42] An early River Brethren confession, consisting of seven articles of faith, can quite easily be mistaken for an early Mormon manifesto.[43] Both groups, a consequence of their strong sectarian leanings, see themselves as a 'peculiar people' on par with the ancient Israelites. The River Brethren took the name, after all, of Brethren in Israel. Both nonetheless patterned their church government after that in the New Testament, believing that theirs was the only true church, Protestant Christianity falling prey to the 'believe-only' heresy.[44] There are other parallels: belief in the inability to be saved alone, 'deacons' or 'visiting brethren' who visit members to 'see that all differences and difficulties are properly settled', 'district councils' and 'General Conference', the Lord's Supper as a memorial to the death of Christ, and even foot washing. River Brethren

[41] Beulah Stauffer Hostetler, *American Mennonites and Protestant Movements* (Scottsdale, PA, 1987).

[42] Cited in Carlton O. Wittlinger, 'The Origin of the Brethren in Christ', *MQR*, 48 (1974), p. 64.

[43] See Martin H. Schrag, 'Influences Contributing to an Early River Brethren Confession of Faith', *MQR*, 38 (1964), pp. 344–86.

[44] Martin H. Schrag, 'The Original and Classical Brethren in Christ Concept of the Church', *MQR*, 46 (1972), p. 133.

occupy a middle ground between colonial Mennonites and antebellum revivalists. Mormonism, according to some, also stands betwixt and between orthodox Calvinism and radical Arminianism.[45]

The Susquehanna and a host of parallels notwithstanding, the River Brethren simply made too many concessions to Evangelical revivalism, in particular the pre-eminence of the prebaptismal new birth, to be a likely or suitable antecedent for Mormonism in the final analysis.[46] Indeed, much of the debate between Evangelicals and Mormons, and between Anabaptists, revolved around the issue of believers' baptism, the significance of the ordinance, the proper mode and so on. And while such theological hairsplitting may seem to us moderns much ado about nothing, even the slightest variation for these marginal and marginalized 'rebaptizers' was the basis for profoundly distinct religious groupings. Here we see the flip side of sectarianism, for such groups agree on the substantive issues but fragment, often, because of minor disagreements. Baptism proved at least as big a hurdle to Anabaptists confronting other Anabaptists as language and culture for outsiders like the Mormons who hoped to convert Anabaptists to their cause. On this point, those heirs of Anabaptism on the American frontier who would join the Mormons would first have to arrive at the Mormon understanding of 'things-soteriological' on their own. In this, the frontier proved to be Mormonism's greatest ally in the mission among wayward Mennonites.

Mennonites believe in believers' baptism for the remission of sins, but pour rather than 'dunk' as a rule. River Brethren and Dunkers also believe in believers' baptism for the remission of sins in accordance with Mennonite teaching but insist upon trine immersion baptism (three times forward). The Dunkers, in concert with Mennonite teaching, believe that baptism should follow repentance and faith in Christ, unlike the River Brethren who share the Evangelical view that the spiritual new birth cleanses sin and thus baptism is a first act of obedience of all such 'babes in Christ'. Yet, unlike Evangelicals, River Brethren did not dispense with baptism, insisting upon a particular mode as well – three times forward. Once backwards, on the other hand, is the Baptist understanding – which is said to have the full support of Scripture. All of the above, with the exception of Pedobaptists, reject infant baptism as an abomination of the established church. The Mormon practice is once backwards in concert

---

[45] See in this connection, Marvin S. Hill, *Quest for Refuge: The Mormon Flight from American Pluralism* (Salt Lake City, UT, 1989), p. 21, and Vogel, *Religious Seekers and the Advent of Mormonism*, pp. 215–20.

[46] See in this connection, Martin H. Schrag, 'The Brethren in Christ Attitude Toward the "World": A Historical Study of the Movement from Separation to the Increasing Acceptance of American Society' (PhD diss., Temple University, 1967).

with orthodox Baptist teaching. However, Mormonism's radical, anti-evangelical predilections make Baptists unlikely Mormons and vice versa. The Church of the Brethren or Dunkers, and not the River Brethren for the same reason, are another matter, especially when one considers that radical Dunker splinter groups had adopted the single or Baptist mode, as well as other American 'heresies' (universalism in particular) gravitating to either the Campbellites or the Mormons shortly thereafter. Clearly, by the time Mormons and Dunkers met on the American frontier they were theologically indistinguishable on the important matter of the mode and significance of baptism. Mormonism had about as little chance of success among the more orthodox, eastern Dunkers of Alexander Mack[47] fame as they would among the Mennonites later on. However, those Dunkers who broke with Mack and subsequently with George Wolfe and Joseph Hostetler, imbibing both Baptist and Universalist beliefs, constituted a missionary harvest not unlike that going on in England at the time when Mormon missionaries converted entire congregations of dissenters and independents.

Donald F. Durnbaugh notes that

> In the course of their journeys, Mormons encountered Brethren ... some of whom were won to the cause. This was the case with the influential Abraham Hunsaker (Hunsiker) family of Adams County, Illinois, and the Pfautz family of Pennsylvania, near Waynesboro, which was the site of an attempted Mormon colony in the mid-1840s under the leadership of Sidney Rigdon. ... Mormon historians have noted that a number of Utah settlers bore typical Brethren names: Hoff, Groff, Hess, Harley, Rodebaugh, Preuss (Price), Koch (Cook), and the like. ... A well-documented link with the Brethren occurred in the Clark family. Joshua Reuben Clark, an active Mormon, was the son of Hendricks Clark, a noted Dunker minister who lived near South Bend in St Joseph County, Indiana.[48]

And yet Mormon–Dunker dialogue was not less acrimonious than the Mormon-Campbellite polemic. Dunkers who converted to Mormonism, such as Mary McMinn of Philadelphia, were summarily excommunicated.[49]

Brethren worship and policy has much in common with that of Mormonism. Mormonism and Brethren are believers' churches which

---

[47] See William G. Willoughby, *Counting the Cost: The Life of Alexander Mack, 1679–1735* (Elgin, 1979).

[48] Durnbaugh, *Fruit of the Vine*, p. 178. See in this connection, Glenn Willett Clark, 'The Woman in the Wilderness: Reflections on a Mormon Family's Dunker Roots', (McLean, VA, 1986), also David B. Eller, 'Church of Jesus Christ of Latter-Day [sic] Saints', *The Brethren Encyclopedia*, p. 298.

[49] Durnbaugh, *Fruit of the Vine*, p. 179.

ridicule infant baptism. Both are highly patriarchal in nature and prone to excommunicate female pretenders to the throne. Both feature kitchens in their places of worship. Their respective ecclesiastic offices are similar in title and function – deacons, bishops and elders in both perform similar duties – and these church leaders are set apart to perform their church work by 'the laying on of hands' and serve without compensation. Both anoint the sick. Annual Conference is an important occasion in both faith communities where church policy is discussed and decisions put to the membership for a sustaining vote (also more ritualistic than democratic). Originally, both hoped to bring Christianity to the Indians and unite Christendom under a single banner. Church discipline is considered by both to represent a court of 'love'. And some in the Brethren church, like the Mormons, even speculate that baptism of/for those in paradise exists.[50] The differences are few but important – the threefold immersion baptism and love feast, the holy kiss, and refusing to swear oaths or perform military duty are Brethren beliefs and practices to which Mormons, as a rule, do not subscribe. Notably, as Rufus D. Bowman has shown, Brethren would be forced to compromise their peace witness in order to avoid persecution during the First World War.[51]

Those Dunkers who gravitated to Mormonism were a very particular and, indeed, peculiar strain of American Anabaptism. I have already discussed briefly the important role which Dunkers played in the emergence of the Restorationist movement in America. Alexander Campbell, whether he chose to accept it or not, owed a debt to the Church of the Brethren. At the same time, Campbell's decidedly Southern and uniquely Universalist theology caused a rift in Brethren circles. In the 1820s, Brethren argued the merits of trine immersion baptism versus the single or Baptist mode. In 1821, the Annual Meeting of the Somerset Country, Pennsylvania Brethren resolved to accept the single mode in principle. The objective of all such doctrinal revisionism was to smooth the way for an ecumenical union with Campbell's Disciples of Christ and other radicals. Adam Hostetler and other 'Universalist' Brethren broke with the 'old connexion in Pennsylvania' about this time, establishing a church of their own in Kentucky of some two thousand souls. Adam's nephew Joseph Hostetler and Peter Hon began deliberations with Campbell who convinced them of the truth of single immersion and other decidedly Baptist beliefs and practices. Campbell would fail miserably in his attempt to win Peter Keyser and Pennsylvania Brethren to

---

[50] Ibid., pp. 103–26.
[51] Rufus D. Bowman, *The Church of the Brethren and War, 1708–1941* (New York, 1971).

the Restorationist cause, but far away in Kentucky and along the vast reaches of the Ohio frontier dissenting Brethren like Hostetler and Hon were easily plucked from the tree of the eastern conference and re-grafted onto the stump of American Protestantism. Hostetler and Hon convinced their wayward, Anabaptist brethren to join forces with the Campbellites. The Quaker and nominal Brethren, John Wright, and his followers filled out the ranks of the so-called 'Christian Connection'.[52] Recognizing a clear and present danger, the more orthodox Eastern Conference of Brethren closed ranks and refused to make any more concessions to other 'Americanizers' who might happen by.

Anabaptist converts to Mormonism came from the same pool of disgruntled, frontier Universalist Brethren roaming the western reaches of America in search of a new sectarian vision which better suited the new social, economic and political reality. The American melting pot forced many to choose between Anabaptism and America, Christianity and Christendom. For those Anabaptists on the frontier who subscribed to the biblicist understanding but had fallen out of favour with ortho-doxy, Campbell was a logical and unavoidable choice. However, for that more radical faction, stubbornly anti-evangelical, resolutely sectar-ian, those incorrigible mystics of Anabaptist dissent who refused to become Protestants or Catholics, Mormonism represented a last and final refuge from American pluralism and Christian ecumenism.

Conclusion

What can we conclude from all of this? Mormon and Mennonite apolo-gists who contend that enough parallels do not exist to make any kind of case for a Mormon–Anabaptist nexus are mistaken. Another strategy of differentiation is required. Indeed, it might be argued that modern Mormons, not unlike their Mennonite counterparts, have abandoned their spiritualism to the point, in the Mormon case, of a soft biblicism thus making the prospect of Mennonite conversions to Mormonism less problematic from a purely theological standpoint. The old linguistic and cultural barriers in the 1990s are not quite what they were in the 1890s, either. (Not many years ago, I attended the wedding of a Mennonite woman and a Mormon male – a friend of the family. Both had served missions for their respective churches and I witnessed their marriage in a Mennonite church in Alberta. I later heard that she had converted to Mormonism and they were to be sealed/married in an LDS

---

[52] See Durnbaugh, *Fruit of the Vine*, pp. 172–7.

temple.) Well on its way to becoming a *bona fide* evangelical denomination, Mormonism is increasingly reluctant to acknowledge its radical roots – lest American attitudes harden once more, conversions drop off and the church atrophy. Suffice it to say that for those who insist Mormons are not Anabaptists and vice versa, time is not on their side.

So then, are Mormons Anabaptists? Obviously they are not direct lineal descendants of the sixteenth-century Anabaptist tradition. But this fact should not distract us from the important parallels between these two religious traditions. Once we have jettisoned the preconceptions of established normative visions of early Anabaptism and Mormonism, these parallels come more clearly into focus. And recognition of the homologous trends in Mormon and Anabaptist history will open up new understanding not only of the sectarian religious experience in the abstract, but also of lived Mormon/Anabaptist interaction.

James M. Stayer: Publications

'The Earliest Anabaptists and the Separatist-Pacifist Dilemma', *Brethren Life and Thought*, 10 (Winter 1965), pp. 17–24.

'Hans Hut's Doctrine of the Sword: An Attempted Solution', *MQR*, 39 (1965), pp. 181–91.

'Terrorism, the Peasants' War, and the "Widertäufer"', *ARG*, 56 (1965), pp. 227–9.

'The Münsterite Rationalization of Bernhard Rothmann', *Journal of the History of Ideas*, 28 (1967), pp. 179–92.

'Eine fanatische Täuferbewegung in Esslingen und Reutlingen?', *Blätter für Württembergische Kirchengeschichte*, 68–9 (1968–69), pp. 53–9.

'Thomas Müntzer's Theology and Revolution in Recent non-Marxist Interpretation', *MQR*, 43 (1969), pp. 142–51.

'Melchior Hofmann and the Sword', *MQR*, 45 (1971), pp. 265–77.

Anabaptists and the Sword (Lawrence, KS, 1972; 2nd edition incl. 'Reflections and Retractions', 1976), xxxiii, 375 pp.

Review article on C.-P. Clasen, *Anabaptism, A Social History, 1525–1618*, *MGBl*, 30 (1973), pp. 98–107.

'From Monogenesis to Polygenesis: The Historical Discussion of Anabaptist Origins', co-authored with Werner O. Packull and Klaus Depperman, *MQR*, 49 (1975), pp. 83–121.

'Die Anfänge des schweizerischen Täufertums im reformierten Kongregationalismus', in Hans-Jürgen Goertz (ed.), *Umstrittenes Täufertum, 1525–1975. Neue Forschungen* (Göttingen, 1975), pp. 19–49.

'Reublin and Brötli: The Revolutionary Beginnings of Swiss Anabaptism', in Marc Lienhard (ed.), *The Origins and Characteristics of Anabaptism/Les débuts et les caractéristiques de l'anabaptisme* [Archives internationales d'histoire des idées, 87] (The Hague, 1977), pp. 83–102.

'Reflections and Retractions on *Anabaptists and the Sword*', *MQR*, 51 (1977), pp. 196–212.

'Die Schweizer Brüder. Versuch einer historischen Definition', *MGBl*, 34 (1977), pp. 7–34.

'The Swiss Brethren: An Exercise in Historical Definition', *Church History*, 47 (1978), pp. 174–95.

'Oldeklooster and Menno', *Sixteenth Century Journal*, 9 (1978), pp. 51–67.

'Wilhelm Reublin: Eine pikareske Wanderung durch das frühe Täufertum', in Hans-Jürgen Goertz (ed.), *Radikale Reformatoren, 21 biographische Skizzen von Thomas Müntzer bis Paracelsus* (Munich, 1978), pp. 93–102.

'Let a Hundred Flowers Bloom and let a Hundred Schools of Thought Contend', *MQR*, 53 (1979), pp. 211–18.

'Oldeklooster en Menno', *Doopsgezinde Bijdragen*, N.S. 5 (1979), pp. 56–76.

The Anabaptists and Thomas Müntzer (Dubuque, IA, 1980), vii, 167 pp., co-edited with Werner O. Packull.

'Vielweiberei als "innerweltiche Askese." Neue Eheauffassungen in der Reformationszeit', *MGBl*, 37 (1980), pp. 24–41.

'Polygamy as "Inner-Worldly Asceticism." Conceptions of Marriage in the Radical Reformation', *CUDAN Bulletin*, 12–13 (1980–81), pp. 59–67.

'Thomas Müntzer's Protestation and Imaginary Faith', *MQR*, 55 (1981), pp. 99–130.

'Zwingli before Zürich. Humanist Reformer and Papal Partisan', *ARG*, 72 (1981), pp. 55–68.

'The Anabaptists', in Steven Ozment (ed.), *Reformation Europe: A Guide to Research* (St Louis, MO, 1982), pp. 135–59.

'Wilhelm Reublin: A Picaresque Journey through Early Anabaptism', in Hans-Jürgen Goertz (ed.), *Profiles of Radical Reformers. Biographical Sketches from Thomas Müntzer to Paracelsus* (Kitchener, Ont., Scottdale, PA, 1982), pp. 107–17; also translated pp. 9–24, 29–43 from German.

Review article, 'Luther Studies and Reformation Studies', *Canadian Journal of History*, 17 (1982), pp. 499–505.

'Qui sont les anabaptistes?', *Conscience et liberteé*, 25 (1983), pp. 29–36.

'Wer waren die Täufer?', *Gewissen und Feiheit*, 21 (1983), pp. 36–44.

'The Separatist Church of the Majority. A Response to Charles Nienkirchen', *MQR*, 57 (1983), pp. 151–5.

'The Eclipse of *Young Man Luther*: An Outsider's Perspective on Luther Studies', *Canadian Journal of History*, 19 (1984), pp. 167–82.

'Davidite vs. Mennonite', *MQR*, 58 (1984), pp. 459–76.

Review article on Ulrich Gäbler, *Huldrych Zwingli*, in *MGBl*, 41 (1984), pp. 116–21.

'Zwingli and the "Viri Multi et Excellentes." The Christian Renaissance's Repudiation of *neoterici* and the Beginnings of Reformed Protestantism', in E.J. Furcha and H. Wayne Pipkin (eds), *Prophet, Pastor, Protestant. The Work of Huldrych Zwingli after Five Hundred Years* (Allison Park, PA, 1984), pp. 137–54.

'Neue Modelle eines gemeinsamen Lebens. Gütergemeinschaft im Täufertum', in Hans-Jürgen Goertz (ed.), *Alles gehört allen. Das*

Experiment Gütergemeinschaft vom 16. Jahrhundert bis heute (Munich, 1984), pp. 21–49.

'Radical Early Zwinglianism: Balthasar Hubmaier, Faber's *Ursach* and the Peasant Programmes', in E.J. Furcha (ed.), *Huldrych Zwingli, 1484–1531: A Legacy of Radical Reform*. Papers from the 1984 International Zwingli Symposium, McGill University (Montreal, 1984), pp. 62–82.

'David Joris: A Prolegomemon to further Research', *MQR*, 59 (1985), pp. 350–61.

'Radikaler Früzwinglianismus: Balthasar Hubmaier, Fabers *Ursach* und die Programme der Bauern', *MGBl*, 42 (1985), pp. 43–59.

'The Revolutionary Origins of the "Peace Churches": The Peasants' War and the Anabaptists, the English Civil War and the Quakers', *Brethren Life and Thought*, 30 (1985), pp. 71–80.

'Davidite vs. Mennonite', in Irvin B. Horst (ed.), *The Dutch Dissenters* (Leyden, 1986), pp. 143–59 (lightly revised reprint).

'Was Dr. Kuehler's Conception of Early Dutch Anabaptism Historically Sound? The Historical Discussion of Anabaptist Münster 450 Years Later', *MQR*, 60 (1986), pp. 261–88.

'Was There a Klettgau Letter of 1530?', *MQR*, 61 (1987), pp. 75–6.

'Anabaptists and Future Anabaptists in the Peasants' War', *MQR*, 62 (1988), pp. 99–139.

'Christianity in One City: Anabaptist Münster, 1534–35', in Hans J. Hillerbrand (ed.), *Radical Tendencies in the Reformation: Divergent Perspectives* (Sixteenth Century Essays and Studies, IX) (Kirksville, MO, 1988), pp. 117–34.

'Joris, David', *Theologische Realenzyklopädie*, 17: 1/2 (Berlin and New York, 1988), pp. 238–42.

'The Anabaptists and the Sects', in G.R. Elton (ed.), *The New Cambridge Modern History*, II: *The Reformation, 1520–1559* (Cambridge, 1990), pp. 118–43.

'Münster Anabaptists', 'Peasants' War', 'Reublin, Wilhelm', in Cornelius J. Dyck and Dennis D. Martin (eds), *ME*, vol. 5 (Scottdale, PA, 1990), pp. 606–7, 687–8, 771.

'Thomas Müntzer in 1989: A Review Article', *Sixteenth Century Journal*, 21 (1990), pp. 655–70.

The German Peasants' War and Anabaptist Community of Goods (Montreal and Kingston, Ont., 1991), x, 227 pp. (paperback edition, 1993).

'Noch einmal besichtigt: "Anabaptists and the Sword," von der Radikalität zum Quietismus', *MGBl*, 47/48 (1990–91), pp. 24–37.

'Saxon Radicalism and Swiss Anabaptism: The Return of the Repressed', *MQR*, 67 (1993), pp. 5–30.

'Reformation, Peasants, Anabaptists: Northeastern Swiss Anticlericalism', in Peter Dykema and Heiko A. Oberman (eds), *Anticlericalism in Late Medieval and Early Modern Europe* (Leiden, 1993), pp. 559–66.

'Anticlericalism: A Model for a Coherent Interpretation of the Reformation', in Hans R. Guggisberg and Gottfried G. Krodel (eds), *The Reformation in Germany and Europe: Interpretations and Issues* (Gütersloh, 1993), pp. 39–47.

'Sachsischer Radikalismus und Schweizer Täufertum: Die Wiederkehr des Verdrängten', in Günter Volger (ed.), *Wegscheiden der Reformation. Alternatives Denken vom 16. bis zum 18. Jahrhundert* (Weimar, 1994) pp. 151–78.

're Arnold Snyder, Beyond Polygenesis', *MGBl*, 52 (1995), pp. 151–60.

'The Radical Reformation', in Thomas A. Brady, Jr, Heiko A. Oberman, James D. Tracy (eds), *Handbook of European History, 1400–1600: Late Middle Ages, Renaissance, and Reformation* (Leiden, 1995), vol. 2, pp. 249–82.

'Anabaptists', 'Community of Goods', 'Hubmaier, Balthasar', 'John of Leiden', 'Mantz, Felix', 'Melchiorites', 'Polygamy', in Hans J. Hillerbrand (ed.), *Encylcopedia of the Reformation* (New York, 1996), vol. 1, pp. 31–5, 389–92, vol. 2, pp. 260–63, 350–51, 504–5, vol. 3, pp. 46–7, 292–4.

'Anabaptists and the Sword Revisited: The Trend from Radicalism to Apoliticism', in Harvey L. Dyck (ed.), *The Pacifist Impulse in Historical Perspective* (Toronto, 1996), pp. 111–24.

'Reeling History Backwards: The Anabaptists as a Key to Understanding Thomas Müntzer More Conservatively', Meiji University International Exchange Programs Guest Lecture Series, No. 9 (1995) (Center for International Programs, Meiji University: 1996), 41 pp.

'Review Essay: Anabaptist History and Theology', *MQR*, 70 (1996), pp. 473–82.

'The Passing of the Radical Moment in the Radical Reformation', *MQR*, 71 (1997), pp. 147–52.

'Karl Holls "Luther und die Schwärmer": Vom abenteuerlichen Leben eines Texts', in Norbert Fischer and Marion Kobelt-Groch (eds), *Aussenseiter, Nonkonformisten und soziale Bewegungen zwischen Mittelalter und Neuzeit* (Leiden, 1997), pp. 269–88.

Martin Luther: German Saviour: German Evangelical Factions and the Interpretation of Luther, 1917–1933 (Montreal, forthcoming 2000).

Index